RESEARCH RESOURCES
Annotated Guide to the Social Sciences

Volume 1
International Relations & Recent History
Indexes, Abstracts & Periodicals

John Brown Mason
Professor of Political Science
California State College, Fullerton

Santa Barbara, California
1968

DEMCO

FOR REFERENCE

Do Not Take From This Room

©1968
by
John Brown Mason

All rights reserved. This book or any part thereof may not
be reproduced in any form without the written permission
of the editor.

Library of Congress Catalog Card No. 68-9685

HOFSTRA UNIVERSITY
LIBRARY

American Bibliographical Center-Clio Press
Riviera Campus, 2010 Alameda Padre Serra
Santa Barbara, California 93103

Ref.
Z 7161
.M36
v. 1, copy 1

To

Nan

ACKNOWLEDGMENTS

The editor is greatly obligated to a large number of persons who contributed in various ways to the making of this book over a period of nine years. Ideas and information were gratefully received from historians, political scientists, and librarians, also from students, both undergraduate and graduate, who used the manuscript in its preliminary mimeoprinted form.

Among the many helpful contributors of data and suggestions are Professor Peter Baehr, University of Amsterdam; Dr. Alexander C. Body, Documents Librarian, Western Michigan University; Miss Helen F. Conover, formerly Legislative Reference Library, Library of Congress; Dr. Forrest S. Drummond, Librarian, Los Angeles County Law Library; Dr. Henry J. Dubester, Chief, General Reference and Bibliography Division, Library of Congress; Professor Harold H. Fisher, Chairman Emeritus, Hoover War Library, Stanford University; Dr. Peter Fliess, Professor of International Relations, University of Massachusetts; Dr. William L. Franklin, Chief, Historical Research Division, Department of State; Professor Edward Glick, Department of Political Science, Temple University; Dr. Arthur E. Gropp, Librarian, Columbus Memorial Library, Organization of American States, Washington, D. C.; Miss Dorothy J. Harmon, African Studies Bibliographer, University Research Library, University of California, Los Angeles; Professor Chauncy D. Harris, Department of Geography, University of Chicago; Dr. Frederick H. Hartmann, Alfred Thayer Mahan Professor, Naval War College, Newport, R. I.; Dr. Kenneth Holland, President, Institute of International Education, New York; Professors John Lovell and Leroy Rieselbach, Department of Government, Indiana University; Dr. David Kaser, Editor, *College and Research Libraries*; Dr. Peter Lengyel, Editor, *International Social Science Journal*, UNESCO, Paris; Dr. Richard Mönnig, Inter Nationes, Bonn.

Miss Patricia Annoni, Acting Editor, *Catholic Periodical Index*; Professor Willard A. Beling, Middle East/North African Program Coordinator, University of Southern California; Leonard Bushkoff, American Review Editor, *Balkan Studies*; Dr. Jost Delbrück, LL.M., Institut für Internationales Recht, University of Kiel; Mr. R. A. Duis, Associate Head, Reports Department, The Rand Corporation, Santa Monica, California; P. W. Esterhuysen, Secretary, The Africa Institute, Pretoria, Republic of South Africa; Professor Stephen Fischer-Galati, Editor, *East European Quarterly*; Professor M. A. Fitzsimons, Editor, *Review of Politics*; Mr. Nils Petter Gleditsch, Assistant Secretary, International Peace Research Institute, Oslo, Norway; Teg C. Grondahl, Executive Director, American Universities Field Staff, New York; Richard Hudson, Editor, *War/Peace Report*, New York; V. M. Kabes, Executive Secretary, International Commission of Jurists, Geneva, Switzerland; P. Kryukov, Executive Secretary, *International Affairs*, Moscow; Professor Charles A. McClelland, School of International Relations, University of Southern California formerly Editor, *Background: Journal of the International Studies Association*; Professor Klaus Mehnert, Editor, *Osteuropa*; Edouard Morot-Sir, Cultural Counselor, Representative in the United States of the French Universities, French Embassy, Washington, D. C.; Dr. Günter Olzog, Publisher, *Literaturverzeichnis der Politischen Wissenschaften*, Munich; Mrs. Barbara Phillips, Assistant Editor, *Asian Survey*, University of California; M. S. Rajan, Associate Editor, *International Studies*, New Delhi; Professor R. John Rath, Editor, *Austrian History Yearbook*; Baren Ray, Editor, *Afro-Asian and World Affairs*, New Delhi; Miss Eloise ReQua, Director, Library of International Relations, Chicago; Miss Mary Ryan, Head, Government Publications Service, University Research Library, University of California, Los Angeles; Mr. Shiro Saito, Sinclair Library, and Mr. S. McCabe, Orientation Center, University of Hawaii; Miss Agatha Schmidt, Research Director, *National Review*; Mr. Sheng Wei, Editorial Department, *China Reconstructs*, Peking; Mrs. Sara Shepherd, Institute of International Studies, University of Claifornia, Berkeley; Latif Ahmed Sherwani, The Pakistan Institute of International Affairs, Karachi; J. Simmonds, Ministry of Overseas Development, London; Alison Smith, Joint Editor, *African Affairs,* Institute of Commonwealth Studies, Oxford; Dean Fred A. Sondermann, Colorado College, Editor, *International Studies Quarterly*; Dr. William B. Stern, Los Angeles County Law Library, Chairman, Committee on Foreign Law Indexing; Dr. Albert C. Stillson, Head, Arms Control and Disarmament Bibliography Section, Reference Department, General Reference and Bibliography Division, Library of Congress; Mr. A. Vogel, Bibliography Division, U.S. Information Agency, Washington, D.C.; Mr. Hermann Volle, Editor, *Europa Archiv,* Bonn; Wang Tsien-wu, Secretary General, Union Research Institute, Kowloon, Hong Kong; Wang Wei, Editor, *Free China Weekly,* Taipei; Miss Ilse Wartberg, The Atlantic Institute, Boulogne-sur-Seine, France; Dr. Carl M. White, Program Specialist in Library Administration, Overseas Development Program, Ford Foundation; H. L. White, Librarian, National and John Balnaves, Principal Librarian, Bibliographical Services Section, National Library of Australia; Mr. Harry N. M. Winton, Chief Documents Reference Section, Dag Hammarskjold Library, United Nations, New York; and Mrs. Margaret E. Wodehouse, Editor, *Canadian Periodical Index.*

The editor is grateful to his colleagues at the California State College at Fullerton for helpful criticism and encouragement when the job of finishing this work seemed endless. They include Professors Charles G. Bell, Anne T. Feraru, and Lee R. Kerschner of the Department of Political Science; and Giles T. Brown, Dean of Graduate Studies, of the Department of History. Professor Ivan L. Richardson, Chairman, Department of Political Science, provided assistance and helpfully adjusted teaching schedules. Valuable help was received from members of the Library staff, especially Mr. Cecil Roberts and Mr. Donald W. Keran. Miss Diane Nixon, now a graduate student at the Library School of the University of Southern California, and Mr. James Sullivan, provided indispensable aid during long hours of research and checking data. Miss Nixon also contributed the Indexes of Titles and of Names.

To President William B. Langsdorf special appreciation is due for the grant of a semester's research leave which provided time for pulling together the thousands of data and details which go into the making of a reference work.

It has been a pleasure and professional privilege to work with Dr. Eric H. Boehm, Director of the American Bibliographical Center-Clio Press, and Mr. Lloyd Garrison, Editor, Clio Books. They have been liberal contributors of ideas, efforts, and time.

John Brown Mason

California State College
at Fullerton
August 15, 1968

PREFACE

THE USE OF RESEARCH RESOURCES

Research Resources is designed as a comprehensive, interdisciplinary guide to the literature of international relations and recent history. It is designed for use of upper and lower division students, graduate students, and professors.

Research Resources provides worldwide coverage, carefully annotated, of hundreds of research aids—both books and periodicals. It acquaints students with the character and scope of some 150 periodicals containing articles on international relations and recent history, including journals devoted to translations of foreign language material, and the characteristics of leading American and foreign newspapers and usefulness of the various types of research aids and efficient ways of utilizing them. An appended section on New and Ceased Publications enables the reader to keep abreast of constant changes in the periodical and reference field.

Students can use *Research Resources* as a guide through the maze of research material in their libraries. Upper division students can use this work to build and refine their knowledge of research resources and to improve their search methods. Graduate students will find *Research Resources* contains useful refresher information on familiar tools. Professors can use it as a convenient guide to information needed for new courses, for updating old courses, or to design new approaches to old subjects.

The relationship between science, government and international relations is included in the coverage. References to selected areas of education are of special value to the teacher and teacher-to-be. Annotations have been furnished in the field of ethics, philosophy, and religion since so many students today relate the study of international relations and history to the quest for a purpose in life and for an understanding of the basic character of government and politics.

Abbreviations

FREQUENCY OF PUBLICATION:

A	annual
B	biennial
BM	bimonthly
BW	biweekly
D	daily
Irr.	irregular
M	monthly
Q	quarterly
SA	semiannual
SM	semimonthly
W	weekly
5 x w	five times a week
3 x y	three times a year

GENERAL:

biblio.	bibliography
comp(s).	compiler(s)
cum(s).	cumulative, cumulation(s)
ed(s).	editor(s)
LC	Library of Congress
p(p).	page(s)
vol(s).	volume(s)

TABLE OF CONTENTS

PART III
BOOKS

PART V
U. S. GOVERNMENT PUBLICATIONS

PART VI
THE PRESS: AMERICAN AND FOREIGN

INTRODUCTION

STUDY AND RESEARCH IN INTERNATIONAL RELATIONS

THE SCATTERED SOURCES

This book provides a selective guide to the extensive literature in the field of international relations and related areas. Sources in these fields are so widely scattered that scholars can find and make use of only part of those available. The book is designed to help students and researchers make a more complete and comprehensive search in less time.

In 1964 the Carnegie Endowment for International Peace commissioned a study, "The State of Bibliography in International Relations: Analysis and Recommendations." The work was published by the American Bibliographical Center-Clio Press in 1965 under the title *Bibliographies on International Relations and World Affairs*. The editor of the study, Dr. Eric H. Boehm, reached the following conclusions:

> 1. The bibliographic situation is chaotic. We found an astounding multiplicity of different bibliographic sources. It appears that there is not a single field of knowledge in which it is so difficult to find out about published material as the field of international relations.
>
> 2. Not a single bibliography covers as much as twenty percent of the published materials. For example: the best bibliography of books on international relations, the *Foreign Affairs Bibliography*, which is published every ten years, covered an average of less than 800 books per year in its most recent edition. It appears from the Library of Congress' statistical breakdowns that the number of books on international relations cataloged annually is roughly ten times the 800 figure: 8,000 to 10,000—more probably the latter—plus or minus twenty percent. . . . Even if one makes allowance for the fact that many of these books are of popular appeal and might not interest a serious scholar, the disproportion between the number of books captured bibliographically in the *Foreign Affairs Bibliography*—the largest general bibliography of books—and the number of such books cataloged per year in the Library of Congress should give us pause for thought. Thus, even with stringent rules for quality, the amount captured bibliographically is not enough to permit one to speak of bibliographical control.
>
> 3. Growth in bibliography has generally taken the form of a proliferation of bibliographies rather than substantial increases in titles in any one bibliography.

It is impossible to find a way through the labyrinth of books, articles, documents, and book reviews without the help of indexes and related research tools. It is nearly impossible to go straight to source materials without a guide to the existing maze of bibliographies, indexes, abstracts, and book reviews. Familiarity with available research tools, knowledge of their possibilities and limitations, is as important as possessing them. The researcher needs to know the right tools for whatever job he sets out to do.

THE INTERDISCIPLINARY ASPECT

The student of international relations and related fields finds most of his material in the documents and literature of political science. That discipline has specialized more than any other social science in the study of international affairs.

However, the political scientist looks outside his immediate area and works beyond the traditional approach. His studies overlap the other social sciences. The resources and findings of history expand his understanding of the past; the data and conclusions of economics and geography aid his diagnosis of the present; sociology helps him understand contemporary societies; both sociology and psychology open avenues of analysis of individual and group behavior. Many cultural anthropologists have joined sociologists in studying modern society, while sociologists work with anthropologists to examine the problems of developing societies in the modern world. The institutions and practices of law—disturbingly backward in the international field—present their own problems and opportunities. Finally, education, as an independent discipline, is indispensable to mankind's progress.

THE BEHAVIORAL APPROACH

The "behavioral revolution" has deeply influenced the development of political science in the last generation, including the study of international relations. According to Professor Heinz Eulau of Stanford University:[1]

> Gradually ... and particularly after the rise of fascism in Italy and Germany, there was a realization that [the post-World War I] preoccupation with institutional and legal gadgetry had neglected the realities of international life. While concern with international organization has continued and was, in fact, reinforced by the setting up of the United Nations and its affiliates, making it a matter of continued scholarly effort, the focus shifted to "international politics." International relations was increasingly seen as a "struggle for power" in a world of nationalism and imperialism in which the problems of "national interest" and "security" represent the hard facts of life. International relations was now seen as a function of foreign policies, and there was a growing tendency to examine the motivations of peoples and policy-makers, their capacity and willingness to carry through on commitments, and all those factors—economic, military, geographic, demographic, and even psychological—which determine this capacity. In other words, the shift of emphasis was from description of formal international structures and prescriptions on how to cure the world's ills to closer observation of international processes and their determinants. There was a tendency to break down the separation of international from domestic policy, and a new awareness of the close relationship between national ideologies and national objectives.
>
> In general, the newer tendencies seem to fall into three categories: first, theoretical efforts to describe and explain international politics on the highest level of analytical generality; second, studies, both theoretical and empirical, of the foreign-policy process and its determinants; and third, attempts to relate both foreign policies and resulting patterns of international relations to the complex interaction of cultural and personality factors. Of the three categories, the last is probably the oldest. It relies on interviews and quantitative analysis of mass communications as tools of inquiry. Closely related are studies of important elites and the elite behavior in the international arena .
>
> The second group of studies is primarily concerned with the conditions and consequences of the foreign-policy making process and those circumstances which affect the course of policy, such as technological developments, environmental conditions, ideological commitments, and changes in the social structure. The distinction between the ends and means of policy, as well as between the internal and external policies of states, calls attention to such problems as the receptivity of policy-makers to communications, or the role of the military in strategic planning in relation to foreign policy.
>
> Finally, there has been increasing realization that, just as in other areas covered by the social sciences, progress in the study of international politics may require more general theories, or at least conceptual schemes of some generality, within which the great number and range of variables of international life can be systematically related and given meaning. A number of such theoretical schemes have been advanced, along with more specific models, among them system analysis schemes, game-theoretical, de-

---

[1] Heinz Eulau, "Political Science," in Carl M. White and Associates, *Sources of Information in the Social Sciences. A Guide to the Literature.* (Totowa, New Jersey, The Bedminster Press, 1964), pp. 383-85. Quoted by permission of the author and publisher.

cision-making and communication models, field theory, and experiments in simulation. At this time, most of these efforts remain unrelated, though there is a growing feeling that integration of diverse theories is the next step.

STUDY AND RESEARCH IN RECENT HISTORY

The research materials of recent history are as widely scattered as those of international relations. Often, they are identical. Where the solid tomes of history once presented the story of political and diplomatic events, they now offer a more diversified picture of life in various aspects, of persons engaged in many activities, and of governments active in fields as widely divergent as the people whose welfare they protect and promote.

The post-World War II restoration of stolen art and the current effort to save Egyptian temples and sculpture from the backed-up waters of the Nile are history as much as the wars in Algeria, Korea, and Vietnam. The achievements of the Marshall Plan in Europe and the problems of developing nations in Asia, Africa, and South America interest historians as much as the naval battles of World Wars I and II. Advances in architecture and the natural sciences, and the impact of modern music and drama on society are researched to pinpoint developments and to expand human understanding of what has happened in past generations and what is going on today. Oral history creates and preserves records of events as experienced by men and women still living. History is no longer confined to the political and diplomatic arena. It is as wide and deep as life.

The variety of subjects which attract and puzzle modern historians bring them into cooperation with scholars in other social sciences—with students of every discipline and field of inquiry. Students of other disciplines, in turn, look to the historian for seasoned interpretations of the record of the past. They may not agree on causes and meanings, but each contributes to a better, composite understanding of history. The fury of Nazism, the tenacity of communism, and the stoicism of the Viet Cong are historical factors which can be understood better if the tools, methods, and skills of psychology, sociology, and anthropology are also used. The pride, perseverance, and push of nationalism; the intolerance of racism; the motivating force of patriotism and religion; the steady growth of scientific inquiry; and the persistency of conflict are also factors which can be understood, explained, or examined only through the interdisciplinary cooperation of scholars with different backgrounds, viewpoints, knowledge, and methods. No one discipline or approach can claim a monopoly on human knowledge—their efforts must be coordinated or their findings will disintegrate into meaningless fragments.

Interdisciplinary efforts in the study of international relations may develop along the traditional approaches, which are indispensable to historical inquiry, or they may merge into the behavioral approach which historians are beginning to explore for new possibilities in a search for deeper and clearer insights.

PART I
INDEXES AND ABSTRACTS
PUBLICATIONS

ARTICLES OFFER FACTS AND IDEAS

The number of periodicals has grown rapidly in recent decades. Consequently, the importance of periodical indexes has grown. Today many researchers would be helpless without them. Indexes to periodicals save researchers from being buried under an avalanche of periodicals—magazines, scholarly reviews, yearbooks, and other serial publications.

On many topics information can be found only in periodicals. Some subjects may not be extensive enough or important enough for a book. Perhaps the available source material is insufficient for a book-length study. Or, a needed book may still be in preparation, unavailable to the scholar, while articles on the same subject have already appeared in periodicals. A scholarly book usually takes years of research and writing, and may take a year or more to publish after it has been written. Significant events, discoveries, or developments may be so recent that only periodicals have been able to publish information about them. An unknown person may become newsworthy, and only periodicals will produce articles about him.

Articles also bring books up-to-date, correct and improve their contents, by presenting new material. They may present new interpretations or syntheses, or present new arguments against old ones. They may reveal inadequate research or slanted views on the part of an author. Some periodicals print the full text of documents which have been discovered recently or which are of recent origin and thus keep scholars informed of current developments.

Indexes

Information contained in thousands of articles would be difficult to find, even inaccessible, if there were no bibliographies or indexes to periodical and serial literature. Such publications, regardless of their general scope or specialized focus, are useful research tools.

Indexes are published weekly, monthly, quarterly, annually, and decennially. Some cover several decades. Some are current, like the weekly *Bulletin of the Public Affairs Information Service,* or less current, like the annual *International Bibliography of Political Science.* Some are retrospective, like the *Foreign Affairs Bibliography* which covers ten years in a single volume. Periodical cumulations increase the usefulness of indexes.

The services of indexes and other bibliographies according to one observer:[1]

> . . . may be limited to selection, organization and listing; but often further information is supplied by discussing the literature item by item. This type of discussion, annotation, may be expository, critical or promotional.

Most indexes concentrate on certain categories of subjects, but many overlap coverage of materials and periodicals. No index covers all periodicals, even those within a single discipline. Indexes list authors, titles, and topics of published articles under classified headings and subheadings which may be cross-referenced. They also list the number of pages and the date of publication of articles. Only a few indexes list so-called "small items," such as short editiorials, which appear in various sections of periodicals. If these are important to a researcher he will find it necessary to check each issue for them. Other indexes list books, bibliographies, pamphlets, leaflets, maps, and illustrations. Some indexes to behavioral publications adopt modified indexing methods suited to their particular purpose. Such modifications require the researcher to be thoroughly familiar with the type of information found in a given

[1]White, Carl M. and Associates, *Sources of Information in the Social Sciences,* p. 12.

index and to search more than one for more comprehensive coverage. Index users should carefully read special instructions concerning scope and method whenever they appear.

Indexes sometimes change their names and alter their type and extent of coverage. They may add or drop subject areas, and they may increase or decrease the number of periodicals covered. The *International Index,* for example, made important changes in coverage in 1955. In 1965 it changed its name as well as its coverage of subject fields. New indexes appear from time to time and others cease publication.

Researchers should look in indexes for broad subject areas as well as specialized or restricted topics. For example, an article may include useful data on several colonies located on three continents yet it may be indexed in a single entry, "colonialism." An article on a particular colony may include information on forced labor, native troops, nationalism, natural resources, tropical diseases, education, the work of UNICEF, etc., but it may not be listed under all these topics.

Titles are frequently too general to be useful in describing the content of books or articles. An article titled "Impressions of Africa" may include worthwhile information on political or economic developments in a key African country even when it sounds like a simple travelogue. In such cases the reader can only hope that the indexer has completely listed and cross-referenced the content under appropriate headings and subheadings. Better yet he may complete his search by scanning the article itself.

Different language usages make research more difficult. Many English words have different meanings in England, in old or new Commonwealth countries, in Eire, and in the United States. Spanish terminology varies from country to country. *The University of Michigan Index to Labor Union Periodicals* recognizes another language problem in this introductory statement:

> If the headline contains too much jargon, or too many slang phrases, which the indexers think may be unfamiliar to the average user of the Index, it has been reworded or omitted to give a clearer picture of the contents of the article.

The contents of general indexes have been broadened in recent years, and the number of specialized indexes has increased. The number of both has grown so large that the researcher must learn—by examining various indexes and through experience—which are most valuable to him.

Abstracts Publications

Several journals abstract as well as index articles. Abstracts journals serve a dual purpose: they index current literature in a given field and they digest important articles and books. Abstracts publications vary in length and quality. They may cover semipopular as well as highly technical and specialized subjects. Abstracts of periodical literature are prepared by the authors in some cases and by professional abstracters in others.

Good abstracts provide an objective summary of articles without critical or editorial evaluation (in this regard they differ from book reviews). They indicate the scope of the article, the thesis or point of view of the author, his sources and new interpretations of old facts or other contributions to scholarship. Abstracts may be a sufficient source of information and, in any case, they serve as a guide to material that should be studied in its entirety. Abstracts omit the documentation and bibliographies found in the original works.

Users of abstracts publications will find subject and author indexes, and cumulative indexes when they are provided, useful in locating material. Categorical cross-references are also helpful. The editors of abstracts publications are usually careful to ensure that the abstracts submitted by contributors represent, accurately and completely, the content and purpose of the original articles, and their indexes usually reflect the care and accuracy of their publications. However, the user should check the original article before he uses an abstract reference to make an important point. Abstracters, no matter how competent and accurate, are limited because their comments must be brief and selective.

The careful researcher will use abstracts as a guide to periodical literature, but will always refer to the original articles—which are almost always available in microfilm, reprint, or in the serial collection of a library.

CHAPTER 1.

GENERAL INDEXES

Many periodicals of general, rather than specialized coverage contain facts and ideas useful in the study of international relations and recent history. Nonspecialized magazines frequently publish factual information and editorial comment useful in presenting researchers a well-balanced view of world events. Much of this material is not duplicated elsewhere, and much is of special value to the researcher.

For a complete list of index periodicals see Ulrich's *International Periodicals Directory*, 11th edition, Eileen C. Graves, ed. (580). The section on "General Bibliography" (Ulrich's, Vol. II, pp. 647—654) refers to other sections such as "Agriculture" or "Labor and Industrial Relations." The section on "Ceased Publications" (pp. 941—945) contains information on periodicals which have stopped publication since Ulrich's previous edition. In special cases it may be necessary to consult earlier editions of Ulrich's for information on periodicals which have not been in print for some time. Appendix 2, "New and Ceased Publications" refers to information on current changes in publications.

1. *Nineteenth Century Readers' Guide to Periodical Literature. 1890—99.* with supplementary indexing, 1900—22. New York: H. W. Wilson Co., 1944. 2 vols.

Indexes 51 periodicals of general interest, 14 of them beyond 1899 until they were included in other Wilson indexes. "Some are covered by Poole, but the Wilson indexing is more thorough; many anonymous articles are identified" (A. J. Walford, *Guide to Reference Materials* (602), p. 47) thus revealing the early work of many subsequently famous writers and illustrators.

2. *Poole's Index to Periodical Literature. 1802—1881,* revised edition, Boston: Houghton, 1891. 2 vols. Supplements: 1882—1908, 5 vols.

This "pioneer index" covers some 470 American and English periodicals. Subject and title index; no author entries. See Walford, *Guide*(602), p. 48, for additional information.

3. READERS' GUIDE TO PERIODICAL LITERATURE. 1900 —. SM; M (July—Aug.); cums. Q, A (B prior to 1966). $25.00. H. W. Wilson Co., 950 University Ave., Bronx, N. Y. 10452.

Currently indexes approximately 130 U. S. publications—primarily general and nontechnical—selected for their usefulness in reference work. Selections represent all important subject areas. Author, subject, and title index; illustrations, maps, portraits, and bibliographies are noted. Book reviews until 1904. Specific subject headings, subheadings and cross-references are used throughout. In 1907 most references to specialized scholarly publications were transferred to the *International Index to Periodicals* (37) which was succeeded, in 1965, by the *Social Sciences & Humanities Index* (43).

4. SUBJECT INDEX TO PERIODICALS. 1915—61. Q.

Formerly appeared as the *Athenaeum Subject Index* (1915—18). Not published 1923—25. Indexes 400 British periodicals, most nonspecialized. Includes some American and Commonwealth journals. Superseded by special subject indexes, including the *British Humanities Index* (27).

5. VERTICAL FILE INDEX: A Subject and Title Index to Selected Pamphlet Material. 1932 —. M (Sept.—July); A cum. discontinued 1965. $8.00. H. W. Wilson Co., 950 University Ave., Bronx, N. Y. 10452.

Published as *Vertical File Service Catalog*, 1932—54. According to the publisher the list includes "current, available pamphlets, booklets, leaflets, and mimeographed material arranged alphabetically by subject, with titles, paging, publishers, publication dates, descriptive notes, and prices or conditions under which they may be obtained." Lists free pamphlets. Title index. Provides helpful references to material not listed elsewhere.

Foreign embassies in Washington, D. C., can be addressed for information published by their respective governments. Books, pamphlets, and periodical publications are usually free. Their value for research ranges from nil (except for the study of propaganda) to very good. Many slanted foreign government publications are useful because they indicate what views the respective governments wish to propagate and what they are trying to cover up by silence.

6. WISSENSCHAFTLICHER LITERATURANZEIGER. 1962 —. BM. DM 5.10. Verlag Rombach & Co., 78 Freiburg, Rosastrasse 9, Germany.

Formerly *Neuer Literatur Anzeiger.* Devoted exclusively to reviews of German books and foreign books in German translation in all fields including history and politics, economics, law, political science, and psychology. Covers reference works and atlases.

CHAPTER 2.

SPECIALIZED INDEXES

Section A. Bibliography

7. BIBLIOGRAPHIC INDEX: A Cumulative Bibliography of Bibliographies. 1938 —. SA; A and 3-yr. cums. Sold on service basis. H. W. Wilson Co., 950 University Ave., Bronx, N. Y. 10452.

Indexes by subject current bibliographies published separately as books, parts of books, pamphlets, and articles, both in English and foreign languages. Also indexes bibliographical lists of 40 or more items. Covers 1,600 American and selected foreign periodicals. Includes references to new editions and supplements.

When a bibliography covers a wider field than is indicated by the title, the wider field is indicated by the subject heading under which the bibliography is entered.

This publication informs the student about bibliographies published on given subjects. Coverage is sufficient for some topics and serves as an introduction to fields which should be researched in specialized subject matter indexes.

8. BIBLIOGRAPHY, DOCUMENTATION, TERMINOLOGY. 1961 —. BM. Free. UNESCO, Department of Documentation, Libraries and Archives, Place de Fontenoy, 75 Paris (7e), France.

Worldwide reports on new publications and developments. This publication supplements R. L. Collison, *Bibliographical Services Throughout the World* (608).

9. BULLETIN OF BIBLIOGRAPHY AND MAGAZINE NOTES (see 1262). Includes bibliographies in all fields, predominantly in literature.

Section B. Biography

10. BIOGRAPHY INDEX: A Quarterly Index to Biographical Material in Books and Magazines. 1946 —. Q; A and 3-yr. cums. $20.00. H. W. Wilson Co., 950 University Ave., Bronx, N. Y. 10452.

References to biographical material in 1,500 periodicals indexed in other Wilson indexes, current works of collective biography, books containing incidental biographical material, works of individual biography and autobiography (all in English), and selected obituaries of national and international interest published in the *New York Times*. Refers to living and deceased persons of current or historical importance. Bibliographies and portraits are indicated when they appear in the indexed material. All listed persons are Americans unless otherwise noted. Indexed by names and by professions or occupations.

Section C. Book Reviews

11. BOOK REVIEW DIGEST. 1905 −. M (except Feb. and July); A cum. Sold on service basis. H. W. Wilson Co., 950 University Ave., Bronx, N. Y. 10452.
Index of selected book reviews in 75 American and English periodicals, mostly of a general character. Brief quotations from some reviews, reference to others.

12. BOOK REVIEW INDEX. 1965 −. M; Q, A cums. $24.00. Gale Research Co., Book Tower, Detroit, Mich. 48226.
Index to reviews published in over 200 general, specialized, and scholarly periodicals, including some Canadian and English publications and such newspapers and review publications as the *Christian Science Monitor, Guardian, New York Review of Books, New York Times, London Times Literary Supplement,* and in the now defunct *New York Herald Tribune.* The name of the reviewer is listed if the review is signed. Reference to 105,000 reviews and 51,000 titles in 1966. Citations of new reviews appear within an average of five weeks following publication.

13. INDEX TO BOOK REVIEWS IN THE HUMANITIES. 1960 −. A (Q to 1963). Phillip Thomson, Box 606, Detroit, Mich. 48206.
The term humanities as used here includes the social sciences. Indexes about 700 periodicals primarily in English. Several thousand book titles covered in each issue. Cumulative index beginning with Vol. 2.

Section D. Indexes to Individual Periodicals

14. LIFE. 1936 −. SA. Time, Inc., Rockefeller Center, New York, N. Y. 10020.
Indexes subjects, authors, titles of articles, and pictures.

15. *The Nation. Volumes 1–105, New York, 1865–1917, Index to Titles and Contributors.* New York: New York Public Library, 1951, 1953.
Vol. I: Index of Titles. Vol. II: Index of Contributors.

16. NATIONAL GEOGRAPHIC MAGAZINE. 1889 −. A; A cums. National Geographic Society, 17th and M Sts., N.W., Washington, D. C. 20036.
Subject, author, and title indexes. Separate index to maps.

17. NEWSWEEK. 1933 −. SA. Newsweek, Inc., 444 Madison Ave., New York, N. Y. 10022.
Subject index.

18. TIME. 1923 −. SA. Time, Inc., 540 N. Michigan Ave., Chicago, Ill. 60611.
Subject index.

19. U. S. NEWS AND WORLD REPORT. 1933 –. SA. U. S. News and World Report, Inc., 2300 N St., N.W., Washington, D. C. 20007.
Subject, author, and title index.

Section E.   Miscellaneous Subjects

The study of contemporary international relations ranges as wide topically as it does geographically. International relations studies branch out in new and often unexpected ways into old subject fields which traditionally were considered apart and separate from world affairs. Consequently, many important contributions are found through indexes to specialized non-social science publications dealing with agriculture, art, business, education, engineering, military affairs, religion, and the sciences.

20. AGRICULTURAL INDEX. 1916–64. M. Sold on service basis. H. W. Wilson Co., 950 University Ave., Bronx, N. Y. 10452.

21. AIR UNIVERSITY LIBRARY INDEX TO MILITARY PERIODICALS. 1949 –. A and 3-yr. cums. Free on exchange basis. Air University Library, Maxwell Air Force Base, Ala. 36112.
Formerly *Air University Periodical Index* (1949–62). "A subject index to significant articles, news items and editorials appearing in 69 English language military and aeronautical periodicals not indexed in readily available commercial indexing services" (editorial statement). Entries under International Cooperation, International Law, International Politics, and International Relations. Cross-references to international aspects of aviation, nuclear power, and space. Subdivisions under names of countries.

22. AMERICAN BEHAVIORAL SCIENTIST. 1957 –. M (Sept.–June). $9.00. The American Behavioral Scientist, Sage Publications, Inc., 275 Beverly Drive, Beverly Hills, Calif. 90212.
Includes *New Studies* (38) which provides information on recent publications in the social and behavioral sciences.

23. APPLIED SCIENCE AND TECHNOLOGY INDEX. 1958 –. M. Sold on service basis. H. W. Wilson Co., 950 University Ave., Bronx, N. Y. 10452.
Formerly the *Industrial Arts Index* (32).

24. BIBLIOGRAPHY OF AGRICULTURE. 1942 –. M. Free. Library, U. S. Department of Agriculture, Washington, D. C. 20250.

25. BIBLIOGRAPHIC SURVEY: The Negro in Print. 1965 –. BM. $7.25. Negro Bibliographic and Research Center, Inc., 117 R St., N. E., Washington, D. C. 20002.
According to the publisher the bibliographic reports are not confined to any particular year, yet the publication tries to keep up with current materials. Past materials are largely incorporated into special feature issues, such as "Focus on Negro History." Material on other minority groups is included.

26. BIOLOGICAL AND AGRICULTURAL INDEX. 1964 –. M. Sold on service basis. H. W. Wilson Co., 950 University Ave., Bronx, N. Y. 10452.

27. BRITISH HUMANITIES INDEX. New series 1954 –. Q (2 parts); A cum. 204s; 168s cum. only (special price to members). Library Association, Chaucer House, Malet Place, London W. C. 1, England.

28. BUSINESS PERIODICALS INDEX. 1958 –. M. Sold on service basis. H. W. Wilson Co., 950 University Ave., Bronx, N. Y. 10452.

29. GOVERNMENT-WIDE INDEX TO FEDERAL RESEARCH AND DEVELOPMENT REPORTS (GWI). 1965 –. BW. $22.00. Clearinghouse for Federal Scientific and Technological Information, Springfield, Va. 22151.

GWI indexes *USGRDR* (44). It serves as a guide to new unclassified U. S. Government-sponsored research and development reports in various technical fields. Issued concurrently with *USGRDR* which covers the behavioral and social sciences. Documents are indexed by subject, author, source, report number, and contract number.

Section 05 covers the behavioral and social sciences, including administration and management; documentation and information technology; economics, history, law, and political science; personnel selection, training, and evaluation; psychology (individual and group behavior); and sociology.

With few exceptions these reports are available to the public from the Clearinghouse.

30. *Index of Selected Publications of The Rand Corporation, 1946–1962.* Santa Monica, Calif.: Rand Corporation, 1962. Available without charge to government, academic, and other nonprofit organizations. Charge is made to commercial organizations.

Superseded by *Selected Rand Abstracts* (41).

31. INDEX TRANSLATIONUM: International Bibliography of Translations. 1932–40. Q. New series 1949 –. A. UNESCO, Place de Fontenoy, Paris (7e), France.

Old series published in Paris by the International Institute of Intellectual Cooperation.

Translations are listed by country in which published and by subject under ten major headings. Complete bibliographical information, including the original language, title, publisher, and date, when available. Both series have indexes to authors, publishers, and translators. Vol. 16 covers 81 languages, 69 countries, and 53,143 translations. Statistical summary by countries.

32. INDUSTRIAL ARTS INDEX. 1913–57. M. H. W. Wilson Co., 950 University Ave., Bronx, N. Y. 10452.

See *Applied Science and Technology Index* (23).

CHAPTER 3.

INDEXES AND ABSTRACTS IN THE SOCIAL SCIENCES

Section A. Social Sciences and Public Affairs: General

33. BIBLIOGRAPHIE DER SOZIALWISSENSCHAFTEN: Internationale Dokumentation der Buch- und Zeitschriftenliteratur des Gesamtgebiets der Sozialwissenschaften. 1905 –. A (formerly M). Vandenhoeck and Ruprecht, Göttingen, Germany.

Annual author and subject indexes. Title varies (see Winchell, *Guide to Reference Books* (603), p. 344).

34. BIBLIOGRAPHIES OF SELECTED RAND PUBLICATIONS. Single copies available at no charge. Rand Corporation, Reports Department, 1700 Main St., Santa Monica, Calif. 90406.

(Note: "Papers" referred to below are abstracts.)

SB-1001 AFRICA. August 1967. Lists 1 report, 2 Rand memoranda, 11 papers.
SB-1002 COMMUNIST CHINA. November 1967. Lists 3 books, 21 Rand memoranda, 50 papers.
SB-1006 SOVIET AGRICULTURE. September 1966. Lists 8 Rand memoranda, 2 papers.
SB-1012 FOREIGN AID. December 1967. Lists 4 books, 11 reports, 15 Rand memoranda, 23 papers.
SB-1013 EAST-WEST TRADE. September 1966. Lists 12 Rand memoranda, 11 papers.
SB-1015 FOREIGN POLICY ISSUES. September 1966. Lists 2 books, 1 report, 11 Rand memoranda, 22 papers.
SB-1017 THE COUNTER-INSURGENCY BACKGROUND. September 1967. Lists 5 books.
SB-1018 LATIN AMERICA. November 1967. Lists 1 book, 15 Rand memoranda, 10 papers.
SB-1022 SYSTEMS ANALYSIS. November 1967. Lists 247 publications selected from 1,500 Rand studies. Subject and author indexes.

See Index for other Rand publications.

35. BULLETIN ANALYTIQUE DE DOCUMENTATION POLITIQUE, ÉCO-NOMIQUE ET SOCIALE CONTEMPORAINE. 1946 –. 8 x y. 20 Fr ($4.80). Presses Universitaires de France, 108 bd. Saint-Germain, Paris (6e), France.

Publication of the Fondation Nationale des Sciences Politiques.

Selective index to some 1,200 French and other journals on economic, political, and social topics. Annual subject index.

Covers documents of national governments and international public organizations and 3,000 to 4,000 articles on political, economic, and social questions in over 1,000 French and other leading periodicals in various European languages. Brief annotations or abstracts. Annual list of periodicals indexed. Cross-references 700 to 800 items per year.

Replaced the *Bulletin Bibliographie de Documentation Internationale Contemporaine*. 1926–40.

36. DOCUMENTATION IN THE SOCIAL SCIENCES.

This is the series title for the *International Bibliography of the Social Sciences* (94), sponsored by UNESCO and prepared by the International Committee for Social Science Documentation. It consists of four international bibliographies: Economics, Political Science, Social and Cultural Anthropology, and Sociology listed below (57, 87, 46, 93).

The purpose of this program according to the foreword is "to supply each social science discipline with the basic bibliographical instruments essential to it."

The annual volumes list and classify all important published contributions from all countries, in all languages. They include books, articles from thousands of journals, and many reports of national governments and international public organizations published in duplicate form, with special attention given to fugitive official publications (i.e., publications of transient interest printed in limited quantity).

The materials are listed under hundreds of subject headings (in both English and French). Each volume contains author and subject indexes.

37. INTERNATIONAL INDEX TO PERIODICALS. A Guide to Periodical Literature in the Social Sciences and Humanities. 1907 –. Q (A cum.). Sold on service basis. H. W. Wilson Co., 950 University Ave., Bronx, N. Y. 10452.

This publication started as a supplement to the *Readers' Guide to Periodical Literature* (3), covering additional periodicals especially of a scholarly nature.

Indexes 163 American and British, plus some Canadian journals. Pre-1940 volumes cover a number of foreign language periodicals. Coverage of geography, history, labor, political science, and public opinion was increased after 1955. Author and subject index. Indexes book reviews from scholarly journals.

Superseded (1965) by the *Social Sciences and Humanities Index* (43).

38. NEW STUDIES: A Guide to Recent Publications in the Social and Behavioral Sciences. 1965 –. M (Sept.–June). $5.00. American Behavioral Scientist, Sage Publications, Inc., 275 Beverly Drive, Beverly Hills, Calif. 90212.

This publication is the monthly bibliographic section of the *American Behavioral Scientist* (22) published separately. It covers 360 journals and reviews, including almost 100 foreign publications in all of the social and behavioral sciences as well as books and pamphlets. Approximately 100 items are selected and annotated for each issue by the staff of the *ABS*.

The *ABS Guide to Recent Publications in the Social and Behavioral Sciences* (632), published in 1965, and the *Recent Publications in the Social and Behavioral Sciences* serve as cumulative indexes to this publication. The ABS Guide supplement is an annual publication.

39. PUBLIC AFFAIRS INFORMATION SERVICE: BULLETIN. 1915 –. W (Sept.–July); BW (Aug.); cums. 5 x y. Weekly and cumulated Bulletins including Annual $100.00; cumulated Bulletins including Annual $50.00; Annual Bulletin alone $25.00. Robert S. Wilson, 11 W. 40th St., New York, N. Y. 10018.

Known as *PAIS*, this selective but comprehensive index lists by subject the latest books, pamphlets, government publications, reports of public and private agencies, yearbooks, and other useful material, also many articles from over 1,000 periodicals, in the fields of economics, social conditions, public administration, and international relations. Author entries only for the most important authors. Excellent country entries and good cross-references.

Lists collective biographical works chiefly in its section "Directories-Biographical."

40. *Publications of the Social Science Department, The Rand Corporation, 1948–1967*. RM-3600-4. I.C.C. Graham and E. Breese, comps. Santa Monica, Calif.: Rand Corporation, 1967. Available free of charge to government agencies, academic and public libraries, and nonprofit organizations; others $15.00.

A bibliography of unclassified books, reports, Rand memoranda, papers, and translations issued by, or books published for the Social Sciences Department of the Rand Corporation since its inception in 1948. The list of books is separate. Deposit Libraries are listed. Items unavailable in Deposit Libraries and also out of print have not been included. A few superseded items have also been omitted.

41. SELECTED RAND ABSTRACTS. 1963 –. Q; A cums. Free to agencies of the government, academic and public libraries, and nonprofit organizations; $15.00 to others. Rand Corporation, Reports Department, 1700 Main St., Santa Monica, Calif. 90406.

Succeeds *Index of Selected Publications of the Rand Corporation, 1946–1962* (30).

A comprehensive index-guide for unclassified publications of the Rand Corporation, including studies on international affairs.

42. SOCIAL SCIENCE ABSTRACTS: A Comprehensive Abstracting and Indexing Journal of the World's Periodical Literature in the Social Sciences. 1929–33. 5 vols. Social Science Abstracts, Columbia University, New York, N. Y. 10027.

Published as a monthly journal under the auspices of the Social Sciences Research Council. Abstracts some 70,000 articles from more than 4,000 journals in various languages in the fields of human geography, cultural anthropology, history, economics, political science, sociology, and statistics. Annual author and subject indexes. Volume 5 is an author and subject index for the previous four volumes and includes an extensive list of periodicals in various social sciences.

43. SOCIAL SCIENCES & HUMANITIES INDEX. 1907 –. Q; A cums. Sold on service basis. H. W. Wilson Co., 950 University Ave., Bronx, N. Y. 10452.

Succeeds the *International Index to Periodicals* (37). The new title is more indicative of the coverage of the index.

Author and subject index to currently 209 periodicals in the social sciences and humanities, including publications in the fields of anthropology, area studies, economics, geography, history, political science, religion and theology, sociology, plus many periodicals of general scholarly interest.

44. U. S. GOVERNMENT RESEARCH AND DEVELOPMENT REPORTS (USGRDR). (U. S. Department of Commerce.) 1965 –. BW. $30.00. Clearinghouse for Federal Scientific and Technical Information, Springfield, Va. 22151.

Supersedes *Bibliography of Scientific and Technical Reports,* 1946–1954, and *U. S. Government Research Reports (USGRR),* 1955–1964.

Abstracts of unclassified reports from the Atomic Energy Commission, National Aeronautics and Space Administration, the U. S. Department of Defense, and other government agencies, resulting from both in-house and contract research. *USGRDR* announces all new government research and development reports released for sale to the public by the Clearinghouse. Each issue covers over 1,000 new documents. Document entries are arranged by subject matter under 22 subject headings. *USGRDR* covers the total research and development input to the Clearinghouse.

The format allows quick scanning of reports by title. Cross-references include title, price, and corporate author. An edge index locates specific subject fields, and where the accession (stock) number is known, a report locator list precedes the report.

USGRDR is indexed in *Government-Wide Index to Federal Research and Development Reports (GWI)* (29).

Section B. Anthropology

45. BIENNIAL REVIEW OF ANTHROPOLOGY. Bernard J. Siegel, ed. 1959 –. B. Stanford University Press, Stanford, Calif. 94305.

Describes and evaluates papers and monographs. International coverage. Includes bibliographies. Subject index.

46. INTERNATIONAL BIBLIOGRAPHY OF SOCIAL AND CULTURAL ANTHROPOLOGY. 1955–. A. Aldine Publishing Co., 320 W. Adams St., Chicago, Ill. 60606.

Indexes 3,500 to 5,000 items per year, arranged in 9 general categories.

Section C. Communications

47. PUBLIZISTIK-WISSENSCHAFTLICHER REFERATEDIENST. 1966 –. Q. (plus Supplement) DM 61. Westdeutscher Verlag, Opladen, Germany.
Edited by the Institut für Publizistik der Freien Universität Berlin.
Between 1,500 and 2,000 bibliographical references covering some 100 German and foreign journals and information services in the fields of public opinion, communications, etc. Author and subject indexes in each issue, cumulative annual indexes in the Supplement.

Section D. Conflict Resolution, Disarmament and Peace

48. ARMS CONTROL AND DISARMAMENT: A Quarterly Bibliography of Current Literature. 1965 –. Q. $2.00. Superintendent of Documents, Washington, D. C. 20402.
Prepared by the Arms Control and Disarmament Bibliography Section, General Reference and Bibliography Division, Reference Department, Library of Congress, through the support of the U. S. Arms Control and Disarmament Agency.
This bibliography comes close to being a general international relations inventory.
Abstracts and annotations of current literature in English, and beginning with Vol. 2, in the French, German, and Russian languages. Also abstracts and annotates current literature in all languages published in English translation. Sources include trade books, monographs, selected government publications of the United States and other countries, publications of national and international organizations and societies, and approximately 1,700 periodicals. Publications that do not lend themselves to abstracting, such as certain Government reports, schematic representations, and congressional hearings, are described in annotations. Articles in newspapers and newsmagazines are not covered except for highly pertinent items that attempt more than the reporting of day-to-day events.
Subject headings include The International Political Environment (general analyses of basic factors in world politics and foreign policies of states and international political organizations), The Strategic Environment (including modern war, modern weaponry, national security policies and military strategies of states and international political organizations), Consequences of National Defense Policies and War (general, political, military, economic, ethical and social, biological), Institutions and Means for the Maintenance of Peace (international law, international organizations, international peace and security forces and other processes, plans, and proposals), The Historical Background, General Analyses and Basic Approaches, and Specific Problems and Related Measures.
Author and subject indexes in each quarterly issue are both cumulated in the fourth number of each volume (Preface, p. iii).

49. PEACE RESEARCH ABSTRACTS. 1964 –. M. $60.00 to institutions, $30.00 to individuals. Canadian Peace Research Institute, Clarkson, Ontario, Canada.
Published with assistance from UNESCO and the Canadian National Commission for UNESCO, this is an official publication of the International Peace Research Association. Formerly *Peace Research Abstracts Journal.*
Abstracts of articles, pamphlets, and books on world affairs published worldwide since 1945. Includes some 9,000 references a year, under 360 classifications, from over 600 journals on both sides of the Iron Curtain. The periodical endeavors to abstract retroactively publications issued prior to its first issue (June 1964) while

publishing abstracts of current work. It also reprints abstracts published in a dozen other periodicals (mostly European). See list in the Annual Index.

Researchers should study "The Classification System of Peace Research Abstracts Journal" on p. 2 of the separate *Coding Manual.*

Monthly author index; subject index cumulated quarterly and annually.

Section E. Development and Technical Aid

50. TECHNICAL CO-OPERATION: A Monthly Bibliography. 1964 −. M. U. K. Ministry of Overseas Development Library, The Library, Eland House, Stag Place, Victoria, London, England.

This bibliography is issued as a result of one of the recommendations of the Bridges Committee (Report of the Committee on Training in Public Administration for Overseas Countries. H.M.S.O., 1963) which proposed the establishment of a documentation center on development administration overseas. Most of this bibliography is devoted to official (including unpublished) papers of the Commonwealth. Reports and bulletins submitted by foreign institutes and organizations concerned with technical aid to foreign countries are also listed. (Editorial statement, February 1966.) Information is provided on how these publications may be obtained.

There is also a *Supplement,* No. 1., 1965.

Section F. Economics

51. DOCUMENTATION ÉCONOMIQUE: Revue Bibliographique. 1934 −. BM. $11.00. Presses Universitaires de France, 108 bd. Saint-Germain, Paris (6e), France.

Prepared by the Institut National de la Statistique et des Etudes Économiques and the Association de Documentation Économique et Sociale, with aid from the Centre National de la Recherche Scientifique. Abstracts of articles in some 200 American, Dutch, English, French, German, Greek, Italian, Portuguese, Spanish, Swedish, and Russian periodicals; covers *inter alia,* bibliography and documentation, biography, statistical year books, demography, economic activities, and international relations. No index.

52. ECONOMIA INTERNAZIONALE. 1948 −. Q. $9.60. Istituto di Economia Internazionale, Via Garibaldi 4, Genoa, Italy.

One section of this learned journal consists of abstracts of important articles; another section has an extensive bibliography. Both are international in scope.

53. ECONOMIC ABSTRACTS: Semi-monthly Review of Abstracts on Economics, Finance, Trade and Industry, Management and Labour. (Library of the Economic Information Service, Ministry of Economic Affairs.) 1953 −. SM. f 30 ($8.35). Martinus Nijhoff, 9 Lange Voorhout, The Hague, Netherlands.

Text in Dutch, English, French and German; Dutch abstracts summarized in English.

54. *Economics Department Publications, 1948–1962: An Author Index of the Open Literature, with Abstracts.* RM-2800-2. H. Porch, comp. Santa Monica, Calif.: Rand Corporation, 1967. Available without charge to government agencies, academic and public libraries, and nonprofit institutions. Charge to others.

55. *Economics Department Publications, 1963–1966: An Author Index of the Open Literature, with Abstracts.* RM-2800-02 (Supplement). H. Porch, comp. Santa Monica, Calif.: Rand Corporation, 1967. Available without charge to government agencies, academic and public libraries, and nonprofit institutions. Charge to others.

56. *Index of Economic Journals.* (American Economic Association.) Homewood, Ill.: Irwin, 1961–1962. 5 vols.
English language articles in major economic periodicals, published between 1896 and 1959. Author index. Articles arranged by subject.

57. INTERNATIONAL BIBLIOGRAPHY OF ECONOMICS. Jean Viet, ed. 1952 –. A. Aldine Publishing Co., 320 W. Adams St., Chicago, Ill. 60606.
Prepared by the International Committee for Social Sciences Documentation.
Part of the UNESCO sponsored *Documentation in the Social Sciences* (36). Bibliography of books, articles, and government and international official reports (including mimeographed material). Categories include Economic Activity and International Economics, with sections on international economic cooperation and technical and financial assistance. Author and subject indexes.

58. JOURNAL OF ECONOMIC ABSTRACTS. 1963 –. A. Harvard University Press, 79 Garden St., Cambridge, Mass. 02138.
Published under the auspices of the American Economic Association. Lengthy abstracts from some 35 contributing journals.

59. UNIVERSITY OF MICHIGAN INDEX TO LABOR UNION PERIODICALS. 1960 –. M. $125.00. Bureau of Industrial Relations, Graduate School of Business Administration, University of Michigan, Ann Arbor, Mich. 48104.
A monthly subject index to materials from a selected list of 50 newspapers and journals published by major labor unions in the United States and Canada. Brief abstracts and numerous cross-references. Headings include Imports and Exports, International Affairs, International Labor Activities, National Defense, Natural Resources, and Population. References to labor movements in various countries.

60. WORLD AGRICULTURAL ECONOMICS AND RURAL SOCIOLOGY ABSTRACTS. 1959 –. Q. $22.50. Commonwealth Agricultural Bureaux, Farnham Royal, Bucks, England.
Published by the Commonwealth Agricultural Bureaux in cooperation with the International Association of Agricultural Economists and the International Association of Agricultural Librarians and Documentalists.
Each issue includes some 1,000 classified abstracts and author, subject, and geographical indexes. A List of Serial Publications is provided with annual supplements. Review articles from time to time.

Section G. Geography

61. BIBLIOGRAPHIE GÉOGRAPHIQUE INTERNATIONALE. 1891 –. A (Irr.). Centre National de la Recherche Scientifique, 13, Quai Anatole-France, Paris (7e), France.
The most comprehensive and important of the annual geographic bibliographies, covering all aspects of geography. Brief annotations. Author index.

Title varies slightly; the first 24 volumes (1891–1914) were issued as part of annual supplements to the *Annales de Géographie*.

62. GEOGRAPHICAL ABSTRACTS: Parts C and D. K. M. Clayton, ed. 1960 –. 6 x y. 54s. Geo Abstracts, University of East Anglia, University Village, Norwich, NOR 77 H, England.
Published in four parts: Part C is Economic Geography; Part D is Social Geography and Cartography (includes political geography and military geography). Abstracts from over 1,000 serials and many books. Over 6,000 abstracts in 1967. Worldwide coverage planned.

Section H. History

63. AMERICA: HISTORY AND LIFE. A Guide to Periodical Literature. Eric H. Boehm, ed. Q (3 nos. of abstracts and 1 index per year). Price based on service rate principle. Clio Press for the American Bibliographical Center, Riviera Campus, 2010 A.P.S., Santa Barbara, Calif. 93103.
Abstracts of articles on 1) the history of the United States and Canada, and 2) all aspects of current American and Canadian life, including international relations, law, foreign relations, peace, World Wars I and II, also general bibliography and other research aids. Some 600 U. S. and Canadian and 900 foreign periodicals, primarily in the social sciences and humanities, are surveyed, also *Festschriften*. See *Historical Abstracts* (67). From about 50,000 articles surveyed, published throughout the world, some 3,000 abstracts are prepared annually. The "cue" indexing system speeds search by using mnemonic, topical, geographic, and chronological data. The cues precede each abstract to supplement the usual type of classification. Examples of cues: IRL (International Relations and Law), FOR (Foreign Relations), NAT (Nationalism), and PAX (Peace, Peace Movements, Pacifism). (A list of cues with an explanation of main, secondary, and subordinate cues may be ordered free of charge.) Many authors are identified with their institutions. Cross-references are arranged alphabetically by cues. Subscribers to *America: History and Life* may utilize its Periodicals Information Service for data on periodicals and, at cost, reprints or photocopies of the original articles.

64. *Bibliographie zur Zeitgeschichte*.
A supplement to *Vierteljahrshefte für Zeitgeschichte* (221).

65. ANNUAL BULLETIN OF HISTORICAL LITERATURE. (Historical Association, London.) 1911 –. A. William Dawson, London, England.

66. Historical Association, London. *General Index*, vols. 1–12, 1911–1922. London: William Dawson, 1923. 68 pp. (U. S. distribution: Banner Press Publications, Box 20189, Birmingham, Ala. 35216.)

67. HISTORICAL ABSTRACTS: Bibliography of the World's Periodical Literature. Eric H. Boehm, ed. 1955 –. Q (3 nos. of abstracts and 1 index per year). Price based on service rate principle. Clio Press for the American Bibliographical Center, Riviera Campus, 2010 A.P.S., Santa Barbara, Calif. 93103.
Abstracts of the world's periodical literature (including yearbooks and some *Festschriften*), covering the period 1775–1945, in many languages, in the fields of political, diplomatic, economic, social, cultural, and intellectual history; methodology and

research methods; historiography; the philosophy and interpretation of history; as well as documents, bibliographical articles, and review articles (as distinct from book reviews). Articles on the period after 1945 are abstracted only if they furnish a pre-1945 historical background as an essential part of the article or if they present significant historical source material on the pre-1945 period. Covers over 1,300 periodicals, including "peripheral" journals which publish historical articles occasionally. Includes a section on bibliographical news. *List of Periodicals* abstracted is published separately. Annual author, biographical, and subject index. Cross-references. Beginning in Vol. 11 (1965): expanded subject and geographic index, showing all facets of articles with abbreviations (cues) plus chronological entries. Two cumulative indexes, Vols. 1–5 (1955–1959) and Vols. 6–10 (1960–1964).

68. DAS HISTORISCH-POLITISCHE BUCH: ein Wegweiser durch das Schrifttum. 1953 –. 10 x y. DM 18. Musterschmidt-Verlag, Postfach 421, Göttingen, Germany.
A journal of book reviews in history and political science. Index.

69. INTERNATIONAL BIBLIOGRAPHY OF HISTORICAL SCIENCES. 1926 –.
A. H. W. Wilson Co., 950 University Ave., Bronx, N. Y. 10452.
Edited for the International Committee of Historical Sciences.

70. JAHRESBIBLIOGRAPHIE DER BIBLIOTHEK FÜR ZEITGESCHICHTE/ WELTKRIEGSBÜCHEREI. 1961 –. A. Bernard & Graefe, Verlag für Wehrwesen, Stuttgart, Germany.
Superseded *Bücherschau der Weltkriegsbücherei*, 1921–1929.

Section I. International Relations

Note: For references to PEACE see CONFLICT RESOLUTION, DISARMAMENT AND PEACE

71. ARMS CONTROL AND DISARMAMENT (see 48).

72. BACKGROUND: Journal of the International Studies Association. 1962–1966. Q; A biblio. University of Southern California, Los Angeles, Calif. 90007.
The first issue each year (since 1963) includes a bibliography of some 2,000 selected, nonannotated books and articles published in English worldwide. Annual bibliographies are found in the following categories: 1) Bibliographies, Inventories, Surveys; 2) Textbooks and Readings; 3) Conceptual Schemes, Theory, Ideas; 4) The International System and World Affairs; 5) Institutions and Organizations of Foreign Policy-Making; 6) Foreign Policy and Diplomatic History; 7) United States Foreign Policy; 8) Peace and War: Research and Policy; 9) Crises-Conflict Areas; 10) International Organizations; 11) Law, International Law; 12) International Communication: Flow of the News, Opinion and Propaganda, Intelligence Functions; 13) Education in International Affairs; 14) Ideology; 15) Attitudes and Images: Factors and Relationships of Personality, Culture, Nationalism, and Race; 16) Integration and Community Formation: Political, Economic, and Social; 17) National Development and Foreign Aid: Political, Economic, and Social; 18) International Trade.
Successor to *Background on World Politics* (73); succeeded in turn by the *International Studies Quarterly* (255). See *Background* (243) for statement on journal contents.

73. BACKGROUND ON WORLD POLITICS. 1957–1962. Q. Center for Foreign Service Studies, Baylor University, Waco, Tex. 76706.

"Serving the generalists by condensing the specialists." Contains digests of articles from 205 American and foreign periodicals specializing in military, scientific, economic, political, and social developments (excludes conventional political science journals) relating to national policy-making processes, techniques of pursuing foreign policies, and the attitudes, traditions, and values of the world's peoples and their leaders.

Superseded by *Background: Journal of the International Studies Association* (243).

74. CUMULATIVE CHECKLIST. 1963 –. A. United Nations, Room 1059, New York, N. Y. 10017.

Replaces the monthly checklist of the *United Nations Document Index* (85).

75. CUMULATIVE INDEX. 1950 –. A. United Nations, Room 1059, New York, N. Y. 10017.

Replaces the monthly index of the *United Nations Document Index* (85).

From Vol. 1 (1950) to date, it consists of separately issued parts: *Part 1*, a consolidation of the 12 monthly indexes and *Part 2*, a consolidated list by symbol of all documents and publications issued by the United Nations (including the International Court of Justice) and received by the Dag Hammarskjold Library during the year. Indicates the languages in which publications were issued. Includes a consolidated list of mimeographed documents republished in the *Official Records* and other publications, a list of sales publications, a list of new document series symbols, and a list of libraries and United Nations Information Centres receiving United Nations material.

76. CURRENT ISSUES: A Selected Bibliography on Subjects of Concern to the United Nations. 1965 –. SM. United Nations, Room 1059, New York, N. Y. 10017.

This bibliography succeeds the *List of Selected Articles* (82) last published in September 1963. It is also prepared in the General Reference Section of the Dag Hammarskjold Library. The first issue includes citations to articles selected from periodicals received by the Library during the period August 1963 through September 1965, as well as to selected books and microfilms. The selection is confined to literature dealing with the work of the United Nations and its specialized agencies, and with subjects of current or recent concern to them. Even within these limits, the bibliography is not comprehensive. Publications of the United Nations and its specialized agencies are not covered by this bibliography.

No indexes.

Items are listed under the following general headings (plus numerous subheadings): General Introduction; International Organization; United Nations Charter; General; Peace-keeping Operations; Principal Organs (Relations with Other Organizations, U. N. Children's Fund, U. N. Conference on Trade and Development, U. N. High Commissioner for Refugees, U. N. Institute for Training and Research); Specialized Agencies; Non-Governmental Organizations; Economic Questions (Land Reform, Permanent Sovereignty over Natural Resources, Population Growth and Economic Development, Migration, Population Control); Legal Questions (including many international relations and law questions); Political and Security Questions; Scientific and Technological Questions; and Social and Humanitarian Questions.

77. EXTERNAL RESEARCH. 1952 –. SA. U. S. Department of State, Bureau of Intelligence and Research, External Research Staff, Washington, D. C. 20520.

Lists published and unpublished works, completed or in progress, by faculty and graduate students throughout the country.

The spring list covers studies currently in progress; the fall list covers recently completed studies. Separate issues for USSR and Eastern Europe; Asia; Western Europe, Great Britain, and Canada; Middle East; Africa; American Republics; International Affairs.

78. INTERCOM: An Information Service for Citizen Education and Activity in World Affairs. 1959 —. BM. $5.00. Foreign Policy Association, 345 E. 40th St., New York, N. Y. 10017.

A unique shortcut to information on world affairs. Regularly featured are New Books on World Affairs, Pamphlets and Paperbacks, and bibliographies on the special topic featured in a given issue, such as "U. S. in the UN," "Western Europe and the Atlantic Community," "Focus on Human Rights," and "Focus on Trade." Items range in depth from adult education for the general public to scholarly publications. Much material, such as study kits or reading guides, is not indexed or listed elsewhere. Free materials are listed. Brief Book reviews. *Intercom* selects the "most useful, significant, newsworthy materials, programs and information services from hundreds of sources—voluntary organizations, United Nations, U. S. and foreign governments, business firms, education and research institutions" (Publisher's note).

79. INTERNATIONAL INFORMATION SERVICE. 1963 —. Q. $10.00. Library of International Relations, 660 N. Wabash Ave., Chicago, Ill. 60611.

Formerly the *World in Focus* (1941—1951).

A selective annotated guide to documents (national governments and international organizations), books, and articles on contemporary political, economic, and social developments in all parts of the world including developing areas. Includes atlases, yearbooks, bibliographies, and directories. Covers a wide variety of American, foreign, and international organization publications. Cross-references and brief annotations. Strong bibliographic section. Geographic index. Addresses of periodicals cited.

80. INTERNATIONAL POLITICS: A Selective Monthly Bibliography. 1956 —. M. U. S. Department of State, Washington, D. C. 20520.

Some 300 to 400 selected articles, plus some monographs, demonstrating the relation of American foreign policy to the affairs of other countries. Most of the articles are in English.

81. INTERNATIONAL RELATIONS DIGEST OF PERIODICAL LITERATURE. 1950—1963. M. Bureau of International Relations, University of California, Berkeley, Calif. 94720.

82. LIST OF SELECTED ARTICLES. 1949—Sept. 1963. M. Dag Hammarskjold Library, United Nations, New York, N. Y. 10017.

References to articles only on the U. N., its specialized agencies, and topics currently before the General Assembly.

Nos. 1—9 were titled *Selected List of Periodical Articles in the United Nations Headquarters Library*.

Succeeded *Monthly List of Selected Articles* (84), originally a publication of the League of Nations and continued by the United Nations. Succeeded, in turn, by *Current Issues* (76).

83. MONTHLY LIST OF BOOKS CATALOGUED IN THE LIBRARY OF THE UNITED NATIONS. 1928 –. M. League of Nations, Geneva, Switzerland (1928-1945); United Nations, New York, N. Y. 10017 (1946–).

Selected books relating to questions studied by organs of the United Nations and formerly by the League of Nations. Some 3,000 to 4,000 items per year. Includes a section listing reference works. Full bibliographical details. Lists no League or U. N. publications. Bilingual (English and French). Annual index of authors and main entries.

Copies are also issued on thin paper, printed on one side, to be cut and mounted on cards to serve as indexes on special questions.

84. MONTHLY LIST OF SELECTED ARTICLES. M. League of Nations, Geneva, Switzerland (1929–1945); United Nations, New York, N. Y. 10017 (1949 –).

Current articles on political, legal, economic, financial, and social problems selected from 2,500 periodicals. Some 7,000 classified entries a year. International coverage. No annotations. No cumulations or annual indexes.

See the comparable monthly publication, *List of Selected Articles* (82), published by the United Nations Library in New York and its successor *Current Issues* (76).

85. UNITED NATIONS DOCUMENTS INDEX. 1950 –. M; A cums. United Nations, Room 1059, New York, N. Y. 10017.

Lists and indexes documents and publications of the United Nations, including the International Court of Justice, except restricted and internal papers and press releases. Volumes 1 to 13 (1950–1962) included documents and publications of specialized agencies which are no longer covered since Volume 14 (1963). Volumes 1 to 13 include an annual *Cumulated Index* and *Cumulated Checklist* issued separately. From Volume 14 the monthly issues were superseded and replaced by the separately issued *Cumulative Index* (75) and the *Cumulative Checklist* (74).

Section J. Political Science

86. *Cumulative Index to the American Political Science Review, Volumes 1–57: 1906–1963.* Kenneth Janda, ed. Evanston, Illinois: Northwestern University Press, 1964. xxvi, 225 pp.

Professor Janda has used and improved the IBM-developed KWIC (Key-Word-In-Context) index technique. It produces three types of output: an alphabetic listing of previously defined Keywords in the titles, a complete bibliography of titles alphabetized by senior authors, and an alphabetic cross-reference for authors (p. x).

Read the Introduction to effectively use Index.

See *American Political Science Review* (370).

87. INTERNATIONAL BIBLIOGRAPHY OF POLITICAL SCIENCE. 1952 –. A. Aldine Publishing Co., 320 W. Adams St., Chicago, Ill. 60606.

Prepared by the International Committee for Social Science Documentation in cooperation with the International Political Science Association. Extensive, but selective bibliography of articles, books, serials, monographs, *Festschriften,* government and international official documents (including mimeographed items) in many languages; 4,000 to 5,000 items per year. Covers 1,000 to 1,400 periodicals and other publications issued during a given year, with one to two year delay. Beginning with Vol. 4, listed items abstracted in *International Political Science Abstracts* (88) are indicated by "[Abstract No. . . .]." Political science is interpreted broadly to include many nonlegal publications, occasional references to book reviews of items of special importance or controversial interest. Meaningless titles are explained, for instance, "U.S.A. and Western Europe" is shown to be concerned with "Suez Crisis and American-European Relations."

Author and subject indexes; cross-references; list of abbreviations of periodicals covered.

88. INTERNATIONAL POLITICAL SCIENCE ABSTRACTS. 1950 –. Q. $7.70. Basil Blackwell, 4 Broad St., Oxford, England.

Prepared by the International Political Science Association in cooperation with the International Committee for Social Sciences Documentation and with the financial assistance of UNESCO.

Abstracts in English or French of articles in some 150 periodicals in political science and other social sciences, published in all parts of the world, classified in six major categories: 1) Political Science; 2) Political Theory; 3) Government and Public Administration; 4) Governmental Process; 5) Public Opinion, Parties, Groups, and Elections; 6) International Relations; and 7) Area Studies. Subject index in each issue; cumulative subject and author indexes in issue No. 4 of each volume; list of periodicals covered.

89. LITERATUR-VERZEICHNIS DER POLITISCHEN WISSENSCHAFTEN. Hermann Berber, ed. 1952 –. A. Isar Verlag, Munich, Germany.

Published for the Hochschule für Politische Wissenschaften, Munich.

Covers German Federal Republic publications primarily but includes some from the German Democratic Republic. References are carefully annotated.

90. NEUE POLITISCHE LITERATUR: Berichte über das internationale Schrifttum. 1956 –. Q. DM 30. Europäische Verlagsanstalt, Elbestrasse 46, 6 Frankfurt am Main, Germany.

Published 1952–1955 as *Politische Literatur.*

This journal is limited to book reviews and review articles in political science and recent history, concentrating on German, French, and English publications. Annual index. Bibliographies discontinued in 1965.

Section K. Population

91. POPULATION INDEX. 1935 –. Q. $10.00. Office of Population Research, Woodrow Wilson School of Public and International Affairs, Princeton University, 5 Ivy Lane, Princeton, N. J. 08540.

Aside from a few articles in each issue in section "Current Items," this journal consists of a topically arranged and annotated bibliography of demographic articles, bibliographies, bulletins, reports, books, and the like, on a worldwide and interdisciplinary basis. According to the editors, "Selection is on the basis of intrinsic merit, current interest, and paucity or richness of the literature for the various areas and problems. Coverage is less complete in peripheral fields, selection less rigid in under-developed areas." Includes lists of new periodicals, official statistical publications, and charts. Geographic and author indexes. Annual cumulative index.

Section L. Sociology

92. CURRENT SOCIOLOGY. (International Sociological Association.) 1958 –.
3 x y. 35s. Basil Blackwell, 4 Broad St., Oxford, England.
Formerly published in Paris by UNESCO (1952–57).
The first four volumes of the UNESCO periodical published a classified world
bibliography and trend reports on special subjects in alternate issues. In 1955 the
bibliography function was turned over to a separate publication, *International Bibliography of Sociology* (93). *Current Sociology* "now contains an analysis of trends
shown by published research on some aspect of sociology, supported by a lengthy
(300–1,000 items) annotated bibliography" (White, *Sources,* p. 210). Covers subjects such as rural sociology in Southeast Asia, political sociology, and social factors
in economic growth.

93. INTERNATIONAL BIBLIOGRAPHY OF SOCIOLOGY. 1951 –. A. Aldine
Publishing Co., 320 W. Adams St., Chicago, Ill. 60606.
Includes some 300 to 500 items a year. Classified in detail. Worldwide coverage
includes documents of governments and international organizations.
Vols. 1–4, 1951–54, were published in *Current Sociology* (92).
Formerly published in Paris by UNESCO (1952–1961).

94. INTERNATIONAL BIBLIOGRAPHY OF THE SOCIAL SCIENCES.
See *Documentation in the Social Sciences* (36).

95. SOCIOLOGICAL ABSTRACTS. 1952 –. 8 x y. $100.00 to institutions and
libraries. Separate categories are available to individuals at $5.00 per subject area.
List of subject categories free on request. Sociological Abstracts, 2315 Broadway,
New York, N. Y. 10024.
This periodical is published under the cosponsorship of the International Sociological Association, the Eastern Sociological Society, the American Sociological Association, and the Midwest Sociological Society.
There are 23 subject categories including: Methodology, Social Psychology, Political Interactions, Economic Development, Sociology of the Arts, Demography, and
Mass Phenomena. Abstracts articles from 110 sociological journals published in 18
languages and 400 other social science journals published worldwide.

Chapter 4

INDEXES AND ABSTRACTS IN FIELDS RELATED
TO THE SOCIAL SCIENCES

Section A. Education

96. ANNUAL EDUCATIONAL BIBLIOGRAPHY. 1955 –. A. International Bureau of Education, Geneva, Switzerland.
Annotated list of bibliographies.

97. EDUCATION ABSTRACTS. Vols. 1–16. 1949–65. Q (Irr.). UNESCO, Education Clearing House, Paris, France.

Published as *Fundamental Education Abstracts,* 1949–51. Devotes each issue to a particular educational topic. Bibliographies on education in various countries.

98. EDUCATION INDEX. 1929 –. M (Sept.–June); A cums. Sold on service basis. H. W. Wilson Co., 950 University Ave., Bronx, N. Y. 10452.

Indexes some 200 educational periodicals by subject. Includes proceedings, yearbooks, bulletins, and monographs published primarily in the United States but including some from Canada and Great Britain. Includes material on all phases of education. Lists publications indexed in each issue with bibliographical information.

Section B. Law and Related Subjects

See Miles O. Price and Harry Bitner, *Effective Legal Research* (693). Discusses types of legal periodicals and the use of indexes to legal periodicals.

99. INDEX TO FOREIGN LEGAL PERIODICALS AND COLLECTIONS OF ESSAYS. 1960 –. Q (3 issues plus A cum.); 3-yr. cum. William D. Murphy, 2900 Prudential Plaza, Chicago, Ill. 60601.

This is the only index to the legal periodical literature of the world outside the Common Law Sphere. Published under the direction of the Committee on Foreign Law Indexing of the American Association of Law Libraries. Articles from more than 300 legal periodicals and essay collections are indexed according to subject, author, country, and geographic names. Book reviews are also indexed.

References to foreign and international law as well as to international organizations, including topics related to common markets, social reforms in Latin America, and the evolution of legal life in developing nations. Many foreign language articles have summaries in English. A Special Union List of indexed periodicals, including photocopy and interlibrary loan facilities is available.

The bound volumes are entitled *Index to Foreign Legal Periodicals.*

100. *Index to Legal Periodical Literature,* Los Angeles: Parker and Baird, 1939. 6 vols.

Covers American, English, Canadian, and British colonial legal periodicals, from 1791 to 1932. Subject and brief author indexes in each volume.

According to Price and Bitner, *Effective Legal Research* (p. 276), the first three volumes (1791–1908) are indispensable. Since 1908 the *Index to Legal Periodicals* (101) is more useful, considerably more inclusive in its periodical coverage, and better kept up-to-date.

101. INDEX TO LEGAL PERIODICALS. 1908 –. M (Oct.–Aug.); A cum.; 3-yr. cum. since 1926. Sold on service basis. H. W. Wilson Co., 950 University Ave., Bronx, N. Y. 10452.

Covers leading articles, notes, case comments, and book reviews in more than 275 English-language legal periodicals; also reports of bar associations and judicial councils. Each issue includes a subject and author index, table of cases, and (since 1940) a book review index. Articles are chosen for listing by a committee of the American Association of Law Libraries, which also establishes the policies for indexing.

Note: Several legal journals have issued cumulative indexes covering their own respective periodical: *Columbia Law Review* (1–10); *Harvard Law Review* (1–40);

Michigan Law Review (1—10); and *Yale Law Journal* (1—38). According to Price and Bitner, *Effective Legal Research* (p. 277), the separate indexes of law reviews provide considerably closer indexing than the *Index to Legal Periodicals.*

For articles published prior to the publication of this index see the *Index to Legal Periodical Literature* (100) which covers the period 1791—1932.

102. INDEX TO PERIODICAL ARTICLES RELATED TO LAW. 1959 —. Q. $7.50. Stanford University, Law Library, Stanford, Calif. 94305.

Index to articles related to law and its effect on agriculture, business, education, medicine, and other vital subjects, including international affairs, selected from general and scholarly (rather than legal) journals and magazines throughout the world. All are in English except for one French-Canadian periodical. The editors state that this index brings together articles scattered throughout more than fifteen other indexes, plus some that are not included in any other indexing service. All articles listed in either the *Index to Legal Periodicals* (101) or the *Index to Foreign Legal Periodicals* (99) are excluded.

List of journals indexed. Author index.

Section C. Psychology

103. PSYCHOLOGICAL ABSTRACTS: Nonevaluative Summaries of the World's Literature in Psychology and Related Disciplines. 1927 —. M. $30.00. American Psychological Association, Inc., 1200 17th St., N. W., Washington, D. C. 20036.

Covers some 800 journals in English and foreign languages; also books, monographs, and other nonserial documents. Students of international relations will be especially interested in the subject headings, General and Social Psychology and Cultural and Social Processes but will want to check others. See also section on Bibliographies and Reviews.

Monthly author and subject indexes, plus annual cumulative indexes and a list of journals abstracted. For other abstracts and index publications in psychology see White, *Sources of Information in the Social Sciences,* (643), pp. 298—304. See also *Psychological Index* (104).

104. PSYCHOLOGICAL INDEX, 1894—1935: An Annual Bibliography of the Literature of Psychology and Cognate Subjects. Psychological Review Corporation, Princeton, N. J. 08540. 42 vols.

According to White, *Sources* (643) pp. 298—304, this index was begun as a supplement to the *Psychological Review,* continuing Benjamin Rand's *Bibliography of Philosophy, Psychology and Cognate Subjects.* Extensive coverage of the literature of psychology and allied fields, both books and articles, in many languages. Classified subject list and author index. See Volume 30 for a list of some 350 indexed periodicals.

Discontinued after 1935. See *Psychological Abstracts* (103) for subsequent years after 1927.

Section D. Religious Affairs, Ecumenics

105. CATHOLIC PERIODICAL INDEX. 1930 —. Q; B cum. Sold on service basis. Catholic Library Association. 461 W. Lancaster Ave., Haverford, Pa. 19041.

Cumulative author and subject index to 130 selected Catholic periodicals from the

United States, Australia, Canada, several European countries, and Vatican City; also selected articles from an additional 100 journals. Only a few of the 213 titles are indexed by other periodical indexes. While emphasizing theology and religion the publisher states that some 70 percent of the entries deal with other subject areas, including the social sciences and international relations. Only a few of the titles covered are indexed anywhere else.

106. RELIGIOUS AND THEOLOGICAL ABSTRACTS. 1958 −. Q. Religious and Theological Abstracts, Inc., Myerstown, Pa. 17067.

Bibliographic guide to some 150 scholarly periodicals in the fields of religion and theology, published in the United States and abroad, of various religious persuasions, including non-Christian. Brief abstracts prepared by Protestant, Roman Catholic, and Jewish scholars. More than 1,200 abstracts in each volume. Includes articles concerned with religious and theological aspects of international relations. Annual index. Cumulative index published in 1967.

CHAPTER 5

INDEXES AND ABSTRACTS FOR GEOGRAPHIC AREAS AND COUNTRIES

Section A. Africa

107. AFRICANA NEWSLETTER. 1963−64. SA. Hoover Institution on War, Revolution, and Peace, Stanford University, Stanford, Calif. 94305.

Includes bibliographic articles, lists of reprints, microfilms, and information on Africa Library collection.

Merged in 1965 with the *African Studies Bulletin* of the African Studies Association of the United States.

108. CURRENT BIBLIOGRAPHY ON AFRICAN AFFAIRS. 1962 −. M (BM to 1968). $20.00 per year to institutions; $15.00 to individuals. African Bibliographic Center, P. O. Box 13096, Washington, D. C. 20009.

Evaluation and reviews of current domestic and foreign publications, and announcements on forthcoming publications. They include documents published by governments and international organizations, scholarly books, and journal articles, as well as an author index.

Beginning in January 1968 these features are supplemented by original scholarly articles, bibliographic essays, and special bibliographies.

109. UNITED STATES AND CANADIAN PUBLICATIONS ON AFRICA, 1962 −. A. $3.00 each; 1964 $5.00. Peter Duignan, ed.; Liselotte Hofmann, comp. Hoover Institution on War, Revolution, and Peace, Stanford University, Stanford, Calif. 94305.

The first issue of this comprehensive bibliography covering 1960 was published by the African Section of the Library of Congress in 1962; the following issues are published by the Hoover Institution.

The preface for the 1963 edition states, "We have attempted to include all books, pamphlets, and articles, published in the United States and Canada during the calendar year 1963 on Africa south of the Sahara (Morocco, Algeria, Tunisia, Libya, and

Egypt are not covered). Editions of books from American branches of British publishing houses and foreign works republished by American publishers are also included. In general, we have omitted news articles, editorials, book reviews, or notes."

Classification by topics and countries (including anthropology, economics, history, politics, and the race question). Section on bibliographies includes both books and articles. Contains list of theses. Author index in each volume.

Section B. Asia

110. JOURNAL OF ASIAN STUDIES. (Association for Asian Studies, Inc.) 1941 —. 5 x y. $15.00 (including Bibliography). Department of History, Duke University, Durham, N. C. 27708.

Includes in each October issue the "Bibliography of Asian Studies" which covers 3,000 to 5,000 books and articles on Asia in general and individual Asian countries. Also covers economics, geography, history, politics, and other social sciences. Author index.

Formerly published under the title of *Far Eastern Quarterly*.

111. SOUTHERN ASIA SOCIAL SCIENCE BIBLIOGRAPHY; with annotations and abstracts. 1959–(beginning with No. 8). A. Research Centre on the Social Implications of Industrialization in Southern Asia, Calcutta, India. *Social Science Bibliography: India* (1952–1958) and *South Asia Social Science Abstracts* (1954–1958), both published by UNESCO, were merged in 1959 to form this new publication. The volume numbering system of the former was continued.

Index and abstracts of books, pamphlets, and articles published in English in India, Pakistan, Ceylon, Burma, Indonesia, Malaya, Singapore, the Philippines, and Thailand, and in French in Vietnam. Author and subject indexes.

Section C. Australia

112. AUSTRALIAN PUBLIC AFFAIRS INFORMATION SERVICE: A Subject Index to Current Literature. 1945 —. M (except Dec.); A cum. A. $8.88. National Library of Australia, Canberra, Australia.

A guide to current material on Australian political, economic, social, and cultural affairs. Covers Australian and overseas periodicals. Sections on Australian subjects from books published outside Australia which do not qualify for *Australian National Bibliography* are included; also some annual reports of government agencies and other important organizations.

Section D. Canada

113. CANADIAN INDEX TO PERIODICALS AND DOCUMENTARY FILMS. 1948–1964. M; cum., 1948–1959. Canadian Library Association, Ottawa, Canada. Author and subject indexes.

Succeeded old *Canadian Periodical Index, 1928–47* (115) and continued as the new Canadian Periodical Index, 1965 — (114).

114. CANADIAN PERIODICAL INDEX. 1965 –. M. Subscription rates upon request. Canadian Library Association, Ottawa, Canada.
Author and subject indexes. In 1967, covered 84 periodicals, including 18 in French. Book reviews listed.
Formerly *Canadian Index to Periodicals and Documentary Films* (113).

115. CANADIAN PERIODICAL INDEX. 1928–47. Public Libraries Branch, Ontario Department of Education, Toronto, Canada.
Covers some 30 to 40 Canadian journals.
Continued as the *Canadian Index to Periodicals and Documentary Films* (113).
Cumulated in 1966 by the Canadian Library Association, Ottawa, Canada, 3 vols.

Section E. Latin America

116. BRITISH BULLETIN OF PUBLICATIONS ON LATIN AMERICA, THE WEST INDIES, PORTUGAL AND SPAIN. 1949 –. SA. 12s 6d. Bailey Bros. & Swinfen Ltd., Warner House, 48 Upper Thames St., London E. C. 4, England.

117. DOORS TO LATIN AMERICA. (Inter-American Bibliographical and Library Association.) A. Curtis Wilgus, comp. 1954 –. Q. $2.00 to individuals; $3.00 to libraries. Inter-American Bibliographical and Library Association, P. O. Box 538, North Miami Beach, Fla. 33160.
List, with brief annotations, of books, monographs, and pamphlets recently published in the United States on various Latin-American subjects including international relations and related topics, both historical and current.

118. *Index to Latin American Periodical Literature, 1929–1960.* Boston: G. K. Hall & Co., 1962. 8 vols.
Prepared by the Columbus Memorial Library, Pan American Union. Some 250,000 entries of authors and subjects. Prior to 1951 only entries by subject were listed except for well-known authors. Covers about 3,000 periodical titles, mostly Latin-American, including national gazettes.
See *Index to Latin American Periodicals* (119) for years following 1960.

119. INDEX TO LATIN AMERICAN PERIODICALS. (Columbus Memorial Library, Pan American Union.) 1961 –. A. (Q to 1963). $16.00. The Scarecrow Press, Inc., 52 Liberty St., Metuchen, N. J. 08840.
Indexes more than 200 periodicals in the social sciences and humanities, concentrating on current material. Cross-references; no annotations. Most of the text is in Spanish, but English translations of Spanish subject headings are listed in each issue.
Most of the periodicals included here are also indexed in the *Index to Latin American Periodical Literature, 1929–1960* (118).
The number of entries has been increased since the publication became an annual in 1963.

120. INTER-AMERICAN REVIEW OF BIBLIOGRAPHY. 1951 –. Q. $3.00. Division of Philosophy and Letters, Pan American Union, 17th and Constitution Ave., N. W., Washington, D. C. 20006.
Official organ of the Inter-American Committee on Bibliography.
Selected list of some 2,000 items a year under 21 subject headings, including

General and Miscellaneous, Agriculture, Bibliography, Economics, Education, Geography, History, International Relations, Labor and Social Affairs, Law, Political Science, Reference Works, and Sociology. Includes documents, books, monographs, articles, and book reviews. Text in English, French, Portuguese, and Spanish. No annotations. Separate list of the publications of the Organization of American States and its specialized agencies. List of new journals in the last issue of every year. Annual author index. No cross-references.

Section F. New Zealand

121. INDEX TO NEW ZEALAND PERIODICALS, 1940–49. New Zealand Library Association, Wellington, New Zealand.
Function taken over by *Index to New Zealand Periodicals and Current National Bibliography of New Zealand Books and Pamphlets* (123).

122. INDEX TO NEW ZEALAND PERIODICALS AND CURRENT NATIONAL BIBLIOGRAPHY OF NEW ZEALAND BOOKS AND PAMPHLETS. 1950 –. A. New Zealand Library Association, Wellington, New Zealand.

123. INDEX TO NEW ZEALAND PERIODICALS AND CURRENT NATIONAL BIBLIOGRAPHY OF NEW ZEALAND BOOKS AND PAMPHLETS. 1940 –. A. $5.25. National Library Service, Private Bag, Wellington, New Zealand.
Annual cumulation.

Section G. Soviet Russia and Eastern Europe

124. AMERICAN BIBLIOGRAPHY OF RUSSIAN AND EAST EUROPEAN STUDIES. Fritz T. Epstein, ed. 1956 –. A. Indiana University Publications, Russian and East European series. Indiana University, Bloomington, Ind. 47401.
Formerly, the *American Bibliography of Slavic and East European Studies.*
Some 1,300 to 1,800 references per year to books and articles in the humanities and social sciences published in English outside of the Soviet Union and of the Eastern European countries.
Sections cover bibliography and sources, reference works, biographies, travel and description, anthropology and archaeology, geography, history, international relations, public affairs, law and government, economics, science, sociology, philosophy, ideology and religion, education, linguistics, literature and the arts, and folklore.
No annotations. Biobibliographical index and author index. List of journals covered. Includes book reviews and reprints, including paperbacks.
The preface of each volume should be consulted for minor editorial changes from year to year.

125. CURRENT DIGEST OF THE SOVIET PRESS. 1949 –. W. $200.00. Joint Committee on Slavic Studies, 351 Riverside Dr., New York, N. Y. 10025.
Each issue contains a complete listing of one week's content of *Pravda* and *Izvestia*, translations from these two dailies, and selected articles from approximately 60 other

Soviet publications. Texts of all major speeches and documents are included, either in full translation or condensed objectively by competent editors. Material is arranged by subject matter.

The translations are presented as documentary materials without elaboration or comment. They state the opinions and views of the original authors, not of the Joint Committee on Slavic Studies appointed by the American Council of Learned Societies and the Social Science Research Council. These materials are published in order that they may be of direct assistance to persons engaged in the research and interpretation of public affairs (Editorial statement).

Indexes are issued weekly and cumulated quarterly. They cover this periodical and the English-language journal *International Affairs* (Moscow), and include material of international content not principally involving the Soviet Union. Charts and illustrations.

126. SOVIET PERIODICAL ABSTRACTS: Asia, Africa, and Latin America. 1961 –. Q. $7.50. Slavic Languages Research Institute, Inc., 1 Seymour Place, White Plains, N. Y. 10605.

Formerly published as part of *Selective Soviet Annotated Bibliographies.*

This periodical is published to give an idea of the Soviet view of political, economic, and social developments in the countries of Asia, Africa, and Latin America. It selects and abstracts articles published in current Soviet periodicals. All titles in the field which appear in *Narody Azii i Afriki* (Peoples of Asia and Africa) are included; the choice from other journals is selective. The purpose of the abstracts is to present the view of the original authors and not that of the Slavic Languages Research Institute, Inc. Whenever translations of titles are available in the *Current Digest of the Soviet Press* (125) or from the Joint Publications Research Service at the time of publication they will be noted (Editorial statement, March 1966).

The journals included are from the fields of economics, the social sciences, law, and philosophy. (See appended list of journals used in each issue.) Both national and regional publications are covered. Only a few of them are available in English translation.

The material is classified as follows: General Spheres of Ideological Conflict—International Affairs and International Conferences; Socialism: The International Worker, Communist and Liberation Movement; Socialism: The Socialist Camp and the Soviet Union; Colonialism; The Developing States; Research and Publications. Asia. Africa. Latin America. Annual index.

127. SOVIET PERIODICAL ABSTRACTS: Soviet Society. 1961 –. Q. $7.50. Slavic Languages Research Institute, Inc., 1 Seymour Place, White Plains, N. Y. 10605.

Formerly published as part of *Selective Soviet Annotated Bibliographies.*

This periodical is published to facilitate a survey of current developments in Soviet society. It selects and abstracts articles published in current Soviet periodicals on matters concerning education, sociology, public administration, philosophy, and non-governmental institutions, with a view to giving a picture of the problems and issues discussed and the intensity and depth of discussion. Articles from the daily press are included only when they serve to point up the importance accorded to a subject. The purpose of the abstracts is to present the view of the original authors and not that of the Slavic Languages Research Institute, Inc. Whenever translations of titles listed are available in the *Current Digest of the Soviet Press* (125) or from the Joint Publications Research Service at the time of publication, they will be noted (Editorial statement, May 1966).

The journals included are from various disciplines and fields of study, and are both national and regional publications.

The material is classified as follows: Education–General; Elementary, Secondary, and Higher Education and Teacher Training; Sociology–General; Labor and the Rural Population; The Nationalities and Religion; Ideology; Public Administration–General; The Soviets; Non-Governmental Organizations–The Party; The Komsomol and Other Public Organizations.

List of journals and newspapers covered; glossary of terms; annual index.

PART II
PERIODICALS

Chapter 6.

PERIODICALS SPECIALIZING IN INTERNATIONAL RELATIONS AND RECENT HISTORY

Section A. Alliances

128. NATO LETTER. (NATO Information Service.) 1953 –. M. Free. Distribution Planning, Office of Media Services, U. S. Department of State, Washington, D. C. 20025.
Thorough documentation and bibliography relating to NATO and the North Atlantic Community.

129. SEATO RECORD. 1962 –. BM. Public Information Office, SEATO Headquarters, P. O. Box 517, Bangkok, Thailand.
Features significant events in Southeast Asia, as well as activities of the organization and its member nations. It reports statements which reflect attitudes on policies related to SEATO's role as a defensive organization (Editorial statement).

Section B. Atlantic Community

130. ATLANTIC COMMUNITY QUARTERLY. 1963 –. Q. $5.00. Atlantic Council of the United States, 1616 H. St., N. W., Washington, D. C. 20006.
Articles by scholars, high-ranking officials of U. S. and foreign governments and international organizations, Congressmen, and so forth, from both sides of the Atlantic, concerning the problems and prospects of developing a true community. Widely divergent opinions. Special features are: Letters from Readers, Source Material, and Atlantic Bibliography. (The latter covers books and magazine articles of note, briefly annotated.)

131. ATLANTIC STUDIES-ÉTUDES ATLANTIQUES. 1964 –. A. 25 Fr ($5.00). Atlantic Institute-Institut Atlantique, 24 Quai du 4-Septembre, Boulogne-sur-Seine, France.
Brief reports on political, economic, military, arms control, social, juridical, and cultural studies, planned or in progress, which are focused on the relations and coordination of policies among the Atlantic countries, on their relations with the developing nations, and on their relations with the socialist states.
List includes the pertinent projects of Atlantic-area international organizations, among them OECD, NATO, the Atlantic Treaty Association, the Council of Europe, the European Communities, the Western European Union, and the Atlantic Institute (Editorial statement).
Text and titles in English and French. Also brief abstracts of studies recently published, mentioned as ongoing research in earlier issues of *Atlantic Studies*. Published semiannually until the fall of 1968. Index by author and organization.

Section C. Commonwealth of Nations

132. COMMONWEALTH JOURNAL. 1961 –. BM. 2s per no. Commonwealth Journal, 13 Northumberland Ave., London W. C. 2, England.

Formerly published as *Royal Commonwealth Society Journal.* Includes book reviews. Index.

133. JOURNAL OF COMMONWEALTH POLITICAL STUDIES. 1961 –. SA. 30s. Leicester University Press, Leicester, England.
Includes book reviews.

134. ROUND TABLE: A Quarterly Review of Commonwealth and World Affairs. 1910 –. Q. 40s. Round Table Ltd., 166 Piccadilly, London W. 1, England.
Cumulative index: 1910–1935.

Section D. Conflict Resolution, Disarmament and Peace

135. ARMS CONTROL AND DISARMAMENT–ANNUAL REVIEW. D. G. Brennan, Hudson Institute, and Robert Maxwell, Pergamon Press, eds. 1967 –. A. $20.00. Hudson Institute, Croton-on-Hudson, N. Y. 10520; and Pergamon Press, Headington Hill Hall, Oxford, England, or 122 E. 55th St., New York, N. Y. 10022.
Published under the joint auspices of the Hudson Institute and Pergamon Press, with an international board of consulting editors.
Articles, reviews, factual material, and bibliographies in the field of arms control and disarmament, broadly understood to include political, technical, economic, legal, and theoretical aspects of arms control. Intended to inform the general interested public of recent developments and current thinking in the field, and to serve as a medium of communication among scholars and others actively concerned with the subject.
Some articles are written by senior government officials with substantial responsibilities for the arms-control policies of their respective countries, others by specialists in the field.
Editors provide opinion in the form of signed or unsigned editorials or special articles, or comments on articles in the *Review,* for the purpose of stimulating discussion and controversy.
Includes book reviews, lists of relevant papers and books, and factual material such as national military budgets and force levels (Publisher's statement).
Supersedes *Disarmament and Arms Control* (138).

136. C.A.I.P. NEWS. 1938 –. 10 x y. Free with membership; nonmembers $2.00. Catholic Association for International Peace, 1312 Massachusetts Ave., N. W., Washington, D. C. 20005.
Includes book reviews.

137. CURRENT THOUGHT ON WAR AND PEACE: A World Affairs Digest of Literature and Research in Progress on Current International Issues. L. Larry Leonard, ed. 1960 –. Irr. Wisconsin State University, Oshkosh, Wis. 54901.
Summaries of recent significant books, articles, government and U. N. documents, as well as reports and memoranda for limited circulation, and accounts of research in progress. Fields covered are political science, sociology, psychology, communications, anthropology, and economics.

138. DISARMAMENT AND ARMS CONTROL: An International Quarterly Journal to Facilitate the Exchange of Ideas on Disarmament and Arms Control within the

International Community. 1963—66. Pergamon Press, 122 E. 55th St., New York, N. Y. 10022.
Published under the direction of a combined American-English editorial board, this journal is directed toward providing analyses for specialists in the field.
Superseded by *Arms Control and Disarmament—Annual Review* (135).

139. DOKUMENTE: Zeitschrift für übernationale Zusammenarbeit. 1945 —. BM. DM 12($4.00). Gesellschaft für übernationale Zusammenarbeit e. V., Hohenstaufenring 11, 5 Cologne, Germany.
Emphasis on European thought and participation in international cooperation. Covers history, politics, and economics.

140. FELLOWSHIP. 1964 —. M. $4.00; $2.50 for students. Fellowship of Reconciliation, Box 271, Nyack, N. Y. 10960.
Contains views congenial to the philosophy of nonviolent and creative solutions to the problems of conflict and war. This has been the publication's general philosophy since it was founded. In its earlier years, when nonviolence and pacifism represented minority positions even more than today, *Fellowship* was more concerned with indoctrination and explication than it was with providing a means of dialogue between opposing views (Editorial statement).
Reviews books and films. Index.

141. FRIEDENS-WARTE: Blätter für internationale Verständigung und zwischenstaatliche Organisation. 1899 —. Irr. (4 nos. per vol.). 36 Sw Fr. Verlag für Recht und Gesellschaft A. G., Bündestrasse 15, Basel, Switzerland.
Includes book reviews. Index for each volume.

142. INTERPLAY OF EUROPEAN/AMERICAN AFFAIRS. 1967 —. M. $6.00 Interplay, Suite 1206, 200 W. 57th St., New York, N. Y. 10019.
An international journal of opinion which reports on issues that divide the two continents in the political, economic, military, and cultural spheres. Superlative contributors.

143. THE JOURNAL OF CONFLICT RESOLUTION: A Quarterly for Research Related to War and Peace. 1957 —. Q. $7.00 to individuals; $8.00 to institutions. Center for Research on Conflict Resolution, University of Michigan, Ann Arbor, Mich. 48104.
The Journal of Conflict Resolution is designed to stimulate and communicate systematic research and thinking on international processes, including the total international system, the interactions among governments and among nationals of different states, and the processes by which nations make and execute their foreign policies. It is our hope that theoretical and empirical efforts in this area will help in minimizing the use of violence in resolving international conflicts.
The editors believe that concepts, data, and methods from all of the social and behavioral sciences are needed for the understanding of problems in this field and for the development of a systematic body of knowledge. Moreover, we believe that relevant insights can be derived from analyses of interaction and conflict, not only directly at the international level, but also at other levels of social organization (Editorial statement).
Articles differ in disciplinary orientation, their level of analysis, their theoretical approach, and the type of research methods used. The wide variety of articles includes reports of empirical research (basic or applied), theoretical analyses, critical

reviews, as well as speculative and programmatic papers with a systematic focus (from the editor's Statement of Purpose). Book reviews.

144. JOURNAL OF PEACE RESEARCH. 1964 –. Q. $4.00. International Peace Research Institute, Universitetsforlaget, University of Oslo, Box 307, Blindern, Oslo 3, Norway.

Edited at the International Peace Research Institute, Oslo. Supported financially by The Aquinas Fund (New York), Institute for International Order (New York), Norwegian Research Council for Science and the Humanities, Swedish Council for Social Science Research, and Ministries of Education of Denmark and of Finland.

The *Journal* is interdisciplinary and international; the editorial board includes Kenneth Boulding and Robert North of the United States.

"The publication is devoted to peace research as research into the conditions for moving closer to 'general and complete peace,' or at least not drifting closer to 'general and complete war.' The two branches of peace research deal with 'negative peace which is the absence of violence, absence of war–and positive peace which is the integration of human society.' The *Journal* as such will never support any specific peace policy. Any article may, of course, in its conclusions favor one policy rather than another, but. . .no valid article is excluded on the basis of the kind of policy it may favor. . . . The articles will be original in the data and/or in the theories they present. They will usually have relevance to the present international situation. . . ." (Editorial statement).

Some articles are heavily documented. Short abstracts in English and in Russian.

145. PEACE RESEARCH REVIEW. 1967 –. 6 x y. $5.00. Canadian Peace Research Institute, Clarkson, Ontario, Canada.

An official publication of the International Peace Research Association.

Each issue contains a critical review in nonspecialized language of such topics as "Alternative Approaches to World Government" or "A History of Disarmament Negotiations." Extensive sections on references and bibliography.

146. PREVENT WORLD WAR III. 1943 –. SA. Free. Society for the Prevention of World War III, Inc., 24 W. 57th St., New York, N. Y. 10019.

Examination of changing conditions in world politics and economics and situations which might lead to a third world war.

147. RECONCILIATION; A Monthly Review of the Things of Peace. 1924 –. M. 14s 6d. Fellowship of Reconciliation. 9 Coombe Rd., New Malden, Surrey, England. Book reviews.

148. SANE WORLD. 1961 –. M. 15c. National Committee for a Sane Nuclear Policy, 17 E. 45th St., New York, N. Y. 10017.

149. SURVIVAL. 1959 –. M. 60s. Institute for Strategic Studies, 18 Adam St., London W.C. 2, England.

Reprints of articles in periodicals and statements of official policy concerning defense and disarmament problems published in various countries, including Soviet Russia and Red China. Worldwide coverage. Book reviews. Index.

150. WAR/PEACE REPORT: Fact and Opinion on Progress Toward a World of Law and Order. 1961 –. M. $5.00. War/Peace Report, 8 E. 36th St., New York, N. Y. 10016.

A liberal journal, with a wide range of contributors including Reinhold Niebuhr,

Hans Morgenthau, Hubert Humphrey, Wilfred Burchett, Herman Kahn, the late Grenville Clark, Soviet Ambassador Valerian Zorin, and Senators Joseph Clark and George McGovern.

Articles written from opposing points of view. Some issues on special topics. Book reviews. Semiannual index.

151. WORLD MARXIST REVIEW: Problems of Peace and Socialism. 1958 –. M. $3.50. Progress Books, 487 Adelaide St., West, Toronto 2b, Canada.

Material related to political science, economics, culture, and international affairs. Edited in Prague, with correspondents on all continents. Published in 33 countries in 25 languages.

Leading Communist contributors.

Section E. Developing Areas

152. DEVELOPMENT DIGEST. 1963 –. Q. Supt. of Documents, Washington, D. C. 20402.

A quarterly journal of excerpts, summaries, and reprints of current materials on economics and social development.

Prepared for the Agency for International Development, U. S. Department of State, by the National Planning Association, Washington, D. C.

153. INTERNATIONAL DEVELOPMENT REVIEW. 1959 –. Q. Free with membership; libraries only $7.50. Society for International Development, 1346 Connecticut Ave., N. W., Washington, D. C. 20036.

Interdisciplinary articles with divergent and occasionally contradictory views by both scholars and practitioners. Directed primarily toward people engaged in work connected with the economic and social development of less developed areas. The *Review* is action-oriented and deals with practical experience or applied theory; includes case histories. Also suggestions of new concepts or approaches (Editorial statement).

Reviews of books and films. Lists of bibliographies and directories. News of the development profession.

154. JOURNAL OF DEVELOPING AREAS. 1966 –. Q. $4.00. Western Illinois University, Macomb, Ill. 61455.

The *JDA'S* objective is to stimulate the descriptive, theoretical, and comparative study of regional development, past and present, in order to promote fuller understanding of man's relationship to the developmental process. Interdisciplinary approach. Some issues will be devoted to specific regions viewed from varied methodological perspectives. Articles invited from scholars in all countries. Most articles in English, some in French (Publisher's prepublication statement).

Bibliography of current periodical literature; News and Notes. Book reviews, occasional review articles. Annual index with October issue. Occasional letters and guest editorials.

155. JOURNAL OF DEVELOPMENT STUDIES: A Quarterly Journal Devoted to Economic, Political and Social Development. 1964 –. Q. 60s. Frank Cass & Co., 8–10 Woburn Wall, London W. C. 1, England.

Particularly concerned with the results of empirical investigations into the processes of economic and political change in developing countries. Includes articles on theoretical topics relevant to the field of development studies. An increasing proportion of articles analyze the efforts of developing countries to establish stable political systems, efficient governmental institutions, and satisfactory international relations. Contributions from analysts in governmental institutions as well as universities; a wide range of nationalities is represented by the contributors. Book reviews.

156. PEACE CORPS VOLUNTEER. 1961 —. M. Division of Volunteer Support, Peace Corps, Washington, D. C. 20525.

157. VENTURE: Socialism and the Developing World. 1949 —. M. 18s. Fabian Society Ltd., 11 Dartmouth St., London S. W. 1, England.
Succeeds *Empire,* founded 1938.
Previously concerned with Commonwealth affairs; now concerned with political and economic affairs of the underdeveloped countries.

Section F. Diplomatic and Counsular Activities

158. DEPARTMENT OF STATE NEWS LETTER. (U. S. Dept. of State.) 1962 —. M. $4.50. Supt. of Documents, Washington, D. C. 20402.
Information on departmental developments of interest to Department of State personnel.

159. DIPLOMATIST: The Review of the Diplomatic and Consular World. 1947 —. M. 84s including supplements. Diplomatist Publications Ltd., 40 Kensington Pl., London W. 8, England.
Social and professional news and articles for the Corps Diplomatique and Consulaire (global). Book reviews.

160. FOREIGN SERVICE JOURNAL. 1924 —. M. $6.00. American Foreign Service Association, 1742 G St., N. W., Washington, D. C. 20006.
Articles on life and work in the foreign service of the United States (not limited to Department of State activities) and on diplomacy and foreign policy. Not an official publication.

Section G. European Community and European Movement

161. COUNCIL OF EUROPE NEWS. 1950 —. BM. Free. Directorate of Information, Council of Europe, Strasbourg, France.

162. COURRIER EUROPÉEN. 1952 —. M. 4 Fr. Organisation Française du Mouvement Européen, 39 rue des Petits-Champs, Paris (1er), France.

163. EUROPÄISCHE BEGEGNUNG: Beiträge zum west-östlichen Gespräch. 1961 —. M. DM 30. Gesellschaft zur Förderung der west-östlichen Begegnung in Europa e. V., Königswörther Str. 2, Hannover, Germany.
Der Remter, West-Ost-Berichte, West-östliche Begegnug, and *Ostdeutsche Monatshefte* combined in 1961 into this single periodical. Features articles on East-West problems, literature, and arts. West-East dialogue. Book reviews.

164. EUROPEAN COMMUNITY. 1954 −. M. Free. European Community Information Service, Farragut Bldg., Washington, D. C. 20006.
Formerly *Bulletin from the European Community.*

165. EUROPEAN REVIEW: Incorporating European-Atlantic Review. 1960 −. Q. 10s. Birket Press Ltd., 64−78 Kingsway, London W. C. 2, England.
Covers politics, finance, technology, and the arts. International editorial board.

166. FORWARD IN EUROPE. 1959 −. BM. Available upon request. Directorate of Information, Council of Europe, Strasbourg, France.
Illustrated account of the work of the Council of Europe.

167. JOURNAL OF COMMON MARKET STUDIES. 1962 −. 4 x y. $5.88. Basil Blackwell, Broad St., Oxford, England.
Articles by specialists on international relations; law; and organization, economics, and politics on the European as well as other common markets. Worldwide range of topics and contributors. Book reviews. Register of current research.

168. MERKUR: Deutsche Zeitschrift für europäisches Denken. 1947 −. M. DM 32. Verlag Kiepenheuer & Witsch, Rondorfer Str. 5, Köln-Marienburg, Germany.
European dialogue.

169. OECD ECONOMIC OUTLOOK. SA. Organization for Economic Co-Operation and Development, Chateau de la Muette, 2 rue André Pascal, F 75 Paris 16e, France.
A periodic assessment of economic trends and prospects in OECD countries, and the developments which influence the course of the world economy (Editorial statement).

170. OECD OBSERVER. BM. Organization for Economic Co-Operation and Development, Chateau de la Muette, 2 rue André Pascal, F 75 Paris 16e, France.
Technical, scholarly articles.

Section H. Foreign Policy

171. AUSSENPOLITIK: Zeitschrift für internationale Fragen. 1950 −. M. DM 42. Deutsche Verlags-Anstalt GmbH., Neckarstr. 12, 7 Stuttgart, Germany.
Articles on foreign policies and world affairs. Chronicle of events. Bibliography.

172. CHRONIQUE DE POLITIQUE ÉTRANGÈRE. 1948 −. BM. 400 BF. Institut Royale des Relations Internationales, 88 av. de la Couronne, Brussels 5, Belgium.
Cumulative index.

173. CURRENT NOTES ON INTERNATIONAL AFFAIRS. 1936 −. M. Free to approved addresses. Department of External Affairs, Canberra, Australia.
Includes articles, notes, official statements, and parliamentary questions and answers. Index.

174. CURRENT REVIEW OF FOREIGN POLICY. 1964 −. Q. 50c per issue. League of Women Voters of the United States, 1200 17th St., N. W., Washington, D. C. 20036.
Published for study groups of the League of Women Voters.

175. DEPARTMENT OF STATE BULLETIN. 1939 –. W. U. S. Department of State, Washington, D. C. 20520.

Provides the public and interested agencies of the Government with (official) information on developments in the field of foreign relations and on the work of the Department of State and the Foreign Service. The *Bulletin* includes selected press releases on foreign policies issued by the White House and the Department; statements and addresses made by the President, the Secretary of State, and other officers of the Department; as well as special articles, some by nongovernmental authors, on various phases of international affairs and the functions of the Department. Information is included concerning treaties and international agreements to which the United States is or may become a party, and treaties of general international interest.

The *Bulletin* published sections titled: List of Congressional Documents Relating to Foreign Policy; List of Current Actions of the Department, in regard to international treaties and agreements; List of Publications of the Department; and Check List of Department of State Press Releases for the previous week. Weekly Index; annual cumulative index.

176. DEUTSCHE AUSSENPOLITIK. 1956 –. M. VEB Deutscher Verlag der Wissenschaften, Taubenstr. 10., 108 Berlin, German Democratic Republic.

Close to the Foreign Office of the German Democratic Republic. Includes texts of documents.

German Foreign Policy (182) is the English-language edition.

177. EXTERNAL AFFAIRS. (Information Division, Department of External Affairs.) 1948 –. M. $2.00. Queen's Printer, Ottawa, Canada.

Editions in English and French. Reference material on Canada's foreign relations and reports on the current activities of the department.

178. EXTERNAL AFFAIRS REVIEW. 1951 –. M. Free. Department of External Affairs, Wellington, New Zealand.

Texts of important statements on foreign policy by members of the government; a record of the principal events of international interest in the month; articles; a survey of the month's activity in the United Nations and its agencies; a calendar of forthcoming conferences; statements of major political importance by world leaders, and statements delivered by New Zealand representatives abroad.

179. FOREIGN POLICY BRIEFS. (U. S. Department of State.) BW. Supt. of Documents, Washington, D. C. 20402.

A concise summary in layman's language of policy and background information based on U. S. Government statements, reports, and documents compiled as an aid to wider public understanding of foreign policy developments, as seen by the Department of State.

180. FOREIGN POLICY BULLETIN. 1920–1960. (Foreign Policy Association.) BW. Kraus Reprint Corp., New York, 1967.

Analysis of current international events and foreign policy. Frequently presented two writers on opposite sides of a controversial issue. Short articles by specialists.

181. FOREIGN POLICY REPORTS. 1925–1950. (Foreign Policy Association.) Kraus Reprint Corp., New York, 1967.

Research studies related to foreign policy carried out during these years.

182. GERMAN FOREIGN POLICY. 1962 –. BM. $4.00. VEB Deutscher Verlag der Wissenschaften, Taubenstr. 10, 108 Berlin, German Democratic Republic.
This is the English-language edition of *Deutsche Aussenpolitik* (176).

183. INTERNATIONAL AFFAIRS. A Monthly Journal of Political Analysis. 1955 –. M. $3.50. All-Union Society "Znaniye," 14 Gorokhovsky Pereulok, Moscow K-64, USSR.
Articles on international affairs. Sections include Our Guest Commentator, Ideology and Foreign Policy, Background Facts, International Commentary, Reviews, Facts and Figures, and Documents.
Originally published in Russian, editions translated into English and French are also available.

184. MIZAN: USSR-China-Africa-Asia. 1959 –. 6 x y. 60s. Also MIZAN SUPPLE-MENT A: Middle East and Africa (Soviet and Chinese Press Reports) and MIZAN SUPPLEMENT B: South-East Asia (Soviet and Chinese Press Reports). 6 x y. 42s each. Central Asian Research Center, 66A King's Rd., London S.W. 3, England. (International Publications, 303 Park Ave., S., New York, N. Y. 10010, agents for subscribers in the United States only).
Aims at providing a balanced view of the policies of the Soviet Union and China toward the developing countries, and in particular the relations of these powers with the countries of Africa, the Middle East, and Southeast Asia.
Published by the Central Asian Research Center in association with St. Antony's College (Oxford) Soviet Affairs Study Group.
Soviet writing on these areas, as a primary source for Soviet views and policies is constantly kept under review (Editorial statement).

Section I. Geography

185. ECONOMIC GEOGRAPHY. 1925 –. Q. $9.00. Clark University, Worcester, Mass. 01610.
This is the leading English-language journal in the field. Index (Vols. 1–25) covers the years 1925–1949. Book reviews.

186. FOCUS. 1950 –. M. (Sept.–June). $2.00. American Geographical Society, Broadway at 156th St., New York, N. Y. 10032.
Each issue contains a brief geographic analysis of a country, region, or topic by a specialist, emphasizing historical influences and the interaction of physical, economic, and social factors. Maps. Short bibliographies.

187. GEOGRAPHICAL JOURNAL. 1893 –. Q. 75s. Royal Geographical Society, 1 Kensington Gore, London S. W. 7, England.
Book reviews. Cumulative index every 20 years.

188. GEOGRAPHICAL REVIEW. 1916 –. Q. $9.50. American Geographical Society, Broadway and 156th St., New York, N. Y. 10032.
Index. Cumulative index every 10 years.

189. INSTITUTE OF BRITISH GEOGRAPHERS. PUBLICATIONS. B. H. Farmer, ed. 1935 –. SA. 50s. London: George Philip and Son Ltd., Victoria Rd., Willesden, London N. W. 10, England.

Papers by academic geographers presented at annual meetings, other scholarly papers, and occasional research monographs published as separate numbers.
Index to Vols. 1–31 (1935–1962) is included in Vol. 31.

190. NATIONAL GEOGRAPHIC MAGAZINE. 1888 –. M. Free with membership; $8.00 to nonmembers. National Geographic Society, 17th and M Sts., N.W., Washington, D. C. 20036.
Nontechnical periodical with articles of general interest. Numerous excellent photographs. Large general-reference maps in color.
Cumulative indexes for 1899–1946 and 1947–1963 with annual supplements. Separate index for maps. A revised index for the years 1888–1946 is scheduled for publication in 1968.

191. NEW GEOGRAPHICAL LITERATURE AND MAPS. 1951 –. SA. 20s. Royal Geographic Society, 1 Kensington Gore, London S.W. 7, England.
Classified list of all articles in 20 major geographic journals and selected items from another 150 periodicals. Also lists new books, atlases, and current maps.

192. REVISTA BRASILEIRA DE GEOGRAFIA. 1939 –. Q. $6.00. Conselho Nacional de Geografia, Av. Beira Mar 436, Rio de Janeiro, Brazil.
Research articles, particularly on the geography of Brazil. Abstracts in English and French. Index for Vols. 1–10 (1939–1948).

193. REVISTA GEOGRÁFICA. Nilo Bernardes, ed. 1941 –. SA. $3.00. Instituto Panamericano de Geografia e Historia, Comissao de Geografia, Av. Franklin Roosevelt, 39, S. 1414, Rio de Janeiro, Brazil.
The leading geographic periodical devoted to the Americas, according to Professor Chauncey D. Harris, Department of Geography, University of Chicago. Articles are rich in documentation and bibliography.

194. SOVIET GEOGRAPHY: Review and Translation. 1960 –. M (Sept.–June). $6.00. American Geographical Society, Broadway at 156th St., New York, N. Y. 10032.
Published by the American Geographical Society with the support of the National Science Foundation to make available in English reports of current Soviet research in geography.
In addition to translations of geographic articles, *Soviet Geography* contains news notes on Soviet political and economic developments of interest to geographers and a survey of Soviet geographic literature.

Section J. History

195. AMERICAN HISTORICAL REVIEW. (American Historical Association.) 1895 –. 5 x y. $15.00. Macmillan Co., 866 Third Ave., New York, N. Y. 10022.
Articles, book reviews. Extensive bibliography entitled "Articles and Other Books Received," classified by periods and countries. Section on Libraries and Archives records their recent major activities, including publications and acquisitions of collections.
Cumulative index every 10 years.

196. AUSTRIAN HISTORY YEARBOOK. R. John Rath, ed. 1965 −. A. $15.00. Department of History and Political Science, Rice University, Houston, Tex. 77001. Outgrowth of the *Austrian History Newsletter.*
Scholarly essays, bibliographies, lists of doctoral dissertations, and news of professional activities and of recent library acquisitions. Scope covers the areas of the former Habsburg Empire. Articles have appended comments from other historians and a final reply from the author. European historians review books by American Scholars, and Americans review those of Europeans.

197. BALKAN STUDIES. 1961 −. SA. $8.00. Institute for Balkan Studies, 2 Vassilissis Sophias, Salonika, Greece.
Articles, book reviews, and reports of scholarly meetings in Europe and the United States concerning the Balkans. Coverage includes the political, economic, and diplomatic history of the modern Balkans and its periphery, including Turkey and Cyprus. Earlier issues were focused primarily on Greece (Editorial statement).
Text is primarily in English, with some articles in French and German.

198. BUSINESS HISTORY REVIEW. (Harvard Graduate School of Business Administration.) 1926 −. Q. $10.00. Baker Library, Soldiers Field, Boston, Mass. 02163.
Formerly the *Bulletin of the Business Historical Society.*
An international journal devoted to the history of business enterprise and the interaction of business and its environment over time. International coverage (Editorial statement).
Cumulative indexes: Vols. 1−15 (1926−41); Vols. 16−35 (1942−61).

199. CANADIAN HISTORICAL REVIEW. 1920 −. Q. $4.00. University of Toronto Press, Toronto, Canada.
Includes in each number a bibliography of books and articles on "Recent Publications Relating to Canada."

200. CENTRAL EUROPEAN HISTORY. Douglas A. Unfug, ed. 1968 −. Q. $7.00 to members, $10.00 to others. Emory University, Atlanta, Ga. 30322.
Sponsored by the Conference Group for Central European History of the American Historical Association.
Articles on research and bibliography. Book reviews. Attention confined to the German-speaking part of Central Europe.

201. COMPARATIVE STUDIES IN SOCIETY AND HISTORY: An International Quarterly. 1958 −. Q. $6.00. Mouton and Co., P. O. Box 1132, The Hague, Netherlands.
The aim of the journal is to combine historical scholarship with the various kinds of analysis that have been developed by the social sciences, especially in sociology and anthropology. Its articles present events, institutions, and processes of change so as to enable new comparisons to be made among societies and across epochs (Editorial statement).
International editorial committee and consulting editors.

202. CURRENT HISTORY. 1914 −. M. $8.00. Current History, Inc., 1822 Ludlow St., Philadelphia, Pa. 19103.
Formerly *Current History of the European War.*
A semipopular periodical with articles on world affairs by specialists. Excerpts

48   RESEARCH RESOURCES

from documents. Book reviews. The Month in Review (a chronology of world affairs).

203. HISPANIC AMERICAN HISTORICAL REVIEW. 1918 –. Q. $6.00, $4.00 to Pan-American subscribers. Duke University Press, Box 6697, College Station, Durham, N. C. 27708.
Articles, book reviews. For information on its early years see R. L. Butler, *Guide to the Hispanic-American Historical Review,* Duke University Press, 1950.
Cumulative index published at irregular intervals.

204. HISTORISCHE ZEITSCHRIFT. 1859 –. BM. DM 48. Verlag R. Oldenbourg, Rosenheimerstr. 145, Munich 8, Germany.
Includes reviews and abstracts of books and articles in current historical periodicals, primarily European and American.

205. HISTORY OF RELIGIONS: An International Journal for Comparative Historical Studies. 1961 –. Q. $8.00. University of Chicago Press, 5750 Ellis Ave., Chicago, Ill. 60637.
One of the primary aims of *History of Religions* is the integration of results of the several disciplines of the science of religion. Studies and discussions on the central themes of the history of religions, methodological studies, and critical surveys and reviews of recent works. The articles deal with the progress made in the general area of the history of religions and with coordinate results in related disciplines, particularly ethnology, sociology, anthropology, and specialized areas of study (Publisher's statement).

206. HISTORY TODAY. 1951 –. M. 50s. Bracken House, Cannon St., London E.C. 4, England.
Assesses the course of human events in all phases—from politics to polar science (Editorial statement).

207. INTERNATIONAL REVIEW OF SOCIAL HISTORY. (Internationaal Instituut voor Sociale Geschiedenis) 1956 –. 3 x y. $8.00. Royal VanGorcum Ltd., P. O. Box 43, Assen, Netherlands.
Worldwide coverage. Book reviews. Text in English, French, and German.

208. JOURNAL OF AFRICAN HISTORY. R. A. Oliver and J. D. Fage, eds. (School of Oriental and African Studies, University of London.) 1960 –. 3 x y. 55s. Cambridge University Press, 200 Euston Rd., London N.W. 1, England; and 32 E. 57th St., New York, N. Y. 10022.
Covers the history of the entire continent of Africa from prehistory to modern times. Includes articles on archaeology, ethnology, and linguistics. Text in English and French.

209. JOURNAL OF AMERICAN HISTORY. (Organization of American Historians.) 1914 –. Q. $8.00. Department of History, Indiana University, Bloomington, Ind. 47401.
The name of the journal was changed in 1964 from *The Mississippi Valley Historical Review* (217) in recognition of a shift in content emphasis from regional to national history. Bibliographic notices.

210. JOURNAL OF CENTRAL EUROPEAN AFFAIRS. S. Harrison Thompson, ed. 1941–1964. Q. University of Colorado, Boulder, Colo. 80302.

211. JOURNAL OF CONTEMPORARY HISTORY. 1966 –. Q. Weidenfeld and Nicolson, 20 New Bond St., London W. 1, England.

Published on behalf of the Institute for Advanced Studies in Contemporary History (associated with the Wiener Library in London).

Research studies, mainly in 20th-century European history. International editorial board. Issues deal with such topics as "International Fascism 1920–1945," "Left-wing intelligentsia between the two world wars," and "1914."

212. JOURNAL OF ECONOMIC HISTORY. 1941 –. Q. $6.00. Economic History Association, 100 Trinity Pl., New York, N. Y. 10006.

The *Journal* aims to bring together the news of economists, historians, statisticians, geographers, and others who find that the story of economic change throws light on their fields of interest or is enriched by their contribution (Editorial statement). Review articles. Lists of recent publications in economic history.

213. JOURNAL OF THE HISTORY OF IDEAS. A Quarterly Devoted to Cultural and Intellectual History. 1940 –. Q. $6.00. Journal of the History of Ideas, Inc., Box 285, City College, New York, N. Y. 10031.

The influence of ideas on historical periods and cultures. Covers all social sciences and the humanities. Coverage includes public opinion and content analysis.

Emphasizes the interrelations of several fields of historical study–the history of philosophy, of literature and the arts, of the natural and social sciences, of religion, and of political and social movements.

214. THE JOURNAL OF MODERN HISTORY. 1929 –. Q. $8.00. University of Chicago Press, 5750 Ellis Ave., Chicago, Ill. 60637.

World history from the Renaissance to the present with the exception of the domestic history of the American Republics. History of the arts and sciences is covered as well as political, diplomatic, military, religious, social, and economic aspects of history. Includes bibliographical and historiographical articles, documents, and reviews of books.

215. JOURNAL OF SOCIAL HISTORY. 1967 –. Q. $10.00. University of California Press, Berkeley, Calif. 94720.

216. JOURNAL OF WORLD HISTORY. (Commission Internationale pour une Histoire du Développement Scientifique et Culturel de l'Humanité.) UNESCO, Paris, 1953 –. 4 x y. $10.00. Éditions de la Baconnière S. A., Neuchâtel, Switzerland.

Published under the auspices of UNESCO with their financial assistance.

Historians from many countries discuss their specialties in articles that form the raw materials for the UNESCO Scientific and Cultural History of Mankind. Text in several languages.

Some issues are devoted to a single topic such as Latin America.

217. MISSISSIPPI VALLEY HISTORICAL REVIEW. See *Journal of American History* (209).

218. PACIFIC HISTORICAL REVIEW. 1932 –. Q. $5.00. University of California Press, Berkeley, Calif. 94720.

Publication of the American Historical Association, Pacific Coast Branch.

219. REVUE D'HISTOIRE DIPLOMATIQUE. 1887 –. Q. 45 Fr. Editions A. Pedone, 13 rue Soufflot, Paris (5ᵉ), France.

220. SLAVONIC AND EAST EUROPEAN REVIEW. 1922 –. SA. $8.40. School of Slavonic and East European Studies, University of London, Malet St., London W.C.1, England.

Until March 1928 entitled *Slavonic Review*. Publication in Great Britain interrupted in 1940 and continued in the United States for seven issues (Vols. XX, XXI, and XXII: American Series I, II, III).

A survey of the peoples of Eastern Europe, their history, economic development, literature, and linguistics. Some documents published in English translation. Cumulative index.

221. VIERTELJAHRSHEFTE FÜR ZEITGESCHICHTE. 1953 –. Q. DM24. Deutsche Verlagsanstalt, Neckarstr. 121, Stuttgart O, Germany.

Published for the Institut für Zeitgeschichte, Munich. Covers Nazi regime and postwar period. Important bibliographic section on recent and current history.

222. ZEITSCHRIFT FÜR GESCHICHTSWISSENSCHAFT. 1953 –. BM. VEB Deutscher Verlag der Wissenschaften, Taubenstr. 10, 108 Berlin, German Democratic Republic.

Section K. International Law and Organization

223. AAUN NEWS. 1928 –. M (BM July–Aug., Dec.–Jan.). Free of charge with membership. American Association for the United Nations, Inc., 345 E. 46th St., New York, N. Y. 10017.

Features United Nations activities, programs, progress, and problems. Superseded by *VISTA* (239).

224. AMERICAN JOURNAL OF INTERNATIONAL LAW. 1907 –. Q. Free of charge with membership; $15.00 to nonmembers. American Society of International Law, 2223 Massachusetts Ave., N. W., Washington, D. C. 20008.

Devoted mainly to contemporary questions of international law and relations. Occasional articles and comments on private international law and domestic law affecting international law and relations between nations. The *Journal* presents varying points of view. Includes Book Reviews and Notes, and a section on official documents. The section titled Periodical Literature of International Law listed articles from 60 to 85 journals from all over the world until it was discontinued in October 1964.

Cumulative index every 20 years.

225. AMERICAN SOCIETY OF INTERNATIONAL LAW PROCEEDINGS. 1907 –. A. American Society of International Law, 2223 Massachusetts Ave., N.W., Washington, D.C. 20008.

226. ARCHIV DES VÖLKERRECHTS. 1948 –. Q. J. C. B. Mohr (Paul Siebeck), 74 Tübingen, Germany.

Articles and reports on international law topics, documents (reprinted in the original language), court decisions. Book reviews.

227. FEDERALIST: A Newsletter. 1951 –. M (10 x y). Free of charge with membership; $2.00 to nonmembers. United World Federalists, Inc., 1346 Connecticut Ave., N. W., Washington, D. C. 20036.

Information on latest developments on Capitol Hill and at the United Nations related to a strengthened United Nations and related matters of international law and foreign affairs. Behind the scenes analytic reporting as well as straight factual monthly commentary (Editorial statement).

228. FREEDOM & UNION: Magazine of the Democratic World. Clarence K. Streit, ed. 1946 –. M (except Aug.). $4.00. Federal Union, Inc., 1736 Columbia Rd., N. W., Washington, D. C. 20009.
Book reviews.

229. INTERNATIONAL AND COMPARATIVE LAW QUARTERLY. 1952 –. Q. 84s including supplements. British Institute of International and Comparative Law, 1 Temple Gardens, London E.C.4, England.

230. INTERNATIONAL COMMISSION OF JURISTS BULLETIN. 1954 –. Irr. International Commission of Jurists, 2, Quai du Cheval-Blanc, Geneva 24, Switzerland.
Concerned with major events–violations and favorable developments–relevant to the application of the Rule of Law.

231. INTERNATIONAL COMMISSION OF JURISTS JOURNAL. 1957 –. SA. $2.00. International Commission of Jurists, 2, Quai du Cheval-Blanc, Geneva 24, Switzerland.
The International Commission of Jurists is a nongovernmental organization which has consultative status with the United Nations and UNESCO. It has National Sections in 45 countries. Scholarly articles deal with the principles of the Rule of Law, and with international and comparative law. Books of interest.
Beginning with the Winter 1965 issue the *Journal* added two features: Digest of Judicial Decisions by Superior Courts of Different Countries on Human Rights Aspects of the Rule of Law; and Studies on the Composition, Jurisdiction and Influence of Supreme and Constitutional Courts of Various Countries.
Text in English, French, German, and Spanish.

232. INTERNATIONAL CONCILIATION. 1907 –. 5 x y. $2.25. Carnegie Endowment for International Peace, United Nations Plaza at 46th St., New York, N. Y. 10017.
Each issue deals with one particular problem in the field of international organization and relations, written by a specialist. Includes documentary material. The fall issue of each year deals with the issues before the United Nations General Assembly.

233. INTERNATIONAL LEGAL MATERIALS: Current Documents. 1962 –. BM. $24.00; $18.00 to members. American Society of International Law, 2223 Massachusetts Ave., N. W., Washington, D. C. 20008.
Provides the reader with 1,200 pages of authentic texts of official documents, selected from new treaties, agreements, legislation and regulations, judicial proceedings (briefs and decisions), official reports, and other official documents, from the United States, other countries, and international organizations. Photo-offset process provides exact reproduction of original documents. Index.
Much of the material is not available in any other form in most libraries, including specialized law libraries. All of it becomes available more quickly in *International Legal Materials* than in other published sources (Editorial statement).

234. INTERNATIONAL ORGANIZATION. Alfred O. Hero, Man. Ed. 1947 –. Q. $6.00. World Peace Foundation, 40 Mount Vernon St., Boston, Mass. 02108.

HOFSTRA UNIVERSITY LIBRARY

Articles on the United Nations, its specialized agencies, and other international organizations. Bibliographies of American and foreign books and articles concerned with international organization and related subjects. Extensive summaries of the activities of the United Nations and other international organizations, with detailed footnote references to the principal documentary material on regional, political, and functional organizations, including the United Nations and its related agencies. Index.

235. INTERNATIONALES RECHT UND DIPLOMATIE. 1956 –. Q. DM 35 ($14.00). Verlag Wissenschaft und Politik, Salierring 14/16, Cologne, Germany.
Text mainly in German with quotations, articles, and documents in English, French, or Russian. Index.

236. JAHRBUCH FÜR INTERNATIONALES RECHT. Eberhard Menzel, ed. 1952 –. A. DM 70. Verlag Vandenhoeck & Ruprecht, Theodorstr. 13, Göttingen,. Germany.
Edited by the Institut für Internationales Recht, University of Kiel, in cooperation with the Forschungsstelle für Völkerrecht und Ausländisches öffentliches Recht, University of Hamburg.

237. JOURNAL DU DROIT INTERNATIONAL. 1874 –. Q. 78 Fr ($13.60). Éditions Techniques, 123 rue d'Alésia, Paris (14e), France.
Text in English and French; occasional documents in German, Russian, and Spanish. Cumulative index every five years; 1874–1955, in eight vols.

238. REVUE DU DROIT INTERNATIONAL, DE SCIENCES DIPLOMATIQUES ET POLITIQUES. 1923 –. Q. Sw Fr 82.50 plus 20% ($23.00). Box 138–1211, Geneva 12, Switzerland.
Text in French, some articles in English and Italian. Includes current bibliography and document section.

239. VISTA. 1966 –. BM. Available to members only (dues $7.00). UNA-USA (United Nations Association of the United States of America), 345 E. 46th St., New York, N. Y. 10017.
Supersedes *AA UN News* (223).
Features United Nations activities, programs, progress, and problems.

240. ZEITSCHRIFT FÜR AUSLÄNDISCHES ÖFFENTLICHES RECHT UND VÖLKERRECHT. 1929 –. Q. $22.00. W. Kohlhammer Verlag, Urbanstr. 12, 7 Stuttgart O, Germany.
Published for the Max-Planck Institut für ausländisches öffentliches Recht und Völkerrecht, Heidelberg. Articles on comparative and international law (the Communist countries included) in English, French, or German, with English summaries of articles written in German. Important documents in their original language. The practice of the German Federal Republic concerning questions of public international law (since 1949) is the subject of detailed reports containing large extracts from official documents. Special numbers, for instance on the International Law Commission's 1966 Draft Articles on the Law of Treaties (October 1967).
List of articles, often with summaries, from some 500 journals and yearbooks published throughout the world. Bibliographic references to U. N. and other documents and books.
Book reviews. Annual subject index; cumulative index to Vols. 1–20 (1929–1960).

Section L. International Relations

241. AMERICAN UNIVERSITIES FIELD STAFF REPORTS. 1952 −. 60 to 100 reports yearly. Subscription rates upon request. American Universities Field Staff, Inc., 366 Madison Ave., New York, N. Y. 10017.

A continuing series of reports on current political, economic, and social developments in world affairs, written by Associates of the American Universities Field Staff (AUFS), a nonprofit educational organization sponsored by a group of American universities and colleges.

Reports are issued in several series based on geographic areas, for instance, West Coast South America Series. They are focused primarily on Asia, Africa, Eastern Europe, and Latin America but do include general problems. The publication is intended primarily for university readers.

242. ATLAS. 1961 −. M. $8.00. Aspen Publishing Co., Inc., 1180 Ave. of the Americans, New York, N. Y. 10036.

The section titled World Press Comment reprints excerpts from articles and editorials on current events and developments selected from 650 newspapers and magazines published all over the world in 25 languages, including those published in small countries or in "unusual" languages. The section titled The World Looks at the U. S. A. presents foreign press comments on this country. Some articles by foreign specialists are reprinted in full under the title World Topics. There are also strong contributions in the cultural field and foreign book reviews.

243. BACKGROUND: Journal of the International Studies Association. Charles A. McClelland, ed. 1962−64. Q. School of International Relations, University of Southern California, Los Angeles, Calif. 90007.

Features "articles and essays which survey and appraise the 'state of the field' in particular aspects or specializations, which introduce or suggest clearly new concepts, conceptual frameworks, models, or theoretical constructions, or which explore the relationships between fields and disciplines in international studies" (Editorial statement).

See *Background* (72) for information on the annual bibliography.

This publication has been superseded by *International Studies Quarterly*. (255).

244. BEHIND THE HEADLINES. (Canadian Institute of International Affairs.) 1940 −. 6 x y. $2.00. Baxter Publishing Co., 228 Bloor St., W., Toronto 5, Canada.

Each issue is devoted to an examination of one current international political or economic topic. This organization also furnishes useful study aids.

245. BRITISH SURVEY: (Main Series). 1939 −. M. 30s. British Society for International Understanding, Benjamin Franklin House, 36 Craven St., London W. C. 2., England.

Editorial policy is to give objective information on history, geography, and economics, and on political, religious, and social developments; to present foreign policy of particular countries; and to provide impartial analyses of international issues. Each number is devoted to one country or one well-defined international topic (Editorial statement).

Annual index. Occasional book reviews and bibliographies.

246. CONFLUENCE: An International Forum. 1952−1959. Q. Summer School of Arts and Sciences and of Education, Harvard University, Cambridge, Mass. 02138.

Contributions by scholars from all over the world who are interested in the meeting of West and East.

247. CURRENT READINGS: A Selection of Recent Magazine Articles. 3 x y. War/Peace Services, Center for War/Peace Studies, 218 E. 18th St., New York, N. Y. 10003.
The Center for War/Peace Studies is a program of the New York Friends Group, Inc.
A bibliography for teachers and professors and for organization programming use. Contains divergent viewpoints and information found in periodicals readily available in public and school libraries.

248. EUROPA-ARCHIV: Zeitschrift für internationale Politik. 1946 –. BW. Hermann Volle, ed. Deutsche Gesellschaft für Auswärtige Politik, Koblenzer Str. 133, 53 Bonn, Germany.
Published by the Forschungsinstitut of the Deutsche Gesellschaft für Auswärtige Politik, formerly known as the Institut für Europäische Politik und Wirtschaft.
Articles and reports by specialists on problems of international, especially but by no means exclusively, European politics and economics. Bibliography of recent publications, including articles. Résumés and texts of selected documents in German, cross-referenced with previously published documents. News. Chronology of world events.
Index, *Sammelregister, 1946–1965,* published in 1966, includes a list of articles and reports, chronological list of documents, and subject and author indexes (323 pp.).

249. FOREIGN AFFAIRS: An American Quarterly Review. 1922 –. Q. $8.00. Council on Foreign Relations, Inc., 58 E. 68th St., New York, N. Y. 10021.
Articles on international affairs by scholars, high government officials and party leaders of various countries, and leading officials of the United Nations and other international public organizations. Section titled Recent Books on International Relations appears in every issue, briefly annotated. Lists of source material include government and international organization documents and pamphlets. The lists are interdisciplinary in character and refer to items published in English and the major Western European languages.

250. HEADLINE SERIES. 1935 –. BM. $4.00. Foreign Policy Association, 345 E. 46th St., New York, N. Y., 10017. Kraus Reprint Series (1935–1951), 1967.
Formerly *Headline Books.*
Analyses of international subjects and areas currently in the news. Written by specialists for the general reader. Maps, charts, discussion guides, and bibliographies.

251. INTERNATIONAL AFFAIRS. 1922 –. Q. 37s 6d. Royal Institute of International Affairs, Chatham House, St. James's Square, London S.W. 1, England.
The principal article in each issue is often contributed by a statesman of world status or other leading personality. Strongly conflicting viewpoints are presented (e.g., by Adam Rapacki, Antonio de Oliveira Salazar, Masayoshi Ohira, Ernesto Che Guevara, and Franz Josef Straus). Some special issues concentrate on certain topics, such as Britain East of Suez (April 1966).
Large book review section. Announcements of new periodicals and recent reference books.

252. INTERNATIONAL JOURNAL: A Canadian Quarterly. 1947 –. Q. $4.00 Canadian Institute of International Affairs, 230 Bloor St., W., Toronto 5, Canada.
Articles on international relations by specialists. Book reviews.

253. INDIA QUARTERLY: A Journal of International Affairs. S. L. Poplai, ed. 1945 –. Q. Rs 14. Asia Publishing House for Indian Council on World affairs, Ballard Estate, Bombay 1, India.

254. INTERNATIONAL STUDIES. A. Appadorai, ed. (Indian School of International Studies, New Delhi). 1959 –. Q. Rs 32 ($8.00). Asia Publishing House, Calicut Street, Ballard Estate, Bombay 1, India (29 E. 10th St., New York, N. Y. 10003).
Articles on international politics, economics, and law as well as on political, economic, and social developments in all parts of the world.
Includes *India and World Affairs: An Annual Bibliography*.

255. INTERNATIONAL STUDIES QUARTERLY: Publication of the International Studies Association. Fred A. Sondermann, ed. 1957 –. Q. $8.00. Wayne State University Press, Detroit, Mich. 48202.
Supersedes *Background* (243) with the same editorial policy.
Features "articles and essays which survey and appraise the 'state of the field' in particular aspects or specializations, which introduce or suggest clearly new concepts, conceptual frameworks, models, or theoretical constructions, or which explore the relationships between fields and disciplines in international studies" (Editorial statement).

256. JOURNAL OF INTERNATIONAL AFFAIRS. 1947 –. SA. School of International Affairs, Columbia University, 409 W. 117th St., New York, N. Y. 10027.
Each issue is focused around a central theme and contains articles written by scholars and statesmen. Book reviews.

257. MODERN AGE. 1957 –. Q. $4.00. Foundation for Foreign Affairs, Inc., 154 E. Superior St., Chicago, Ill. 60611.
International and foreign affairs. Book reviews.

258. ORBIS: A Journal of World Affairs. 1957 –. Q. $6.00. Foreign Policy Research Institute, University of Pennsylvania, 133 S. 36th St., Room 102, Philadelphia, Pa. 19104.
Deals with important issues, events, and trends in international relations, with emphasis on problems in U. S. foreign policy, country and area studies, and analyses of communist strategy, arms control, technology, and military affairs. Occasional articles on theory and methodology in international relations but main emphasis is on current, "practical" problems (Editorial statement).

259. PARLIAMENTARY AFFAIRS: Devoted to All Aspects of Parliamentary Government. 1947 –. Q. 40s. The Hansard Society for Parliamentary Government, 162 Buckingham Palace Rd., London S.W. 1, England.

260. REVIEW OF INTERNATIONAL AFFAIRS. 1950 –. BW. $3.40. Federation of Yugoslav Journalists, Nemanjina 34, Box 413, Belgrade, Yugoslavia.
Covers politics, economics, law, science, and culture.

261. SWISS REVIEW OF WORLD AFFAIRS. 1951 –. M. $6.50. Neue Zürcher Zeitung, Box 660, 8021 Zürich, Switzerland.
Material edited and written by the editorial staff and foreign correspondents of the *Neue Zürcher Zeitung*.

262. UN MONTHLY CHRONICLE. 1964 –. M. United Nations, Sales Section, New York, N. Y. 10017.

Supersedes the *United Nations Review* (1954–1964) which took the place of the *United Nations Bulletin* (1946–1954).

The *Chronicle* and its predecessors are written for the general reader. Every issue contains a record of the month, describing the proceedings, decisions, and resolutions of the main organs and committees in the political, economic, social, legal, and administrative fields. Articles by distinguished contributors deal with various aspects of the work of the United Nations in all parts of the world. A picture section covers events, people, and places. The notes of the month include announcements of international meetings, book reviews, and selected documentation.

263. WORLD AFFAIRS. 1837 –. Q. Free with membership; $4.00 to nonmembers. American Peace Society, 1307 New Hampshire Ave., Washington, D. C. 20036.
Short articles for the nonspecialist. Important book reviews.

264. WORLD AFFAIRS QUARTERLY. 1930–62. Q. School of International Relations, University of Southern California, Los Angeles, Calif. 90007.
Formerly *World Affairs Interpreter*.

265. WORLD POLITICS: A Quarterly Journal of International Relations. (Center of International Studies, Princeton University.) 1948 –. Q. $7.50. Princeton University Press, Princeton, N. J. 08540.
Articles present the results of original scholarly research which has a broad theoretical impact in history, geography, economics, international relations, military affairs, foreign policy, sociology, and political theory (Editorial statement).
Book reviews.

266. WORLD TODAY. New Series 1945 –. M. $5.30. Oxford University Press, Ely House, 37 Dover Street, London W. 1, England.
Published under the auspices of the Royal Institute of International Affairs, Chatham House.
Up-to-date factual information on current world problems written by experts for the general reader; documented.
Annual subject index.

267. ZEITSCHRIFT FÜR GEOPOLITIK. 1924 –. M. DM 30 ($7.50). Verlag des Instituts für Geosoziologie und Politik, 3569 Bellnhausen über Gladenbach, Hessen, Germany.
Book reviews.

Section M. Miscellaneous

268. AFRICAN FORUM: A Quarterly Journal of Contemporary Affairs. 1965 –. Q. $4.00. American Society of African Culture (AMSAC), 401 Broadway, New York, N. Y. 10013.
This journal deals with the political, social, economic, and cultural development of the African nations and the American Negro. Articles are by scholars and national leaders involved in African and American Negro development. Each issue treats a specific topic, e.g., Pan-African Unity, African Socialism, The Military in Africa, The Rhodesian Crisis. The National Minorities section is concerned with intergroup adjustment and the Cultural Notes section is concerned with the cultural development and contribution of the African and American Negro.

269. EUROPA ETHNICA: Vierteljahresschrift für Nationalitätenfragen. Wilhelm Braumüller, ed. 1958 —. Q. S 160 ($6.40). Universitäts-Verlagsbuchhandlung, Servitengasse 5, Vienna 9, Austria.
Text in English, French, and German. Book reviews.

270. JOURNAL OF AMERICAN STUDIES. 1967 —. SA. 50c. Cambridge University Press, 32 E. 57th St., New York, N. Y. 10022.
Published for the British Association of American Studies.

271. FOOD RESEARCH INSTITUTE STUDIES. 1961 —. 3 x y. $7.00. Stanford University, Stanford, Calif. 94305.
Devoted to economic studies related to the production, distribution, and consumption of food in the United States and around the world. The coverage includes such topics as problems of agricultural development in tropical Africa, and studies of grain economies and policies of the European Common Market. Food and agricultural problems are considered in their general economic and political setting, and stress is placed on quantitative methods and on historical perspective (From Editorial statement).
See No. 1, 1966, pp. 95–113, for "Publications of the Food Research Institute: 1959–1965."

272. GDR REVIEW: A Magazine From the German Democratic Republic. 1956 —. M. Price varies according to country. League of the German Republic for Friendship Among the Peoples, 8 Thälmannplatz 8/9, 108 Berlin 8, German Democratic Republic.
Published for the Society for Cultural Relations with Foreign Countries.

273. HUMAN RELATIONS: A Journal of Studies Towards the Integration of the Social Sciences. 1947 —. Q. $12.00. Plenum Publishing Co. Ltd., Ansvar House, London Rd., Wembley, England.
Published under the joint editorial auspices of the Tavistock Institution of Human Relations, London, and the Research Center of Group Dynamics, University of Michigan. Emphasis on the study of group processes and interpersonal relations at all levels, from the family to international societies.

274. ICFTU ECONOMIC AND SOCIAL BULLETIN. 1953 —. 6 x y. $1.80. International Confederation of Free Trade Unions, 37–47 rue Montagne aux Herbes Potageres, Brussels 1, Belgium.
Editions in English, French, German, and Spanish.

275. TECHNOLOGY AND CULTURE. 1960 —. Q. $10.00. University of Chicago Press, 5750 Ellis Ave., Chicago, Ill. 60637.
Articles on the significance of technology and its role in the development of civilization as seen by sociologists, economists, and political scientists, as well as scholars in the humanities and fine arts. The underdeveloped areas of the world are included in the coverage.
Annual bibliography. Book reviews.

276. TECHNOLOGY REVIEW. 1895 —. 9 x y. $7.00. Massachusetts Institute of Technology, Cambridge, Mass. 02139.
A chronicle of achievements and their implications in science, engineering, architecture, management, and the social sciences of M. I. T. The scope of the periodical has been widened recently to focus on broad technological developments, wherever they

originate, in the context of modern economic and social affairs and in the perspective of M. I. T.'s continuing world leadership (Publisher's statement).

277. WORLDVIEW: A Journal of Religion and International Affairs. 1958 –. M. $4.00. Council on Religion and International Affairs, 170 E. 64th St., New York, N. Y. 10021.
Contains essays, symposia (e.g., on selective conscientious objection), excerpts from other periodicals, and book reviews.
Cumulative index every two years.

CHAPTER 7.

PERIODICALS ON GEOGRAPHIC AREAS AND COUNTRIES

Section A. Continents and Regions

AFRICA

278. AFRICA DIGEST. 1953 –. BM. 25s. The Africa Bureau, 65 Denison House, Vauxhall Bridge Rd., London S.W. 1, England.
Survey of events in Africa, arranged by countries and other territorial units and based on English, French, and African newspapers and periodicals, official statements and press releases, interviews, and publications of international public organizations such as the International Development Association (I.D.A.).
Includes many excerpts from newspapers and official statements or reports.
The editor states that he does not necessarily endorse the views of correspondents who provide the reports.

279. AFRICA INSTITUTE BULLETIN. Afrikaans ed. 1961 –; English ed. 1963 –. 10 x y. R 4.80 ($6.72). Box 630, Pretoria, Republic of South Africa.
Memoranda, news background, and analyses of African affairs. Maps and statistics. Reviews and lists of new books and articles. Index.

280. AFRICAN AFFAIRS. (Royal African Society.) 1901 –. Q. Free with membership; £1.14 to nonmembers. Oxford University Press, Press Road, Neasden, N. W. 10, England.
Formerly *Journal of the African Society* (1901–1935) and *Journal of the Royal African Society* (1935–1944).
Articles on African affairs and problems written from professional and academic viewpoints. Coverage on recent African history was supplemented in 1967 when the Journal added special concern for the interaction of Africa with the non-African world. Journal has become increasingly academic in character.
Includes book reviews and bibliographies.

281. AFRICA: POLITICAL, SOCIAL AND CULTURAL. 1964 –. M. 315s; 735s including Series: Economic, Financial and Technical. Africa Research Ltd., 1 Parliament St., Exeter, England. (U. S. Distribution Center: National Agency for International Publications, Inc., 317 E. 34th St., New York, N. Y. 10016.)
Index published quarterly with six-month cumulations.

282. AFRICA REPORT. 1956 –. M (Oct.–Aug.). $6.00. African-American Institute, 345 E. 46th St., New York, N. Y. 10017.
Formerly the *African Special Report* (1956–1961).
Analytical articles by area specialists primarily concerned with the dynamics of political, economic, and cultural developments in contemporary Africa. The section on Correspondence publishes comments and corrections on statements made in articles.
News in Brief is an extensive selective chronicle of events significant in themselves or in relation to African trends drawn from some 250 African, European, and American publications; African radio broadcasts; and informal sources; and refined by the editors (Editorial statement).
Book reviews. Annual index covers, separately: Africa (General), Africa (By Areas), and books reviewed (with authors).

283. AFRICA RESEARCH BULLETIN. SERIES A: POLITICAL, SOCIAL AND CULTURAL SERIES. 1964 –. M. 315s; with Series B: Economic, Financial and Technical, 735s; special rates for African universities and research institutions. Africa Research Ltd., 1 Parliament St., Exeter, England.
Book reviews.
Monthly index; cumulative quarterly and annual indexes.

284. AFRICA TODAY. 1954 –. M (Sept.–June). $5.00. Graduate School of International Studies, University of Denver, University Park Campus, Denver, Colo. 80210.
Articles, editorials, columns, news, book reviews.
Reports by specialists on African movements and the struggle for freedom and racial equality (Editorial statement).
Published by the University of Denver beginning with Vol. 12, 1965.

285. AFRIQUE ET L'ASIE: Revue Politique Sociale et Économique. 1948 –. Q. 15 Fr. Afrique et l'Asie, 13 rue du Four, Paris (6ᵉ), France.

286. AFRO-ASIAN AND WORLD AFFAIRS. 1964 –. Q. Rs 8 ($2.00). Institute of Afro-Asian and World Affairs, 14 Theatre Communication Bldg., New Delhi 1, India.
Review articles, discussions, book reviews, and documents. Index.

287. JOURNAL OF MODERN AFRICAN STUDIES: A Quarterly Survey of Politics, Economics and Related Topics in Contemporary Africa. David and Helen Kimble, eds. 1963 –. Q. $7.50. Cambridge University Press, 200 Euston Rd., London N.W. 1, England; American branch: 32 E. 57th St., New York, N. Y. 10022.
Includes articles on international relations, human geography, social psychology, and literary and cultural topics. Contributions from all over the world, especially from scholars working in African universities.
The Africana section contains notes on centers of African studies, research projects, and reports of conferences. Review articles, book reviews. Annual bibliography and bibliographic articles.

ASIA

288. ASIA: For a Better Understanding Between the United States and the Asian Countries. 1964 –. Q. $4.00. The Asian Society, 112 E. 64th St., New York, N. Y. 10021.

289. ASIAN RECORDER: A Weekly Digest of Asian Events. 1955 —. W. Rs 95 ($20.00). Asian Recorder, C-I/9, Tilak Marg, Box 595, New Delhi 1, India.

Events in Asia are listed and described under each country, arranged alphabetically, with a summary where considered necessary. Events which occur elsewhere and affect Asia are listed separately. News sources are indicated—newspapers, periodicals, radio, embassy, and government departments.

Quarterly and annual index.

290. ASIAN REVIEW: The Journal of the Royal Society for India, Pakistan and Ceylon. John White, ed. 1964 —. Q. 50s. Offices of the Society, 3 Temple Chambers, Temple Ave., London E.C. 4, England.

Formerly *Asian Review and Art and Letters,* formed by the merger of *Art and Letters* and *Asian Review.* The original *Asian Review* was founded in 1886.

Since 1967 much stronger emphasis on contemporary political, economic, and social problems.

Articles with opposing viewpoints; intended for the general reader. Book reviews on South Asian subjects.

291. ASIAN SURVEY: A Monthly Review of Contemporary Asian Affairs. 1961 —. M. $8.00. Asian Survey, University of California, 2234 Piedmont Ave., Berkeley, Calif. 94720.

Published under the auspices of the Institute of International Studies, University of California. Formerly *Far Eastern Survey.* Topical papers in the social sciences on South and Southeast Asia. Special issues each January and February, reviewing events and issues of the previous year in each country in the area. Periodically, other special issues are published, e.g., the August 1967 issue was devoted to Vietnam.

292. COLOMBO PLAN: Co-Operative Economic Development in South and South-East Asia. 1956 —. M. Free. Information Officer, Colombo Plan Bureau, Box 596, 12 Melbourne Ave., Colombo 4, Ceylon.

293. EASTERN ECONOMIST. Gurdip Singh, ed. 1943 —. W. Rs 65 ($15.00). Eastern Economist, A—148 Defence Colony, New Delhi 3, India.

Analysis of economic and financial affairs in India and abroad.

294. EASTERN WORLD: The Asia Monthly. 1947 —. M. 30s. Foreign Correspondents Ltd., 58, Paddington St., London W. 1, England.

Articles by prominent spokesmen of both East and West.

295. JOURNAL OF ASIAN STUDIES. (Association for Asian Studies, Inc.) 1941 —. 5 x y. $15.00 (including Bibliography). Department of History, Duke University, Durham, N. C. 27708.

Formerly the *Far Eastern Quarterly* (until September 1956).

Research articles in all the social sciences and humanities on the countries of East, Southeast, and South Asia from Japan to Pakistan. Historical and contemporary, interdisciplinary. Features include: Book Reviews; Other Books Received.

The valuable annual *Bibliography of Asian Studies,* formerly known as the *Far Eastern Bibliography* (1941 to 1956), is published as the fifth issue of the *Journal* in September. It contains several thousand titles of books and articles published in Western languages during the preceding year. Valuable for the specialist and nonspecialist.

296. MODERN ASIAN STUDIES. C. A. Fisher, ed. 1967 —. Q. $9.50. Cambridge University Press, 32 E. 57th St., New York, N. Y. 10022.

Concerned with Asian societies from the standpoint of the social sciences—modern history, human geography, economics, politics, sociology, and modern litera-ture—when it bears on social and cultural interests. The countries studied lie in an arc from West Pakistan to Japan and include China and South and Southeast Asia. Countries on the periphery are sometimes included.

Editorial policy avoids commitment to any political ideology but the journal wel-comes uninhibited discussion of current issues, including politics, from the point of view of the individual contributor. Contributions from all over the world include authors in diplomacy and business management as well as the academic community (Editorial statement).

Includes original articles, major review articles, and book reviews. Special attention is given to books published in languages such as Japanese, Chinese, or Hindi and not available in English.

297. PACIFIC AFFAIRS: An International Review of the Far East and Pacific Area. 1928 –. Q. $5.00. University of British Columbia, Vancouver 8, Canada.

Covers international relations, politics, economics, and history in the Pacific area and eastern and southern Asia. Book reviews and review articles. Annual index.

298. UNITED ASIA: International Magazine of Afro-Asian Affairs. 1948 –. BM. Rs 12 ($4.00). United Asia, 12 Rampart Row, Bombay 1, India.

AUSTRALIA

299. AUSTRALIAN JOURNAL OF POLITICS AND HISTORY. 1955 –. 3 x y. 42s. University of Queensland Press, St. Lucia, Brisbane, Australia.

300. AUSTRALIAN OUTLOOK. 1947 –. 3 x y. 25s. Australian Institute of Inter-national Affairs, 124 Jolimont Rd., East Melbourne, 3002, Australia.
Articles, book reviews.

301. AUSTRALIAN QUARTERLY. 1929 –. Q. A $3.56. Australian Institute of Political Science, Delfin House, 16 O'Connell St., Sydney, Australia.

302. AUSTRALIA'S NEIGHBORS. 1950 –. 6 x y. 7s 6d. Australian Institute of International Affairs, 124 Jolimont Rd., East Melbourne, 3002, Australia.
Background notes on countries and problems of East Asia and the Pacific.

303. PACIFIC NEIGHBORS. (Australian-American Association.) 1946 –. 3 x y. $1.00. Victorian Secretariat, 405 Collins St., Melbourne, Australia.

304. WORLD REVIEW. 1962 –. 3 x y. 10s 6d. Jacaranda Press Pty. Ltd., 73 Elizabeth St., Brisbane, Australia.
Concise background to world crises, particularly those of direct importance to Australia; expert opinion on the likely impact of international developments on Australia; information and analyses of current events.

LATIN AMERICA

305. AMERICA LATINA. 1962 –. Q. Cr $3000 ($4.00). Centro Latino-Americano de Pesquisas em Ciências Sociais, Av. Pasteur 431, Praia Vermelha, Rio de Janeiro ZC–82, Brazil.
Text in English, French, Portuguese, and Spanish.

Articles on results, methodology, and data analysis of social science field research in Latin America. Also translations of articles published simultaneously in other social science periodicals, particularly in the United States and Europe.

The section on news and documentation reports activities of Latin-American institutions of research and teaching, or institutions of other regions interested in Latin-American problems; meetings and congresses of the social sciences; research and studies undertaken by other institutions.

The documentation section presents book reviews and abstracts of articles of interest to Latin America, published in about 300 social science periodicals; abstracts of documents presented to international conferences; and references to documentation in the social sciences.

306. AMERICAS. 1949 –. M. $4.00. Department of Public Information, Pan American Union, Washington, D. C. 20006.

An official publication of the Organization of American States (OAS) for the general reader in three editions—English, Spanish, and Portuguese—telling about life in the 21 Western Hemisphere republics. Copiously illustrated. Its regular departments include a roundup of excerpts from other hemisphere periodicals, a book review section, and "The OAS in Action."

307. CUADERNOS AMERICANOS: Revista del Nuevo Mundo. 1942 –. BM. $9.00. Av. Coysacan, No. 1035, Apdo. Postal 965, Mexico, D. F.

"A cultural and political review, with a circulation among intellectuals throughout Latin America" (*Atlas*, May 1961, p. 57). Cumulative index, 1942–52.

308. HISPANIC AMERICAN REPORT. 1948–64. M. Institute of Hispanic American and Luso-Brazilian Studies, Stanford University, Stanford, Calif. 94305.

Formerly *Hispanic World Report* (1948–49).

Country-by-country analysis of developments in Spain, Portugal, and Latin America. General developments are covered in the international section. Book reviews. Annual index.

309. INTER-AMERICAN ECONOMIC AFFAIRS. 1947 –. Q. $9.00. Inter-American Economic Affairs, Box 181, Washington, D. C. 20044.

Not confined to economics; includes articles on political science, economic history, etc.

310. JOURNAL OF INTER-AMERICAN STUDIES. 1959 –. Q. $5.00. University of Miami Press, Box 8134, Coral Gables, Fla. 33124.

Articles in English, Spanish, Portuguese, or French on various social science topics. Stress on current developments and recent history. The section titled Nuevas Corrientes presents comments on recent developments taken from books, periodicals, and other sources.

311. LATIN AMERICAN RESEARCH REVIEW: A Journal for the Communication of Research Among Individuals and Institutions Concerned with Studies of Latin America. 1965 –. 3 x y. $9.00 to individuals; $12.00 to institutions and graduate students. Editorial office: University of Texas, Box 7819, Austin, Tex. 78712.

Published by the Latin American Studies Association, with text in English and Spanish.

Topical articles on social sciences and humanities. Current research inventory. News section covering meetings with Latin-American content, institutional news, new and suspended periodicals, libraries and archives (including publications received), movement of professionals, major art exhibits, and necrology.

312. REVISTA INTERNACIONAL Y DIPLOMÁTICA: Documentos y Temas de Política Internacional. 1950 —. M. Mex $36 ($2.89). Francisco Agüera Cenarro, Independencia 72—7o. Piso, Mexico 1, D. F.

MIDDLE EAST AND NORTH AFRICA

313. ARAB NEWS AND VIEWS. 1965 —. SM. Free to subscribers of the *Arab World* and upon request to editors, writers, and officers of educational and business organizations. Arab Information Center, 757 Third Ave., New York, N. Y. 10017.
Current Arab news and attitudes.

314. ARAB WORLD. 1954 —. M. $2.00. Arab Information Center, 757 Third Ave., New York, N. Y. 10017.
The Arab Information Center is an agency of the 13 governments of the League of Arab States.
Articles on political, economic, social, and cultural aspects of the Arab countries. Editorials. Cartoons from Arab newspapers. Illustrations. Includes book reviews.

315. CHRONOLOGY OF ARAB POLITICS. 1963 —. Q. Department of Political Studies and Public Administration, American University of Beirut, Beirut, Lebanon. Index. Text in Arabic and English.

316. JEWISH OBSERVER AND MIDDLE EAST REVIEW. 1952 —. W. 50s. Zionist Review Ltd., Norwich House, 13 Southampton Pl., London W. C. 1, England.
Includes book reviews.

317. MAGHREB DIGEST. Willard A. Beling, ed. 1963 —. M. $12.00. Middle East and North African Program, School of International Relations, University of Southern California, Los Angeles, Calif. 90007.
Contemporary political and economic issues of North Africa. Scholarly articles; survey of French- and Arabic-language periodicals of the Maghreb; chronology of events; and book review section of works in French and Arabic dealing with the Maghreb.

318. MIDDLE EAST DIGEST. 1957—60. M. American Friends of the Middle East, Inc., 1605 New Hampshire Ave., Washington, D. C. 20009.
Superseded by *Viewpoints* (323) and subsequently by *Mid East* (321).

319. MIDDLE EASTERN STUDIES. 1964 —. Q. $9.00. F. Cass and Co. Ltd., 8—10 Woburn Walk, London W. C. 1, England.
Devoted to the study of the Arabic-speaking countries of Southwest Asia and North Africa, together with Israel, Iran (Persia), and Turkey. Scholarly discussion of the political, economic, religious, and legal history of this area since the end of the 18th century, and its literature, social geography, sociology, and anthropology.

320. MIDDLE EAST JOURNAL 1947 —. Q. $7.50. Middle East Institute, 1761 N St., N. W., Washington, D. C. 20036.
Articles on contemporary politics, economics, and social sciences of the Middle East and the modern history of the area. Chronology for the previous quarter for the area as a whole and individually for some 25 countries. Documents. Book reviews.

Bibliography of periodical literature lists some 250 items per issue. List of recent publications and forthcoming books. Communications. Annual index.

321. MID EAST: A Middle East–North African Review. 1966 –. 6 x y. $3.00. American Friends of the Middle East, Inc., 1605 New Hampshire Ave., N. W., Washington, D. C. 20009.
Supersedes *Viewpoints* (323).
Socioeconomic, cultural, and educational developments in the Middle East and North Africa. Area literature and short stories. Book reviews.
The American Friends of the Middle East describes itself as a private organization devoted to improving relations between the United States and all the countries of the Middle East.

322. NEAR EAST REPORT: A Washington Letter on American Policy in the Near East. 1957 –. BW. $7.00. Near East Report, Inc., 1341 G St., N. W., Washington, D. C. 20005.
The *Report* attempts to present an authoritative and factual account of events in the Near East and of American policy toward the Arab states and Israel. "We favor an Arab-Israel peace settlement" (Publisher's statement).
A special survey is published three times each year, e.g., "Iran, A Study of Development" (January 1966), "Israel at 18, Partner in Progress" (May 1966), "The U. S. Commitment in the Near East" (September 1966), "The Arms Race in the Near East" (February 1967), "Myth and Fact, Background to the Arab-Israel War" (August 1967).

323. VIEWPOINTS: Middle East, North Africa. 1961–66. 10 x y. American Friends of the Middle East, Inc., 1607 New Hampshire Ave., N. W., Washington, D. C. 20009.
Superseded *Middle East Digest* (318). News and feature articles on economic, political, and educational developments in the Middle East and North Africa. Book reviews.
Succeeded by *Mid East* (321).

SOVIET RUSSIA AND EASTERN EUROPE

324. AMERICAN SLAVIC AND EAST EUROPEAN REVIEW. See *Slavic Review* (342).

325. AMERICAN-SOVIET FACTS. 1964 –. 5 x y. Free. National Council of American-Soviet Friendship, Inc., 156 Fifth Ave., New York, N. Y. 10010.
Presents life and activities in the Soviet Union and material on American-Soviet relations. Reprinted wholly or in part from the *New World Review* (335).

326. ANALYSIS OF CURRENT DEVELOPMENTS IN THE SOVIET UNION. 1957 –. W. DM 40 ($10.00). Institute for the Study of the USSR, Mannhardtstr. 6, Munich 22, Germany.
The stated purpose of the Institute is to publish and distribute throughout the world the results of its research on current conditions and trends in the USSR and to train specialists in Soviet affairs.
Editions in English, Russian, and Spanish.

327. CENTRAL ASIAN REVIEW. 1953 –. Q. 60s. Central Asian Research Centre, 66A King's Road, London S.W. 3, England.

Aims at giving a balanced and objective assessment of Soviet writing on social, political, and cultural developments in the Central Asian and Kazakh SSRs and adjacent countries. Maps. Index.

328. CURRENT SOVIET DOCUMENTS. See *Soviet Documents* (552).

329. DONAURAUM: Zeitschrift des Forschungsinstituts für den Donauraum. 1956 –. Q. S 135. Kommissionsverlag, Hermann Böhlaus Nachf., Frankgasse 4, Vienna 9, Austria.
Covers the Danube River area. Book reviews. Index.

330. EAST EUROPE: A Monthly Review of East European Affairs. 1952 –. M. $5.00. Free Europe, Inc., 2 Park Ave., New York, N. Y. 10016.
Includes sections on The Month in Review; Press and Podium (translations from the East European press, periodicals, and radio and reprints of cartoons and press photos); Current Developments; and Book Reviews. Articles by specialists interpreting political, economic, and cultural developments. The magazine has access to the research facilities of Radio Free Europe in Munich.
Editions in English, French, and German.

331. EAST EUROPEAN QUARTERLY. Stephen Fischer-Galati, ed. 1967 –. Q. $6.00. University of Colorado, Hellems 12-E, Boulder, Colo. 80302.
A journal of the social sciences. Contributions by scholars from all nations and disciplines, covering every historical epoch and the many different aspects of people in the Baltic, Adriatic, Aegean, and Black Sea areas. Material also deals with peoples on the periphery of those areas including the Great Russians, the Germans, and the Turks as they affect Eastern Europe. Articles, documents, and book reviews in English, French, and German.

332. EAST WEST DIGEST. 1965 –. M. 30s. Foreign Affairs Publishing Co., 139 Petersham Rd., Petersham, near Richmond, Surrey, England.
Resistance to communism and the countries of the Communist bloc. Political warfare. Subversion. Book reviews.

333. MIZAN (See 184).

334. NEW TIMES. 1943 –. W. 6.60 rub. New Times, Pushkin Sq., Moscow K-6, USSR.
Journal with a large circulation, published in several languages.

335. NEW WORLD REVIEW. Jessica Smith, ed. 1932 –. A (M to fall 1967). N. W. R. Publications, Inc., 156 Fifth Ave., New York, N. Y. 10010.
Supersedes *Soviet Russia Today* (345). Information about the socialist countries, including questions of foreign policy. The policy of the Soviet Union is presented in the form of documents (speeches, decrees, etc.). Other viewpoints from both Communist-led and other countries are presented. Editorial policy is independent and often differs from Soviet positions. Communist and non-Communist contributors. Book reviews.

336. OSTEUROPA: Zeitschrift für Gegenwartsfragen des Ostens. Klaus Mehnert, ed. 1926 –. M. DM 42 ($10.50). Deutsche Verlags-Anstalt, Neckarstr. 121, 7 Stuttgart, Germany.
Scholarly and critical; not hostile toward the Communist bloc in principle;

German-European; objective; more interested in manuscripts with facts and trends than with authors' opinions (Editorial statement).
Bibliography; book reviews.

337. OSTPROBLEME. 1949 –. BW. DM 24. Verlag Wissenschaft und Politik, Salierring 14–16, Cologne, Germany.
Publishes contemporary documents, scholarly analyses, and political commentary dealing with the Soviet Union, the Soviet bloc, and the worldwide Communist movement. Its purpose is to promote understanding of the dynamic aspects of East-West problems. Includes reprints of important articles in Soviet Russian and other Communist publications.

338. POLISH PERSPECTIVES. 1958 –. M. $4.80. Polish Perspectives, P. O. Box 159, Warsaw, Poland.
Sponsored by the Polish Government. Coverage includes international affairs; political, economic, and social relations; and Polish developments of interest to foreign readers. Editions in English and French.

339. POLISH REVIEW. 1956 –. Q. $5.00. Polish Institute of Arts and Sciences in America, 59 E. 66th St., New York, N. Y. 10021.

340. RUSSIAN REVIEW: An American Quarterly Devoted to Russia Past and Present. 1941 –. Q. $6.00. Russian Review, Inc., Box 146, Hanover, N. H. 03755.
A scholarly quarterly devoted to interdisciplinary articles on Russia past and present.
The purpose of the *Review* is to interpret and distinguish the real aims of the Russian people in contrast to those of Soviet communism, and to advance general knowledge of Russian culture, history, and civilization. It draws on scholars, writers, and political leaders of prerevolutionary Russia, and on well-known American and European specialists on Russia (Editorial statement).

341. SBZ-ARCHIV: Dokumente, Berichte, Kommentare zu Gesamtdeutschen Fragen. 1950 –. SM.DM 3 per month. Verlag für Politik und Wirtschaft, Goltsteinstr. 185, 5 Cologne-Bayenthal, Germany.
Documents, reports, and comments. Information on events and developments in the Soviet Zone of Occupation (SBZ), i.e., the German Democratic Republic (GDR). Documented articles by specialists on the political, governmental, economic, cultural, military, and other developments in the GDR, including changes in the party line, East German interpretations of Marxist theory, and in political and governmental leadership. Chronicle of events, complete texts or extensive abstracts from GDR political documents, and extracts from articles on the GDR in the satellite press and periodicals. Issues for earlier years also provide a periodic supplement with the texts of important GDR laws, decrees, and regulations. Charts, book reviews. Annual index.
Note: The German Democratic Republic is, of course, a part of Eastern Europe ideologically rather than geographically.

342. SLAVIC REVIEW: American Quarterly of Soviet and East European Studies. 1941 –. Q. $12.00. American Association for the Advancement of Slavic Studies, Inc., Mt. Royal and Guilford Aves., Baltimore, Md. 21202.
Formerly *American Slavic and East European Review*. Applications for membership may be submitted to the Association at the University of Illinois, 1207 West Oregon Street, Urbana, Illinois 61801.

343. SLAVONIC AND EAST EUROPEAN REVIEW (See 220).

344. SOVIET LIFE. 1956 –. M. $1.90. Embassy of the USSR, 1706 18th St., N.W., Washington, D. C. 20009.
Official publication of the Soviet Union addressed to the American reader. Formerly *USSR*.

345. SOVIET RUSSIA TODAY. See *New World Review* (335).

346. SOVIET STUDIES: A Quarterly Review of the Social and Economic Institutions of the U.S.S.R. (Institute of Soviet and East European Studies, University of Glasgow.) 1949 –. Q. $7.40. Basil Blackwell, Broad St., Oxford, England.

347. STUDIES ON THE SOVIET UNION. 1961 –. Q. DM 24 ($6.00). Institute for the Study of the USSR, Mannhardtstr. 6, 8 Munich 22, Germany.
Replaces the *Caucasian Review, East Turkish Byelorussian Review, Ukrainian Review, Vestnik,* and *Byelorussian Review.* Text in English.

348. SURVEY: A Quarterly Journal of Soviet and East-European Studies. Walter Z. Laqueur and Leopold Labedz, eds. 1961 –. Q. 20s. Ilford House, 133-135 Oxford St., London W.1., England.
Serious discussion of long-term trends in the Soviet bloc, cultural, social, political, and economic. The *Survey* is unique in trying to provide both expertise for the specialist and stimulating material for the general student of contemporary affairs. (Statement taken from "Survey's Objectives.") Special issues provide a detailed examination of a particular subject such as "The Soviet Union" and "The Great Proletarian Cultural Revolution in China."

349. ZEITSCHRIFT FÜR OSTFORSCHUNG: Länder und Völker im östlichen Mitteleuropa. 1952 –. 4 x y. DM 40. N. G. Elwert'sche Universitätsbuchhandlung, Marburg an der Lahn, Germany.
Covers East-Central Europe. Text in German with English summaries. Book reviews. Index.

Section B.   Countries

CANADA

350. DALHOUSIE REVIEW: A Canadian Quarterly of Literature and Opinion. 1921 –. Q. $4.00. Review Publishing Co., Ltd., Dalhousie University, Halifax, N. S., Canada.
Articles written by specialists for the general reader. Subjects include international affairs, history, economics, political science, psychology, and current events of interest to Canadians.

351. QUEEN'S QUARTERLY: A Canadian Review. 1893 –. Q. $5.00. Queen's Quarterly, 524 Humanities Bldg., Queen's University, Kingston, Ont., Canada.
Covers politics and foreign affairs.

CHINA

352. CHINA QUARTERLY. 1960 –. Q. $6.00. Ilford House, 133 Oxford St., London W. 1, England.
Published by the Congress for Cultural Freedom for specialists and general readers. The section titled Recent Developments contains articles on all aspects of contemporary Chinese developments, including texts of documents. Other sections include Comment; Book Reviews; and Quarterly Chronicle and Documentation: 1. Internal Developments, 2. Foreign Relations.

353. CHINA RECONSTRUCTS. 1952 –. M. $3.00. China Welfare Institute, Wai Wen Bldg., Peking 37, People's Republic of China.
Articles on economic, social, and cultural developments in continental China. Popular style.

354. CHINA TODAY. 1958 –. M. NT $120 ($4.00). The Institute for Advanced Chinese Studies, 174, Section 2, Chung Shan North Rd., Taipei, Taiwan, Republic of China.
Current Chinese affairs.

355. FREE CHINA REVIEW. 1951 –. NT $100. James Wei, Box 337, Taipei, Taiwan, Republic of China.
Its purpose is to present Chinese culture and the democratic outlook of the Republic of China to the English-speaking world (Editorial statement).

356. FREE CHINA WEEKLY. 1964 –. W. NT $100. James Shen, Box 337, Taipei, Taiwan, Republic of China.
Published by the Government Information Office to report to the world the latest tidings in the Republic of China, her story, and what she stands for (Editorial statement). Text in English.

357. PEKING REVIEW: A Magazine of Chinese News and Views. 1958 –. W. Pai Wan Chuang, Peking 37, People's Republic of China.
Analysis and commentary on international relations.

INDONESIA

358. INDONESIA. 1966 –. SA. $6.00. Cornell Modern Indonesia Project, 102 West Ave., Ithaca, N. Y. 14850.
Devoted to the study of Indonesia on an interdisciplinary basis. Articles dealing with religion, history, anthropology, education, government and politics, bibliography, and other subjects. The first issue contains a special 70-page supplement of documents relating to the September 30th movement and its aftermath.

JAPAN

359. CONTEMPORARY JAPAN: A Review of Far Eastern Affairs. 1932 –. Q. Yen 5,400 ($15.00). Foreign Affairs Association of Japan, 7 Yuraku-cho 1-chome, Chiyoda-ku, Tokyo, Japan.
Book reviews. Index.

360. JOURNAL OF SOCIAL AND POLITICAL IDEAS IN JAPAN. 1963 –. 3 x y. Free with membership; Yen 1,800 ($5.00) to nonmembers. Center for Japanese

Social and Political Studies, Nihon Shakai Shiso Kenkyusho, 11 Wakagi-chō, Shibuya-ku, Tokyo, Japan.
Book reviews. Index.

PAKISTAN

361. PAKISTAN HORIZON. 1948 —. Q. $3.00. Pakistan Institute of International Affairs, Karachi 1, Pakistan.
Articles, staff studies, documents, chronology, book reviews.

362. STATESMAN: Week-End Review. 1955 —. W. Rs 8.50. M. Owais, Dilkusha Bldg., McLeod Rd., Box 212, G. P. O., Karachi, Pakistan.

CHAPTER 8.

PERIODICALS IN THE SOCIAL
AND BEHAVIORAL SCIENCES

363. ACADEMY OF POLITICAL SCIENCE. PROCEEDINGS. 1910 —. Irr. Free with membership; $3.50 to nonmembers. Academy of Political Science, 413 Fayerweather Hall, Columbia University, New York, N. Y. 10027.
Addresses and discussions of the Academy's meetings on problems of national or international importance. Index.

364. ACTA POLITICA. 1965 —. Q. $4.50; $6.00 to libraries and institutions. J. A. Boom en Zoon, Hoofdstraat 87, Meppel, Netherlands.
Published by the Netherlands Political Science Association. Articles generally in Dutch and summarized in English. Includes international relations topics. Bibliography.

365. AMERICAN ACADEMY OF POLITICAL AND SOCIAL SCIENCE. ANNALS. 1890 —. BM. Free with membership; $2.50 per no. to nonmembers. 3937 Chestnut St., Philadelphia, Pa. 19104.
Each issue is devoted to various aspects of a selected political, economic, or social problem covered by specialists in 15 to 20 articles. Many issues deal with international and foreign affairs. Detailed index for each issue, 5-year cumulative index. Book review section.

366. AMERICAN BEHAVIORAL SCIENTIST. 1957 —. BM (M Sept.—June until June 1967). $14.00 to institutions; $10.00 to individuals. Sage Publications, Inc., 275 South Beverly Dr., Beverly Hills, Calif. 90212.
Supersedes *Prod* (408).
Interdisciplinary approach to the multiple facets of the social and behavioral sciences. Articles on new trends in anthropology, economics, education, geography, history, political science, psychology, sociology, and their interrelationships. Reports on current research developments.
Includes *New Studies* (38).

367. AMERICAN ECONOMIC REVIEW. 1911 —. 5 x y. Free with membership; $10.00 to nonmembers. American Economic Association, 619 Noyes St., Evanston, Ill. 60201.

Official publication of the American Economic Association. Classified lists of new books and recent periodical articles.

368. THE AMERICAN JOURNAL OF SOCIOLOGY. 1895 –. BM. $8.00. University of Chicago Press, 5750 Ellis Ave., Chicago, Ill. 60637.
The oldest journal in the world devoted to sociology is a professional journal of fundamental sociologic analysis, research, and theory. Includes articles in neighboring areas such as cultural anthropology and political science. Research notes, commentary and debates, book reviews, and list of current publications. Special issues are devoted to a single topic of particular interest, with annotated bibliographies.

369. AMERICAN PHILOSOPHICAL SOCIETY PROCEEDINGS. 1938 –. 6 x y. $5.00 per vol. 104 S. Fifth St., Philadelphia, Pa. 19106.
Extends to all academic fields, including history and political science. Cumulative index covers Vols. 1–100 (1838–1957).

370. AMERICAN POLITICAL SCIENCE REVIEW. 1906 –. Q. Free with membership; $12.00 to nonmembers. American Political Science Association, 1726 Massachusetts Ave., N. W., Washington, D. C. 20006.
Official journal of the American Political Science Association.
Scholarly articles, essays, research notes, and bibliographic essays in all fields of political science, including its various international areas. Large section on Book Reviews and Notes. The extended bibliographies of selected articles and documents formerly included in this section were discontinued in 1967. Periodically, lists of doctoral dissertations in political science are published. Communications to the Editor.
See *Cumulative Index to the American Political Science Review, Volumes 1–57: 1906–1963* (86).

371. AMERICAN PSYCHOLOGIST. 1946 –. M. $10.00. American Psychological Association, 1200 17th St., N. W., Washington, D. C. 20036.
Book reviews. Index.

372. AMERICAN QUARTERLY. 1949 –. 4 nos. and 1 supplement per year. $8.00. Trustees of the University of Pennsylvania, Box 30, College Hall, Philadelphia, Pa. 19104.
Official journal of the American Studies Association. Devoted to the study of the total culture of the United States, past and present including politics, society, history, literature, and art. Interdisciplinary. Reviews and bibliographies.

373. AMERICAN SOCIOLOGICAL REVIEW. 1936 –. BM. Free with membership; $10.00 to nonmembers. American Sociological Association, 1001 Connecticut Ave., N. W., Washington, D. C. 20036.
Official journal of the American Sociological Association. Research and scholarly reports cover population, race relations, social psychology, and other areas. Large book review section. Cumulative indexes for 1936–60 and 1961–65.

374. ASSOCIATION OF AMERICAN GEOGRAPHERS. ANNALS. 1911 –. Q. $10.00. Association of American Geographers, 1146 16th St., N.W., Washington, D. C. 20036.
Scholarly articles. Book review articles. Index for Vols. I–XXV (1910–35).

375. BEHAVIORAL SCIENCE. 1956 –. BM. $10.00. Mental Health Research Institute, University of Michigan, Ann Arbor, Mich. 48104.

An interdisciplinary journal containing articles on general theories of behavior and on empirical research specifically oriented toward such theories. Includes abstracts of articles published.

376. BRITISH JOURNAL OF SOCIOLOGY. (London School of Economics.) 1950 –. Q. 50s. Routledge & Kegan Paul Ltd., 68–74 Carter Lane, London E. C. 4, England.
Book reviews. Index. Cumulative index every 10 years.

377. CANADIAN JOURNAL OF ECONOMICS. 1968 –. Q. $10.00. University of Toronto Press, Toronto 5, Canada.
This new journal continues the economics portion of the *Canadian Journal of Economics and Political Science* (378).

378. CANADIAN JOURNAL OF ECONOMICS AND POLITICAL SCIENCE. (Canadian Political Science Association.) 1935–1967. Q. $6.00. University of Toronto Press, Toronto 5, Canada.
Superseded by the *Canadian Journal of Economics* (377), and the *Canadian Journal of Political Science* (379).
Book reviews. Index. Cumulative index every 10 years.

379. CANADIAN JOURNAL OF POLITICAL SCIENCE. 1968 –. Q. $10.00. University of Toronto Press, Toronto 5, Canada.
This new journal continues the political science section of the *Canadian Journal of Economics and Political Science* (378).

380. CANADIAN REVIEW OF SOCIOLOGY AND ANTHROPOLOGY. 1964 –. Q. $6.00. Canadian Anthropology and Sociology Chapter, Canadian Political Science Assoc., University of Alberta, Calgary, Canada.
Book reviews. Index. Text in English and French.

381. COLUMBIA JOURNALISM REVIEW. 1962 –. Q. $6.00. Graduate School of Journalism, Columbia University, New York, N. Y. 10027.
Assesses the performance of journalism in all its forms.

382. ECONOMIC DEVELOPMENT AND CULTURAL CHANGE. 1952 –. Q. $8.00. University of Chicago Press, 5750 Ellis Ave., Chicago, Ill. 60637.
Published under the auspices of the Research Center in Economic Development and Cultural Change, University of Chicago.
Papers deal mainly with the theoretical orientation of significant new data in the fields of economics, anthropology, sociology, history, geography, political science, and ancillary areas of study. The journal is designed for exploratory discussion of the problems of economic development and cultural change (Editorial statement).
Special issues deal with different aspects of one particular problem. Book reviews. List of new books.

383. ECONOMIC JOURNAL. 1891 –. Q. 50s. Royal Economic Society, Sidgwick Ave., Marshall Library, Cambridge, England.
Articles and book reviews. Annotated lists of new books and articles in the principal economic journals of other countries. Cumulative index for Vols. 1–40 (1891–1930).

384. ETHICS: An International Journal of Social, Political, and Legal Philosophy. 1890 –. Q. $8.00. University of Chicago Press, 5750 Ellis Ave., Chicago, Ill. 60637.

The purpose of *Ethics* is to develop and clarify ideas and principles relevant to practical problems—individual, social, political, and international.

Ethics presents a significant sample of the advanced thinking of philosophers, economists, lawyers, political scientists, and sociologists from various countries on topics of practical relevance and general interest (Editorial statement).

Essays, discussions, book reviews, and notes on new books.

385. GENERAL POLITICS: Quarterly of Political Arts and Science. 1967 –. Q. $3.50. John Westburg & Associates, Conesville, Iowa 52739.

This journal aspires to combine the traditions of philosophic values and scientific findings with observations of actual practices of working politicians (Editorial statement).

International affairs and foreign country topics are included.

386. GOVERNMENT AND OPPOSITION. 1965 –. Q. 45s. Wm. Dawson & Sons Ltd., Cannon House, Macklin St., London W.C. 2, England.

Specialists on world politics examine the process of government—the aims and accomplishments of those in power in relation to the opposition, be it adamant or reconcilable (Editorial statement).

Interdisciplinary.

387. HUMAN ORGANIZATION: A Scientific Quarterly for the Study of Developmental Change. 1941 –. Q. $10.00 to institutions; $8.00 to individuals. Society for Applied Anthropology, University of Kentucky, Lexington, Ky. 40506.

Formerly *Journal of Applied Anthropology* (Vols. 1-7).

Descriptive case studies; theoretical, methodological, or other overall approach; social or behavioral setting (government agency, industry, etc.). Also, general approaches to the study of human behavior (intercultural, interpersonal, economic, or other institutional behavior, etc.).

Special issues deal with such subjects as Latin America, the Middle East, and South Asia. Cumulative index every five years.

388. IMPACT OF SCIENCE ON SOCIETY. 1950 –. Q. $2.50. United Nations Educational, Scientific and Cultural Organization (UNESCO), place de Fontenoy, Paris (7ᵉ), France. (UNESCO Publications Center, 317 E. 34th St., New York, N. Y. 10016.)

Basic articles on the social consequences of science by social and natural scientists. Editions in Arabic, English, French, and Spanish.

389. INTERNATIONAL LABOUR REVIEW. 1921 –. M. $6.00. International Labour Office, Geneva, Switzerland.

Includes statistics, bibliographies, and book reviews. Semiannual index.

390. INTERNATIONAL REVIEW OF ADMINISTRATIVE SCIENCES. 1928 –. Q. 500 BF. International Institute of Administrative Sciences, 25 rue de la Charité, Brussels 4, Belgium.

Cumulative index every five years.

391. INTERNATIONAL SOCIALIST REVIEW: The Marxist Theoretical Magazine of American Socialism. 1934 –. BM. $2.50. International Socialist Review Publishing Association, 873 Broadway, New York, N. Y. 10003.

Book reviews. Cumulative index every three years, 1934–1966; annual index beginning in 1967.

392. INTERNATIONAL SOCIAL SCIENCE JOURNAL. 1949 –. Q. $7.00. UNESCO, place de Fontenoy, Paris (7e), France.
Published until 1959 under the name *International Social Science Bulletin.*
Part I of each issue contains up to 10 articles on special topics, such as Population Studies, Peace Research, History and Social Science, and Human Rights in Perspective, together with select bibliographies of recent works in the field in all the principal languages. Topics are selected to cover the various social science disciplines in turn; emphasis is given to subjects of international significance and problems of cross-cultural research. Part II, "World of the Social Sciences," provides information on the organization, personnel, and current activities of social science organizations and research, training, and study centers in all parts of the world. Also includes condensed accounts of key international meetings and news of conferences, meetings, symposia, etc.
The section on Reviews of Documents and Books lists 600 to 700 publications of the United Nations and its specialized agencies each year, with brief annotations. Book list titled Books Received: 200 to 300 titles a year with short annotations.
The No. 2, 1967, issue is devoted to description and discussion of "The Social Science Press" in Brazil, France, India, Japan, Mexico, Poland, United Kingdom, and United States.

393. JOURNALISM QUARTERLY: Devoted to Research in Journalism and Mass Communications. 1924 –. Q. $8.00. Association for Education in Journalism, School of Journalism, University of Minnesota, Minneapolis, Minn. 55455.
Formerly *Journalism Bulletin,* 1924–1928.
Research studies in the field of mass communication, including an international communications section. Features articles on mass communications in U. S. and foreign journals, and a selected annotated bibliography. Book reviews; annotated book lists. Cumulative index for Vols. 1–40.

394. JOURNAL OF POLITICS. 1939 –. Q. $6.00. Southern Political Science Association, Peabody Hall, University of Florida, Gainesville, Fla. 32601.
Worldwide interests. Book reviews.

395. JOURNAL OF SOCIAL ISSUES. 1945 –. Q. $7.00 to individuals; $9.00 to organizations and institutions. Society for the Psychological Study of Social Issues, P. O. Box 1248, Ann Arbor, Mich. 48106.
The Society for the Psychological Study of Social Issues is a group of two thousand psychologists and allied social scientists who share a concern with research on the psychological aspects of important social issues. In various ways, the Society seeks to bring theory and practice into focus on human problems of the group, the community, and the nation as well as the increasingly important ones that have no national boundaries. The *Journal* has as its goal the communication of scientific findings and interpretations in a nontechnical manner but without the sacrifice of professional standards. The *Journal* typically publishes a whole number on a single theme but in 1967 began to include some separate articles on other topics (Editorial statement).

396. JOURNAL OF SOCIAL PSYCHOLOGY. 1930 –. BM. (3 vols. per year) $30.00. The Journal Press, 2 Commercial St., Provincetown, Mass. 02657.
Special attention given to cross-cultural research. Index in second half of each of the three volumes per year.

397. LAW AND CONTEMPORARY PROBLEMS. 1933 –. Q. $10.00. Duke University, School of Law, Durham, N. C. 27706.

Each issue deals with a single topic such as European Regional Communities, Soviet Impact of International Law, International Control of Propaganda, and Population Control. Not limited to legal aspects or to international subjects, although foreign experience is often the subject of individual articles.

398. LAW AND SOCIETY REVIEW. 1967 −. Q. Sage Publications, Inc., 275 South Beverly Dr., Beverly Hills, Calif. 90212.
Articles and research notes by lawyers, social scientists, and other scholars which bear on the relationship between law and the social sciences. Published by the Law and Society Association, a nationwide group drawn primarily from the legal and social science professions, whose purpose is the stimulation and support of research on political, social, and economic aspects of the law (Policy statement).

399. MIDWEST JOURNAL OF POLITICAL SCIENCE. (Midwest Conference of Political Scientists.) 1957 −. Q. Free with membership; $6.00 to nonmembers. Wayne State University Press, 5980 Cass Ave., Detroit, Mich. 48202.
All fields of political science. Book reviews. Cumulative index to Vols. 1−10, 1957−1966, in May 1967 issue.

400. POLITICAL QUARTERLY. 1930 −. Q. 35s. T. Nelson and Sons, Ltd., Parkside Works, Edinburgh 9, Scotland.
Covers all fields of political science.

401. POLITICAL SCIENCE. 1948 −. SA. 8s. School of Political Science and Public Administration, Victoria University of Wellington, Box 196, Wellington, New Zealand.
Studies in all fields of political science. Book reviews.

402. POLITICA SOCIAL. 1947 −. BM. 175 pts. Instituto de Estudios Politicos, Plaza de la Marina Española 8, Madrid 13, Spain.
Formerly *Revista de Estudios Politicos.* Political studies.

403. POLITICAL SCIENCE QUARTERLY. 1886 −. Q. Free with membership; $8.00 to nonmembers. The Academy of Political Science, 413 Fayerweather Hall, Columbia University, New York, N. Y. 10027.
Edited for The Academy of Political Science by the Faculty of Political Science at Columbia University.
Articles on political, economic, and social questions−both historical and contemporary−by authors with widely divergent convictions. Book reviews.

404. POLITICAL STUDIES. (Political Studies Association of the United Kingdom.) 1953 −. 3 x y. 50s. Oxford Univeristy Press, Ely House, 37 Dover St., London W. 1, England.
Scholarly, extensive book reviews. Index; cumulative index at the end of 10 years.

405. POLITISCHE STUDIEN. 1950 −. BM. DM 24 (plus postage) for 6 mos. Günter Olzog Verlag, Thierschstr. 11/15, 8 Munich 22, Germany.
Coverage includes international relations and contemporary history. Section on "Personalien" furnishes detailed biographic data on leading personalities from all over the world. Book reviews.

406. POLITISCHE VIERTELJAHRESSCHRIFT. (Deutsche Vereinigung für Poli-

tische Wissenschaft.) 1960 —. Q. DM 45. Westdeutscher Verlag, Ophovener Str. 1—3, Opladen, Germany.
Journal of the German Political Science Association. Articles; book reviews.

407. POLITY: The Journal of the Northeastern Political Science Associations. 1968 —. Q. $7.00. University of Massachusetts Press, Amherst, Mass. 01002.
Covers all areas of political science.

408. PROD: Political Research, Organization and Design. 1957—58. BM. Princeton, N. J. 08540.
Superseded by *American Behavioral Scientist* (366).

409. PUBLIC ADMINISTRATION REVIEW. 1940 —. Q. $15.00. American Society for Public Administration, 1329 18th St., N. W., Washington, D. C. 20036.

410. PUBLIC OPINION QUARTERLY. 1937 —. Q. $6.00. Columbia University Press, 136 S. Broadway, Irvington-on-Hudson, N. Y. 10533.
Articles on public opinion analysis and related subjects, including voting behavior and propaganda. Book reviews.

411. QUARTERLY JOURNAL OF ECONOMICS. Arthur Smithies, ed. 1886 —. Q. $6.00. Harvard University Press, 79 Garden St., Cambridge, Mass. 02138.
Oldest professional journal in economics in the English language. Cumulative index for Vols. 1—50 (1886—1936).

412. REVIEW OF POLITICS. M. A. Fitzsimons, ed. 1939 —. Q. $5.00. Notre Dame University, Box 4, Notre Dame, Ind. 46556.
Strong emphasis on "philosophical and historical approaches to political realities." Many contributions by non-Catholics. Book reviews.
See M. A. Fitzsimons, "Profile of Crisis, The *Review of Politics,* 1939—1963," *ibid.*, 1963, 25(4): 419—430, which traces the editorial policy of the journal during its first quarter century.

413. REVISTA BRASILEIRA DE ESTUDOS POLITICOS. 1956 —. Sa. $5.00. Universidade Federal de Minas Gerais, C. P. 1301, Belo Horizonte, Minas Gerais, Brazil.

414. REVIEW FRANÇAISE DE SCIENCE POLITIQUE. 1951 —. BM. 30 Fr ($6.60). Presses Universitaire de France, 108 bd. Saint-Germain, Paris (6e), France.

415. SAIS REVIEW. 1957 —. Q. $2.00. School of Advanced International Studies, Johns Hopkins University, 1740 Massachusetts Ave., N.W., Washington, D. C. 20036.
Presents current thought on the theoretical and practical aspects of international relations as well as news items regarding the school.

416. SCIENCE AND SOCIETY. 1936 —. Q. $5.00. Science and Society, Inc., 30 E. 20th St., New York, N. Y. 10003.

417. SOCIAL AND ECONOMIC STUDIES. 1953 —. Q. 40s. Institute of Social and Economic Research, University of the West Indies, Mona, Jamaica, W.I.
Topics related to the West Indies and developing countries generally.

418. SOCIAL FORCES: A Scientific Medium of Social Study and Interpretation. 1922 —. 4 x y. $6.00. University of North Carolina Press, Chapel Hill, N. C. 27515.
Sociology and related subjects, including population, public opinion, and developing nations.

419. SOCIAL RESEARCH: An International Quarterly of Political and Social Science. 1934 —. Q. $7.50. New School for Social Research, 66 W. 12th St., New York, N. Y. 10011.
An interdisciplinary and international journal of political and social science. Its aim is "to explore significant trends in the sciences of man and society." Book reviews.

420. SOCIAL SCIENCE. (National Social Science Honor Society, Pi Gamma Mu.) 1925 —. Q. $2.50. Social Science Publishing Co., 1719 Ames St., Winfield, Kan. 67156.
Book reviews. Index. Cumulative index for Vols. 21—25 (January 1946—October 1950).

421. SOCIAL SCIENCE INFORMATION. 1962 —. Q. $12.00. Mouton & Co., N.V., Box 1132, The Hague, Netherlands.
Published by the International Social Science Council with the financial assistance of UNESCO and the Ecole Pratique des Hautes Etudes, Sorbonne.
This journal supplies interdisciplinary documentation on the progress of research and teaching in the social sciences in various countries—more particularly the organization of research, its aims, methods, and problems—with special emphasis on intercultural comparative research.
Leading articles by specialists from countries all over the world; scientific news; information on international and national organizations, research centers and training institutions, meetings, etc.; reviews of books and new periodicals; and information on the activities of the International Social Science Council, the research program of the European Coordination Centre for Research and Documentation in the Social Sciences (Vienna).

422. SOCIOLOGICAL QUARTERLY. (Midwest Sociological Society.) 1960 —. Q. $5.50. Central Publications, Southern Illinois University, Edwardsville, Ill. 62025.
Book reviews. Index.

423. SOCIOLOGY OF EDUCATION. Leila Sussman, ed. 1927 —. Q. $7.00. American Sociological Association, 1755 Massachusetts Ave., N.W., Washington, D. C. 20036.
Formerly *Journal of Educational Sociology*.
A forum for studies of education by scholars in all the social sciences from all parts of the world. Contributors' papers are evaluated by colleagues in their own field as well as by other social scientists to insure their value to the entire audience. Educational institutions and processes are analyzed from the theoretical perspectives of anthropology, economics, history, political science, psychology, and sociology.

424. SOCIOMETRY: A Journal of Research in Social Psychology. Melvin Seeman, ed. 1937 —. Q. $7.00. American Sociological Association, 1755 Massachusetts Ave., N. W., Washington, D. C. 20036.
Publication of research and theory in social psychology, by both sociologists and psychologists. Occasional review articles deal with major studies or with groups of related works in social psychology.

425. STUDIES ON THE LEFT: An Independent Journal of Research, Social Theory, and Review. 1959 –. BM. $3.50. Studies on the Left, Inc., Box 33, Planetarium Station, New York, N. Y. 10024.

426. WESTERN POLITICAL QUARTERLY. (Western Political Science Association.) Ellsworth E. Weaver, man. ed. 1948 –. Q. $5.00. Institute of Government, University of Utah, Salt Lake City, Utah 84112.

427. ZEITSCHRIFT FÜR POLITIK. (Hochschule für Politische Wissenschaften München.) N. S. 1954. 4 x y. DM 46. Carl Heymanns Verlag KG, Gereonstr. 18–32, Cologne, Germany.
Book reviews. Index.

CHAPTER 9.

PERIODICALS OF GENERAL INFORMATION, OPINION AND COMMENT

Section A. Weekly and Biweekly Journals

428. AMERICA: National Catholic Weekly Review. 1909 –. W. $9.00. America Press, 106 W. 56th St., New York, N. Y. 10019.
Edited by Jesuit Fathers and laymen. Includes articles by non-Catholics.

429. AMERICAN BAR ASSOCIATION JOURNAL. 1915 –. M. Free with membership; $5.00 to nonmembers. American Bar Association, 1155 E. 60th St., Chicago, Ill. 60637.
Articles deal with international law and constitutional law related to the conduct of American foreign relations. Book reviews. Cumulative index for 1915–1923. Fifty-year cumulative index in preparation.

430. AMERICAN OPINION: An Informal Review. 1958 –. M. $10.00. John Rousselot, Belmont, Mass. 02178.
A Birch Society publication. Book and film reviews.

431. BULLETIN OF THE ATOMIC SCIENTISTS: A Journal of Science and Public Affairs. 1945 –. M. $7.00. Education Foundation for Nuclear Science, 935 E. 60th St., Chicago, Ill. 60637.
Articles on the mutual impact of science and public affairs, including international relations. Special issues on such subjects as Loyalty and Security, Disarmament and Arms Control, Civil Defense, and China Today. Book reviews; bibliographies.

432. BUSINESS WEEK. 1929 –. W. $7.00. McGraw-Hill, Inc., 330 W. 42nd St., New York, N. Y. 10036.

433. CANARD ENCHAÎNÉ. 1915 –. W. Paris, France.
Political satire. "No international figure is too exalted, no event or calamity too

grave to escape the wit of the writers and cartoonists of the *Canard Enchaîné*." (*Atlas*, June 1961).

434. CHRISTIAN CENTURY: An Ecumenical Weekly. 1884 —. W. $8.50. Christian Century Foundation, 407 S. Dearborn St., Chicago, Ill. 60605.
   Protestant, nondenominational. Liberal. Strong interest in national and international affairs.

435. CHRISTIANITY AND CRISIS: A Christian Journal of Opinion. 1941 —. BW. $5.00; $3.00 to students and foreign nationals. Christianity and Crisis, Inc., 537 W. 121st St., New York, N. Y. 10027.
   Established by Reinhold Niebuhr and others at Union Theological Seminary to promote United States participation in the struggle against the Nazi threat. Seeks to reflect the Christian mind and conscience as it plays upon the determinative questions of the modern world. It moves into areas where political, economic, and cultural decisions are made and attempts to show that faith is not culturally trivial. Specific international issues include U. S. banking in South Africa, American involvement in Vietnam, revolution in Latin America, cultural revolution in China (Publisher's statement).
   Book reviews. Index.

436. CHRIST UND WELT: Deutsche Wochenzeitung. 1947 —. W. DM 3 per no. Christ und Welt Verlag, Aixheimer Str. 26, 7-Stuttgart-Sillenbuch, Germany.
   Protestant publication specializing in international, foreign, and domestic affairs.
   Reports on political, economic, and cultural developments in Germany and abroad. Liberal and conservative (Editorial statement). Book reviews.

437. COMMONWEAL. 1924 —. W. $9.00 Commonweal Publishing Co., Inc., 232 Madison Ave., New York, N. Y. 10016.
   Edited by Roman Catholic laymen. Liberal. Non-Catholic contributors. Frequent contributions on international topics and American foreign policy.

438. ECONOMIST. J. W. A. Burnet, ed. 1843 —. W. 120s. Economist Newspaper Ltd., 25 St. James St., London S.W. 1, England.
   A leading journal on economic, political, and business subjects including international affairs. Lengthy analyses of key issues. Book reviews. Letters to the editor.

439. I. F. STONE'S WEEKLY. 1953 —. W. $5.00. I. F. Stone's Weekly, 5618 Nebraska Ave., N. W., Washington, D. C. 20015.
   Strongly liberal commentary.

440. MANCHESTER GUARDIAN WEEKLY. 1919 —. W. 41s. Manchester Guardian and Evening News Ltd., 3 Cross St., Manchester 2, England.
   Outstanding paper. Liberal. Political, economic, and other developments.

441. THE NATION. 1865 —. W. $10.00. Nation Co., Inc., 333 Sixth Ave., New York, N. Y. 10014.
   Liberal. Includes international politics, social, and economic affairs. For a complete history of this periodical see its centennial edition, September 20, 1965.
   See *The Nation* (15) for a special index for Volumes 1—105 (1865—1917).

442. NATIONAL GUARDIAN: The Progressive News-Weekly. 1948 —. W. $7.00; $3.50 for students. Weekly Guardian Associates, Inc., 197 E. Fourth St., New York, N. Y. 10009.

Beginning in 1968 will be entitled *Guardian.* Describes itself as "independent-radical."

443. NATIONAL OBSERVER. 1962 –. W. $10.00. Dow Jones & Co., Inc., 200 Burnett Rd., Chicoppe, Mass. 01020.

444. NATIONAL REVIEW: A Journal of Fact and Opinion. William F. Buckley, ed. 1955 –. BW. $9.00. 150 E. 35th St., New York, N. Y. 10016.
Conservative. Public and international affairs.
The *National Review* was a weekly until the fall of 1958; since then the *National Review Bulletin* (445) has been published in alternate weeks. Annual index in last issue.
"*National Review* is out of place, in the sense that the United Nations and the League of Women voters and *The New York Times* and Henry Steele Commager are *in* place. It is out of place because, in its maturity, literate America rejected conservatism in favor of radical social experimentation." (Editorial statement.)

445. NATIONAL REVIEW BULLETIN. William F. Buckley, ed. 1958 –. BW. $10.00. 150 E. 35th St., New York, N. Y. 10016.
Published alternately with *National Review* (444). Semiannual index.

446. NATION'S BUSINESS. 1912 –. M. $23.75 for three years. Chamber of Commerce of the United States, 1615 H St., N. W., Washington, D. C. 20006.

447. NEW AMERICA. Michael Harrington, Norman Thomas, David McReynolds, and Paul Feldman, eds. 1960 –. SM. $4.00. Socialist Party, USA, 1182 Broadway, New York, N. Y. 10001.
News stories; news analysis, discussion, and debate. Writers of many viewpoints, including foreign Socialists. Book reviews.

448. NEW LEADER: A Bi-Weekly of News and Opinion. Myron Kolatch, ed. 1927 –. BW. $8.00. American Labor Conference on International Affairs, 7 E. 15th St., New York, N. Y. 10003.
Deals with United States national and international affairs. Book reviews.

449. NEW REPUBLIC: A Journal of Opinion. 1914 –. W. $8.00. 1244 19th St., N. W., Washington, D. C. 20036.
Liberal, independent.

450. NEW STATESMAN: An independent Political and Literary Review. 1913 –. W. 63s. Statesman & Nation Publishing Co., 10 Great Turnstile, London W. C. 1, England.
Incorporating the *Nation, Athenaeum,* and *Week-End Review.* News and comment from independent radical viewpoint, covering world affairs, political and social matters, books, art, theater, films, etc.
Started by Sidney and Beatrice Webb, joined by George Bernard Shaw.

451. NEW YORKER. 1925 –. W. $8.00. The New Yorker Magazine, Inc., 25 W. 43rd St., New York, N. Y. 10036.
Includes reports from foreign countries; also profiles of eminent persons. "Notes and Comments" in the Talk of the Town section is the *New Yorker's* equivalent of an editorial page.

452. NEW YORK TIMES MAGAZINE. 1896 —. W. $27.00. The New York Times Co., 229 W. 43rd St., New York, N. Y. 10036.
A section of the *New York Times* Sunday edition. Background articles on persons, places, and problems in the current news.

453. PUNCH. 1841 —. W. 105s. Punch Publications, Ltd., 10 Bouverie St., London E.C. 4, England.
Famous British humor magazine. Includes political commentary, international and foreign affairs, generally humorous in treatment. Book reviews.

454. REPORTER: The Magazine of Facts and Ideas. 1949—68. BW. $7.00. Reporter Magazine Co., 660 Madison Ave., New York, N. Y. 10021.
National and international affairs. Liberal.

455. SATURDAY EVENING POST. 1728 —. BW. $3.95. Curtis Publishing Co., 641 Lexington Ave., New York, N. Y. 10022.

456. SATURDAY REVIEW. 1924 —. W. $8.00. Saturday Review, Inc., 380 Madison Ave., New York, N. Y. 10017.
Formerly *Saturday Review of Literature.* A general, rather than literary, review. Strong interest in foreign affairs. Some issues devoted to one subject. Book reviews.

457. SPECTATOR. 1828 —. W. 75s. Spectator Ltd., 99 Gower St., London W.C. 1, England.
Political and literary review. Independent.

458. ZEIT: Wochenzeitung für Politik, Wirtschaft, Handel und Kultur. (U. S. and South African editions.) 1946 — . W. $9.00. Gruner & Jahr GmbH, Speersort 1, Hamburg, Germany. (U. S. subscriptions to: German Language Publishers, Inc., 75 Varick St., New York, N. Y. 10013.)
Leading German weekly with outstanding editorials and reports.

Section B. Monthly, Quarterly And Semiannual Journals

459. AMERICAN SCHOLAR: A Quarterly for the Independent Thinker. 1932 —. Q. $5.00. United Chapters of Phi Beta Kappa, 1881 Q St., N. W., Washington, D. C. 20009.
Contemporary thinking on politics, history, philosophy, the arts, religion, science, and the cultural scene. Book reviews.

460. ATLANTIC MONTHLY. 1857 —. M. $8.50. Atlantic Monthly Co., 8 Arlington St., Boston, Mass. 02116.
Includes economics and political affairs. "Atlantic Report on the World Today" provides background material on current events and problems. Some issues contain special supplements on various foreign countries.

461. THE CENTER MAGAZINE. 1967 —. BM. Free with membership. Center for the Study of Democratic Institutions, The Fund for the Republic, P. O. Box 4068, Santa Barbara, Calif. 93103.

462. CHALLENGE, THE MAGAZINE OF ECONOMIC AFFAIRS. 1952 –. 5 x y. $4.00. Challenge Communications, Inc., 475 Fifth Ave., New York, N. Y. 10017.
Published under the auspices of the Institute of Economic Affairs, New York University.
For laymen; aims to "combine professionalism with practical insight to make economics a living subject for all" (Editorial statement). Coverage includes foreign trade, foreign aid, defense, and national goals.

463. CHRISTIAN SOCIALIST. 1960 –. BM. 5s. Christian Socialist Movement, Kingsway Hall, London W.C. 2, England.
Formerly *C. S. M. News.*

464. COMMENTARY, Incorporating *Jewish Record*: Journal of Significant Thought and Opinion on Jewish Affairs and Contemporary Issues. 1945 –. M. $8.00. American Jewish Committee, 165 E. 56th St., New York, N. Y. 10022.
Includes articles on national and world affairs. Book reviews.

465. CONTEMPORARY REVIEW, Incorporating *The Fortnightly*. 1866 –. M. 53s. Contemporary Review Co., Ltd., 36 Broadway, Westminster, London S. W. 1, England.
Short articles on current political, economic, and cultural events and developments.

466. CURRENT: Significant New Material from all Sources on the Frontier Problems of Today. 1960 –. M. $8.00. Eliot D. Pratt, 905 Madison Ave., New York, N. Y. 10021.
Extended excerpts or summaries from American and foreign newspapers, periodicals, books, documents, reports, pamphlets, and speeches for the information of the concerned citizen and public official. Topics covered range from the sciences to international affairs and American foreign policy.
The Current Readers Service offers to subscribers free copies of brochures on public affairs each month. They are provided by the Library Foundation for Voluntary Organizations, Inc., in cooperation with *Current* so that they may be more available to concerned citizens.
Annual general subject and author indexes.

467. DAEDALUS. 1958 –. Q. $6.50. Journal of the American Academy of Arts and Sciences, 7 Linden St., Cambridge, Mass. 02138.
Has widened its interests in recent years. Now concerned "with the shaping of national policy and opinion and with scholarship in all fields." Each issue devoted to a single topic of major concern. Articles by outstanding writers. Balanced presentation. No editorials. Coverage includes public and international affairs, e.g., special issues on Arms Control, Color and Race, Towards the Year 2000; Work in Progress.

468. DOCUMENTS: Revue des Questions Allemandes. 1945 – . BM. 15 Fr. Documents, 10 rue Saint-Marc, Paris (2e), France.
Specializes on West and East German topics. Book reviews. Index; cumulative index for 1945–47.

469. ENCOUNTER. Stephen Spender and Melvin J. Lasky, eds. 1953 –. M. 50s. 25 Haymarket, London S.W. 1, England.
Monthly magazine of current affairs, literature, and the arts. Articles and book reviews by leading writers.
British and American coeditors. Supported by the Congress for Cultural Freedom until 1964. Semiannual index.

470. FABIAN NEWS. 1891 —. M. 3d per no. Fabian Society, 11 Dartmouth St., London S.W. 1, England.

471. FORTUNE. 1930 —. M. $14. Time, Inc., Rockefeller Center, New York, N. Y. 10020.
Includes coverage of economic, social, and political trends. Every issue has a regular column on international business, and special 14th issue published on September 15 each year contains an annual list of the 200 largest industrial corporations outside the United States.

472. FRANKFURTER HEFTE: Zeitschrift für Kultur und Politik. 1946 —. M. DM 37. Frankfurter Hefte, Reichenbachweg 216, 6243 Falkenstein, Germany.
Catholic; leftist on political and economic questions.

473. FRIENDS JOURNAL. 1955 —. BM. $5.00. Friends Publishing Corp., 152-A N. 15th St., Philadelphia, Pa. 19102.
Index.

474. HARPER'S MAGAZINE. 1850 —. M. $8.50. Harper's Magazine, Inc., 2 Park Ave., New York, N. Y. 10016.
Includes recent history, international affairs, political and contemporary problems.

475. HOCHLAND. 1903 — . BM. DM 16.80 ($4.80). Kosel-Verlag, Kaiser Ludwigsplatz 6, 8 Munich 15, Germany.
Leading Catholic intellectual periodical, edited by laymen.

476. INTERCOLLEGIATE REVIEW: A Journal of Scholarship and Opinion. 1965 —. Four issues during the academic year. $4.00; free to student members and professors. Intercollegiate Studies Institute, Inc., 14 South Bryn Mawr Ave., Bryn Mawr, Pa. 19010.
Strongly conservative. Articles on contemporary problems. The March—April 1966 issue, for instance, included three articles on "Morality and the Modern War." Book reviews.

477. MIDSTREAM: A Monthly Jewish Review. 1955 —. M. $6.00. Theodor Herzl Foundation, Inc., 515 Park Ave., New York, N. Y. 10022.
A Zionist publication. Study and discussion of problems confronting Jews in the world today. Book reviews. Index.

478. MILITARY GOVERNMENT JOURNAL AND NEWS LETTER. 1949 —. M. Free with membership; $4.00 to nonmembers. Military Government Association, 5611 Nevada Ave., N. W., Washington, D. C. 20015.

479. MODERATOR: The National Magazine for the Leading College Student. 1962 —. BM. $3.00; free to certain leaders of campus activities and organizations. Moderator, 1738 Pine St., Philadelphia, Pa. 19104.
Features articles by U. S. student leaders and eminent nonstudents. Covers political, educational, and cultural activities of students. International topics included.

480. MONAT: eine internationale Zeitschrift. 1948 —. M. DM 15. Monat, Schorlemer-Allee 28, Berlin 33, Germany.
Liberal journal of opinion. Outstanding German and non-German contributors.

481. MONTHLY REVIEW: An Independent Socialist Magazine. Leo Huberman and Paul M. Sweezy, eds. 1949 –. M; BM (July–Aug.). $6.00. Monthly Review, 116 W. 14th St., New York, N. Y. 10011.
Leading Marxist (not Communist) economic journal. Includes sections titled Review of the Month, World Events, Correspondence. Articles; book reviews. Index.

482. NATIONAL VOTER. 1967 –. 10 x y. $1.00. League of Women Voters of the United States, 1200 17th St., N. W., Washington, D. C. 20036.
Balanced statements of problems facing the American voter, including the international scene. Presents pros and cons of various issues; nonpartisan.

483. HISTORY AND THEORY: Studies in the Philosophy of History. 1960 – . Irr. $9.00. Wesleyan University Press, Middletown, Conn. 06457. LC 63-47837.
Monographs, reviews, essays, notes and bibliographies principally in four areas: 1) theories of history: cause, law, explanation, generalization, determinism; 2) historiography: studies of historians, historical philosophers, historical figures, and events which illuminate general historiographic problems; 3) methods of history: interpretation, selection of facts, objectivity, social and cultural implications of the historian's method; 4) related disciplines: relationship of problems in historical theory and method to those of economic, psychological, and other social sciences (Publisher's statement).
Cumulative index for Vols. I–V.

484. NEW POLITICS: A Journal of Socialist Thought. 1961 –. Q. $3.50. New Politics Publishing Co., 507 Fifth Ave., New York, N. Y. 10017.
Book reviews. Index.

485. NIEMAN REPORTS. 1947 –. Q. $3.00. Society of Nieman Fellows, 77 Dunster St., Cambridge, Mass. 02138.
Published by the Nieman Alumni Council, representing the newspaper men who have held Nieman Fellowships at Harvard.
Articles on problems of the American and foreign press. Book reviews.

486. PHYLON: The Atlanta University Review of Race and Culture. Tilman C. Cothran, ed. 1940 –. Q. $3.00. Atlanta University, 223 Chestnut St., Atlanta, Ga. 30314.
Includes essays and research articles written within the framework of cultural and racial contacts.

487. POLITISCHE MEINUNG: Monatshefte für Fragen der Zeit. 1956 – . M. DM 18. Verlag Staat und Gesellschaft, Meckenheimer Str. 56, 53 Bonn, Germany.
Includes international relations. Book reviews.

488. POPULATION BULLETIN. 1944 –. 6 x y. $3.00. Population Reference Bureau, Inc., 1755 Massachusetts Ave., N. W., Washington, D. C. 20036.
Studies of the problems of expanding population.
Members of the Population Reference Bureau also receive *Population Profiles,* brief summaries of specific demographic situations, published frequently throughout the year; the annual *World Data Sheet,* giving population facts on 135 countries; and *PRB Selections,* miscellaneous statements of demographic interest published when available. Written for lay readers.

489. POPULATION STUDIES. 1947 –. 3 x y. 60s. Population Investigation Committee, London School of Economics, Houghton St., London W. C. 2, England.

490. PROGRESSIVE. 1909 –. M. $5.00. The Progressive, Inc., 408 W. Gorham, Madison, Wisc. 53703.
Articles represent a variety of opinions consistent with the general policies of this liberal periodical.

491. THE PUBLIC INTEREST. Daniel Bell and Irving Kristol, eds. 1965 –. Q. $5.00. Freedom House, Dept. 5968, 20 W. 40th St., New York, N. Y. 10018.
"Concerned with the problem of American democracy: problems of public policy especially, but also problems of democratic theory as related to the American experience. Broadest possible scope is given to controversy as the proper journalistic and educational form in certain instances. The editors do not care whether a contributor writes from a 'liberal' or a 'conservative' or a 'radical' point of view provided he is enlightening and provocative." (Editorial statement.)

492. RACE. (Institute of Race Relations.) Donald Wood, ed. 1959 –. Q. $6.00. Oxford University Press, Press Rd., London N.W. 10, England.
Articles on all aspects of race relations in different parts of the world. Includes articles on contemporary political problems and contributions from anthropologists, historians, sociologists, and psychologists.
Index for every three volumes.

493. RAMPARTS. 1962 –. M. $8.50. Ramparts Magazine, Inc., 301 Broadway, San Francisco, Calif. 94133.
Originally a left-wing Catholic lay journal, it changed in 1965 into a general gadfly and muckraking magazine on the liberal-to-left side.

494. REVUE DES DEUX MONDES. 1829 –. BM. 80 Fr ($17.00). Revue des Deux Mondes, 15 rue de l'Université, Paris (7ᵉ), France.

495. SOUTH ATLANTIC QUARTERLY. 1902 –. Q. $6.00. Duke University Press, Box 6697, College Station, Durham, N. C. 27708.
Nonregional. Includes social and political issues.

496. SOUTHWEST REVIEW. Margaret L. Hartley, ed. 1915 –. Q. $3.00. Southern Methodist University Press, Dallas, Tex. 75222.
Formerly the *Texas Review* (1915–1924). Regional, national, and international affairs topics.
Index; cumulative index for Vols. 1–50 (1915–65) in preparation.

497. SOUTHWESTERN SOCIAL SCIENCE QUARTERLY. 1920 –. Q. $5.00. University of Texas Press, Austin, Tex. 78712.
Published under the direction of the Southwestern Social Science Association. Formerly *Southwestern Political Science Quarterly*, later *Southwestern Political and Social Science Quarterly*.

498. STIMMEN DER ZEIT: Monatsschrift für das Geistesleben der Gegenwart. 1865 –. M. DM 38.40. Verlag Herder KG, Hermann-Herber-Str. 4, Freiburg, Germany.
Catholic intellectual periodical, edited by Jesuit Fathers.

499. UNITED STATES NAVAL INSTITUTE PROCEEDINGS. 1873 –. M. $7.00. United States Naval Institute, Annapolis, Md. 21402.
Some articles on international affairs. Book reviews. Cumulative index for Vols. 1–27 (1874–1901) and Vols. 28–45 (1902–1919).

500. VIRGINIA QUARTERLY REVIEW: A National Journal of Literature and Discussion. 1925 –. Q. $5.00. University of Virginia, 1 West Range, Charlottesville, Va. 22903.
Not regional in scope. Includes economics and politics by specialists.

501. VITAL SPEECHES OF THE DAY. 1934 –. SM. $8.00. City News Publishing Co., 1 Wolf's Lane, Pelham, N. Y. 10803.
Texts of important public speeches.

502. YALE REVIEW. 1911 –. Q. $5.00. Yale University Press, 28 Hillhouse Ave., New Haven, Conn. 06520.
Articles on current problems and developments in foreign affairs.

Section C. Journals Specializing In Communism

503. COMMUNIST AFFAIRS: A Bi-Monthly Review. 1962 –. BM. $5.00. Research Institute on Communist Strategy and Propaganda, University of Southern California, University Park, Los Angeles, Calif. 90007.
Sections on Background, Developments and Trends, Quotable Quotes from Communist Publications, Biography (of Communist leaders). Book reviews.

504. POLITICAL AFFAIRS: Theoretical Journal of the Communist Party, USA. 1922 –. M. $5.00. Political Affairs Publishers, Inc., 799 Broadway, Rm. 618, New York, N. Y. 10003.

505. PROBLEMS OF COMMUNISM. 1952 –. BM. $2.50 for residents of the U. S.; free outside of U. S. by writing to the nearest office of the U. S. Information Service. Superintendent of Documents, Washington, D. C. 20402.
Editorial office: U. S. Information Agency, Washington, D. C. 20547.
Substantial articles, carefully documented, written by specialists. Worldwide coverage and circulation. Book reviews. Comments by readers in correspondence section.
The purpose of this publication is to provide analyses and significant background information on various aspects of world communism today. Opinions expressed by contributors do not necessarily reflect the views or policies of the U. S. Government (Editorial statement).
Over a period of years various foreign-language editions have carried similar material. Annual index.

506. REPRINTS FROM THE SOVIET PRESS (see 551).

507. SBZ-ARCHIV (see 341).

508. STUDIES IN SOVIET THOUGHT. 1961 – . Q. F 40 ($11.25). D. Reidel Publishing Co., Singel 419, Dordrecht, Netherlands.

Publication of the Institute of East European Studies at the University of Fribourg, Switzerland.

Research papers, notes, reviews, and other writings in English, German, and French on contemporary Soviet philosophy and the philosophy of other Communist countries.

509. WORLD MARXIST REVIEW: Information Bulletin (North American edition). 1958 —. Free with subscription to *World Marxist Review*. Progress Books, 487 Adelaide St. W., Toronto 2b, Canada.
See also *World Marxist Review* (151).

Section D. News and Illustrated Magazines

510. EBONY. John H. Johnson, ed. 1945 —. M. $5.00. Johnson Publishing Co., 1820 S. Michigan Ave., Chicago, Ill. 60616.
The largest Negro periodical in the country. Illustrated. Patterned after *Life*.

511. LIFE. 1936 —. W. $7.75. Time, Inc., Rockefeller Center, New York, N. Y. 10020.
Semiannual index (14).

512. LOOK. 1937 —. BW. $4.00. Cowles Magazine and Broadcasting, Inc., 488 Madison Ave., New York, N. Y. 10022.

513. NEWSWEEK. 1933 —. W. $10.00. Newsweek, Inc., 444 Madison Ave., New York, N. Y. 10022.
Includes signed opinion columns.
Semiannual index; author index (17).

514. PUBLISHERS' WEEKLY: The Book Industry Journal. 1872 —. W. $15.00. R. R. Bowker Co., 1180 Ave. of the Americas, New York, N. Y. 10036.
Weekly list of new publications released by all publishers on various subjects, except government publications, subscription books, dissertations, and periodicals. Also lists books to be published. Articles; editorials.

515. SPIEGEL. 1947 —. W. DM 1.20 per no. Spiegel-Verlag, Presshaus, 2000 Hamburg 1, Germany.
News magazine; mass circulation. Muckraking tendency.

516. TIME: The Weekly Newsmagazine. 1923 —. W. $9.00. Time, Inc., 540 N. Michigan Ave., Chicago, Ill. 60611.
Semiannual and annual subject and author indexes (18).

517. U. S. NEWS AND WORLD REPORT. David Lawrence, ed. 1933 —. W. $8.00. U. S. News and World Report, Inc., 2300 N St., N. W., Washington, D. C. 20007.
This periodical originated as the *United States Daily*, a national newspaper founded by David Lawrence in 1926. It then presented news and analysis of the activities of the government of the United States and other nations. The *Daily* was succeeded in 1933 by the *U. S. News*, a weekly newspaper with the same objective. In 1940 the

U. S. News became a weekly magazine which merged in 1948 with *World Report*, established in 1946, because of a growing realization that national and international news had become inseparable. Semiannual subject and author indexes (19).

Section E. News Digests and Surveys

518. AFRICA DIARY. 1961 –. W. Rs 120 ($25.25). Africa Publications (India), 9-M Bhagat Singh Market, Box 702, New Delhi 1, India.
A weekly diary of African events, with index, country-by-country and for Africa as a whole.

519. AFRICAN RECORDER: A Digest of African Events. Mrs. D. B. Samuel, ed. 1962 –. BW. Rs 65 ($15.00). African Recorder, C-I/9, Tilak Marg, Box 595, New Delhi 1, India.
Reports events country-by-country as well as events relating to Africa outside the continent. Annual and semiannual indexes.

520. ASIAN SURVEY (see 291).
Special issues each January and February review events of the previous year in each country in the area.

521. ASIAN RECORDER: A Weekly Digest of Asian Events. 1955 –. W. Rs 95 ($20.00). Asian Recorder, C-I/9, Tilak Marg, Box 595, New Delhi 1, India.
Events in all the countries of Asia are listed and described under each country, arranged alphabetically, with a summary for each where necessary. External events about Asia are listed under a separate heading. Sources of the news are cited—newspapers, periodicals, radio, embassy, or government departments.
Quarterly and annual index.

522. CHRONOLOGY OF ARAB POLITICS. 1963 –. Q. Department of Political Studies and Public Administration, American University of Beirut, Beirut, Lebanon.
Text in Arabic and English. Index.

523. CONGRESSIONAL DIGEST: Featuring Controversies in Congress, Pro and Con. 1921 –. 10 x y. $10.00. Congressional Digest, 3231 P St., N. W., Washington, D. C. 20007.
Each issue features one major controversy in Congress, with factual background material and pro-and-con arguments selected from speeches, editorials, articles, testimony before Congressional committees, etc. Also a news summary "The Month in Congress."

524. CONGRESSIONAL QUARTERLY SERVICE. WEEKLY REPORT. 1945 –. W. $120.00. Congressional Quarterly, Inc., 1735 K St., N. W., Washington, D. C. 20006.
Weekly reports on major issues, pro-and-con history, politics, outlook. Congressional organization: seniority, committee assignments, leadership posts, background of Members in influential positions; analysis of politics and elections; investigations; the lobbyists: who they are, what they want, what they do about it, what they spend, what they get; court decisions and administrative rulings affecting legislation before

Congress; the President's press conferences, major statements, speeches, and messages (full texts thoroughly indexed); Presidential legislative requests and subsequent congressional action.

When Congress is in session these reports are supplemented by the record of action on bills introduced, their subject matter, and sponsors; Committee hearings and conclusions; floor action; results of Senate-House conferences. Roll-call votes are listed to show the voting record of each Member and his stand (or confirmation of desire not to take a stand) on key issues.

Indispensable for keeping a close check on all congressional and related activities and developments, including foreign affairs.

The *Quarterly Index* indexes all previous issues of the *Weekly Report* for the year (names, subjects). It is the only current cumulative index of congressional and Presidential activities and politics.

525. DEADLINE DATA ON WORLD AFFAIRS. 1955 –. W. $250.00. Deadline Data, Inc., 71 Lewis St., Greenwich, Conn. 06830.

A reference service on cards which reports on the domestic and foreign affairs of every country in the world, every major world issue, and every important subject in the field of international affairs. An information retrieval system for quick access to the sequence of world events. The current file includes more than 12,000 cards on more than 300 index subjects. Weekly supplements of about 50 cards add, update, or revise subjects. Each subject is traced historically. The information is documented. Interpretative editorial comments are identified as to source and date. The principal subject headings are organized alphabetically and chronologically.

Deadline Data is more comprehensive than *On Record* (531) which is based on the former. Index.

526. DOKUMENTATION DER ZEIT, GESAMTDEUTSCHES INFORMATIONS-ARCHIV. 1949 –. BW. Deutsches Institut für Zeitgeschichte, Berlin, German Democratic Republic.

Includes texts of documents, newspaper excerpts, chronologies of events, statistical data, cultural reports, and cartoons; bibliographies on current problems.

527. EDITORIAL RESEARCH REPORTS: A Numbered Series of Independent Pamphlets, Each on a Different Topic. W. $108.00 (including semiannual bound vols.); $2.00 per no. Editorial Research Reports, 1735 K St., N.W., Washington, D.C. 20006.

528. FACTS ON FILE. 1940 – . W. $120.00. Facts on File, Inc., 119 W. 57th St., New York, N. Y. 10019.

Indexed news reference service; condensation of important developments in all fields. Cumulative index published semimonthly, quarterly, and every five years.

529. INTERNATIONAL REVIEW SERVICE: Analysis and Review of International Problems. 1942 –. Irr. $25.00. International Review Service, Inc., 15 Washington Pl., New York, N. Y. 10003.

IRS provides—in brief but comprehensive form—analysis and review of contemporary major international, political, economic, and social problems with full documentation and references, e.g., on Disarmament, Berlin and Germany, China Representation in the United Nations, and Chronology of the United Nations. Each publication is devoted to a single issue, combining an analysis, chronology, appendixes, tables, and maps.

530. KEESING'S CONTEMPORARY ARCHIVES: Weekly Indexed Diary of World Events. 1931 −. W. $40.00 (including general indexes); air mail edition available for an additional $10.50. Keesing's Publications Ltd., 65 Bristol Rd., Keynsham, Bristol, England. (American Representative: Charles Scribner's Sons, New York.)

Weekly condensed reports on important events and developments. Worldwide coverage. Includes texts or extensive summaries of speeches of world's statesmen and documents. Also statistics, charts, maps, obituaries, etc. News sources are indicated. Weekly, biweekly, quarterly, annual, and biannual indexes. Index of 4,000 names a year since 1959-60; published quarterly, annually, and biannually.

Synopsis of important events, June 1918 to June 1931, issued as a supplement in conjunction with Vol. 1; 31 pp.

531. ON RECORD: Today's Vital World Problems. 1963-66. 10 x y. Deadline Data, Inc., 1078 Madison Ave., New York, N. Y. 10028.

Produced by the editors of *Deadline Data on World Affairs* (525).

Topical issues, such as "Laos: Cold War, Battleground" or "Dominican Chaos" chronicle the background on current critical problems, providing data for their evaluation and developments. Extensive quotes from leading American and foreign newspapers, periodicals, and reports (U. S. Government, United Nations, and private). More than one issue on some topics.

532. SBZ-ARCHIV (see 341).

Includes chronology of events in the German Democratic Republic.

CHAPTER 10.

MISCELLANEOUS PERIODICALS

Section A. Book Reviews and Listings

533. THE ACADEMIC REVIEWER. 1967 −. 3 x y. (Sept. to June) funds permitting. Intercollegiate Studies Institute, Inc., 629 Ledge Bldg., Philadelphia, Pa. 19106.

Its purpose is to present for the use of the student brief reviews of noteworthy books and essays to facilitate research and promote sound scholarship (Publisher's statement). Combination of reviews and summaries of articles and books from a wide variety of sources. Conservative point of view.

534. AMERICAN BOOK PUBLISHING RECORD: Monthly Record of American Book Publications Arranged by Subject According to the Dewey Decimal Classification and Indexed by Author and Title. 1960 −. M. $15.50. R. R. Bowker Co., 1180 Ave. of the Americas, New York, N. Y. 10036.

Books listed each week in *Publishers' Weekly* (514) are cumulated monthly to help specialists in various fields. Descriptive annotations arranged by subject fields. Monthly and cumulative annual index.

535. BOOKS ABROAD: An International Literary Quarterly. 1927 −. Q. $4.00. University of Oklahoma Press, Norman, Okla. 73069.

Reviews of foreign books in all fields, published in many languages.

536. CHOICE: A Publication of the Association of College and Research Libraries (a division of the American Library Association). Peter M. Doiron, ed. 1964 –. M. $20.00. American Library Association, 50 E. Huron St., Chicago, Ill. 60611. Editorial offices: 100 Riverview Center, Middletown, Conn. 06457.

Reviews 500 to 600 books each month in the liberal arts field. Reviewers are 2,300 subject specialists from the faculties of junior colleges, colleges, and universities in the United States and Canada. Concise reviews (100 to 200 words) evaluate titles in respect to a subject's bibliography. Special monthly features, e.g., "Politics in the Middle East and North Africa: The Literature of the 1960's." Serves as a helpful introduction to judging new books prior to reviews in the scholarly journals.

537. CUMULATIVE BOOK INDEX: A World List of Books in the English Language. 1898 –. M (except July, Aug., and Dec.); SA and B cums. Sold on service basis. H. W. Wilson Co., 950 University Ave., Bronx, N. Y. 10452.

538. NEW YORK REVIEW OF BOOKS. 1963 –. BW. $7.50. A. Whitney Ellsworth, New York Review, Inc., 250 W. 57th St., New York, N. Y. 10019.

539. NEW YORK TIMES BOOK REVIEW. 1896 –. W. $7.50. The New York Times Co., Times Square, New York, N. Y. 10036.

Title varies. See the *New York Times Index* (1237) for exact citations.

540. PAPERBOUND BOOKS IN PRINT: A Guide to Available Paperbacks Indexed by Author, Title and Subject. 1955 –. M; 3 cums. per year. $23.50; $9.25 per cum. R. R. Bowker Co., 1180 Ave. of the Americas, New York, N. Y. 10036.

541. THE TIMES LITERARY SUPPLEMENT. 1902 –. W. 30s 8d. Times Publishing Co., Ltd., Printing House Sq., London E.C. 4, England.

Book reviews. Annual index of authors and subjects. Unsigned reviews of books in all fields.

542. UNITED STATES QUARTERLY BOOK REVIEW. (Library of Congress.) 1945-1956. Q. Rutgers University Press (1945-1954); Swallow Press, Denver, Colo. (1954-1956).

Formerly the *United States Quarterly Book List* (1945-1950). Unsigned reviews by specialists of a selected number of new American books, with special consideration of the interests of foreign libraries and scholars. Coverage includes the social sciences.

See also *Book Review Digest* (11), *Book Review Index* (12), *Index to Book Reviews in the Humanities* (13), and Part I, Indexes and Abstracts Publications.

Section B. Translation Reports,
Surveys and Journals

U. S. GOVERNMENT-SPONSORED TRANSLATIONS

In recent years publications issued in Communist countries or published in difficult or unusual languages have received special attention as source materials for scholarly research. In the past they were often unknown and unused because they were accessible only to research workers with special linguistic abilities. Many of these materials are now issued in translation by U. S. Government agencies for the use of their officials. A large number of them are made available to the public through the sponsoring agency or by the photoduplication service of the Library of Congress.

543. JPRS REPORTS. 1963 –. Irr. U. S. Joint Publications Research Service, Bldg. Tempo E, 4th and Adams Dr., S. W., Washington, D. C. 20443.

The *JPRS Reports* are primarily translations of articles and other materials published in Communist countries or countries having difficult or unusual languages, with emphasis on Sino-Soviet materials. In 1966, serial titles were published (USSR 42, Eastern Europe 25, Communist China 9, Asia outside of China 7, Latin America 3, Middle East and Africa 2, and International Developments 9). The China series includes the *Communist China Digest*. It is estimated that about 70 percent of these reports are of interest to social scientists. For further details see: Rita Lucas and George Caldwell, "Joint Publications Research Translations," *College and Research Libraries,* March 1964, and Brock Clifton, "English Translations of Foreign Social Science Materials," *Library Journal,* April 15, 1966, pp. 1995–2002.

JPRS Reports are reproduced in the microprinted *United States Government Publications* (nondepository) (547) and listed in the *Monthly Catalog of United States Government Publications* (1196). See also Mary E. Poole, *Index to Readex Microprint Edition of JPRS Reports* (545) and *Technical Translations* (546).

544. *Catalog of Current Joint Publications Research Service Publications* (See 1204).

Full information on the availability of current and past *JPRS Reports* (543).

545. Readex Microprint Corporation. *Index to Readex Microprint Edition of JPRS Reports* (Joint Publications Research Service). Mary Elizabeth Poole, ed. New York, 1964, 137 pp.

This index correlates the JPRS numbers and the *Monthly Catalog* (1196) numbers used in the microprint edition *United States Government Publications* (nondepository) (547). As stated in Winchell's *Guide* (603), p. 158, the use of this index makes it unnecessary to check a report under the author or subject index in the *Monthly Catalog* when the JPRS number is known.

546. TECHNICAL TRANSLATIONS (TT). 1959–67. BW. $12.00. Clearinghouse for Federal Scientific and Technological Information, Springfield, Va. 22151.

Published in cooperation with the Special Libraries Association Translation Center.

Lists translations available from the Clearinghouse formerly known as the Office of Technical Services (OTS), and other American and foreign sources. Social science materials are announced in both the *USGRDR* (44) and *TT,* but see also the *Monthly Catalog of United States Government Publications* (1196) for additional items. Author, journal, and number indexes.

TT was discontinued at the end of 1967 and all U. S. Government-sponsored technical translations are now announced in *U. S. Government Research and Development Reports* (USGRDR) (44). Translations not sponsored by U. S. Government agencies will not be announced by the Clearinghouse. They are now announced in the *Translations Register-Index* (554) and in the European Translations Centre's *World Index of Scientific Translations* (555).

The Clearinghouse continues to provide reference information and attempts to answer specific questions on all translations whether government-sponsored or nongovernment-sponsored.

547. UNITED STATES GOVERNMENT PUBLICATIONS (nondepository). 1953 –. M. Readex Microprint, New York.

Includes all U. S. Government-issued nondepository items, reproduced in full on cards, for use in a Readex Microprint reader. Arranged by *Monthly Catalog* (1196)` number. The *JPRS Reports* (543) are included.

FOREIGN RADIO BROADCAST AND PRESS EXCERPTS

548. FBIS DAILY REPORT: Foreign Radio Broadcasts. 1947 −. 5 x w. Available to university libraries on a subscription basis from the Documents Expediting Project of the Library of Congress. Foreign Broadcast Information Service, P. O. Box 2604, Washington, D. C. 20013.
Includes full translations, as well as excerpts and summaries of foreign radio broadcasts, news agency transmissions, and newspapers. Each issue contains 80 to 90 pages in four sections: 1) Middle East, Africa, and Western Europe; 2) USSR and Eastern Europe; 3) Far East; 4) Latin America. Several supplements a year on Soviet Russia and Eastern Europe.

549. U. S. Consulate General, Hong Kong. The following publications, released by the Press Monitoring Unit of the Consulate General, are among the most extensive and easily accessible materials on Communist China. They are obtained from Chinese mainland sources.

CURRENT BACKGROUND. 1950 −. Irr.
Published whenever suitable material is available but, in general, biweekly. Contains 40 to 60 pages per issue. Articles and documents are grouped according to subject. This is the oldest publication of the Press Monitoring Unit.

EXTRACTS FROM CHINA MAINLAND MAGAZINES. 1955−June 1960. Succeeded by *Selections from China Mainland Magazines.*

SELECTIONS FROM CHINA MAINLAND MAGAZINES. 1960 −. W.
Selections from a large number of mainland periodicals. Each issue contains 40 to 45 pages. The 500th edition was published in December 1965.

SURVEY OF THE CHINA MAINLAND PRESS. 1950 −. 5 x w.
Includes the most important articles from Chinese mainland newspapers. Each issue contains 35 to 45 pages.

Note: Many American embassies and U. S. Information Agency posts abroad issue translations and summaries of the local press—from Austria to the United Arab Republic. Those available to the public may be secured through the External Research Staff, Department of State, Washington, D. C. 20520, or the Photoduplication Service of the Library of Congress.

PRIVATELY PUBLISHED TRANSLATION JOURNALS

In addition to many translations of foreign material published by the United States government there has been a significant increase in recent years in the number and types of private publications devoted to the translation of foreign research data and views.

550. IASP JOURNALS. International Arts and Sciences Press, Inc., 108 Grand Ave., White Plains, N. Y. 10601.

The following journals contain complete translations of important scholarly articles appearing in leading Soviet, Eastern European, and Communist Chinese publications in the social sciences and humanities.

	Subscription prices	
	Libraries, Institutions, Businesses	Individuals associated with subscribing organizations
China Series		
CHINESE LANGUAGE AND LITERATURE. Scheduled for Spring 1969.	$40.00	$15.00
CHINESE ECONOMIC STUDIES. 1967 –. Q.	40.00	15.00
CHINESE EDUCATION. Scheduled for Spring 1968. Q.	40.00	15.00
CHINESE LAW AND GOVERNMENT. Scheduled for Spring 1968. Q.	40.00	15.00
CHINESE STUDIES IN SOCIOLOGY AND ANTHROPOLOGY. Scheduled for Spring 1968. Q.	40.00	15.00
CHINESE STUDIES IN HISTORY AND PHILOSOPHY. 1967 –. Q.	40.00	15.00
Soviet Series		
PROBLEMS OF ECONOMICS. 1958 –. M.	60.00	25.00
SOVIET STUDIES IN WORLD ECONOMICS AND POLITICS. Q.	40.00	15.00
SOVIET PSYCHOLOGY. Q.	40.00	10.00
SOVIET PSYCHIATRY. Q.	40.00	10.00
SOVIET EDUCATION. 1958 –. M.	75.00	25.00
SOVIET LAW AND GOVERNMENT. 1962 –. Q.	40.00	15.00
SOVIET STATUTES AND DECISIONS. 1964 –. Q.	40.00	15.00
SOVIET SOCIOLOGY. 1962 –. Q.	40.00	15.00
SOVIET ANTHROPOLOGY AND ARCHEOLOGY. 1962 –. Q.	40.00	15.00
SOVIET STUDIES IN HISTORY. 1962 –. Q.	40.00	15.00
SOVIET STUDIES IN LITERATURE. 1964 –. Q.	40.00	15.00
THE SOVIET REVIEW. 1960 –. Q.	8.00	8.00
SOVIET STUDIES IN PHILOSOPHY. Q.	40.00	15.00

	Subscription prices	
	Libraries, Institutions, Businesses	Individuals associated with subscribing organizations

Eastern European Series

EASTERN EUROPEAN ECONOMICS. 1962 –. Q.	40.00	15.00
EASTERN EUROPEAN STUDIES IN LAW AND GOVERNMENT. Scheduled for 1968. Q.	40.00	15.00
EASTERN EUROPEAN STUDIES IN SOCIOLOGY AND ANTHROPOLOGY. Scheduled for 1968. Q.	40.00	15.00
EASTERN EUROPEAN STUDIES IN HISTORY. Scheduled for 1968. Q.	40.00	15.00
CZECHOSLOVAK ECONOMIC PAPERS. (Copublished with the Czechoslovak Academy of Sciences.) Scheduled for 1968. SA.	10.00	10.00
CZECHOSLOVAK SOCIAL SCIENCES. (Copublished with the Czechoslovak Academy of Sciences.) Scheduled for 1968. Q.	15.00	10.00
ACTA OECONOMICA. (Copublished with the Hungarian Academy of Sciences.) Scheduled for 1968. Q.	12.00	12.00
NEW HUNGARIAN QUARTERLY. (Copublished with Lapkiado Publishing House in Hungary.) Scheduled for 1968. Q.	10.00	10.00

Soviet and Eastern European Series

SOVIET AND EASTERN EUROPEAN FOREIGN TRADE. BM.	40.00	15.00
THE AMERICAN REVIEW OF EAST-WEST TRADE. (Copublished with Symposium Press, Inc.) M.	50.00	25.00
MATHEMATICAL STUDIES IN ECONOMICS AND STATISTICS IN THE USSR AND EASTERN EUROPE. Q.	40.00	15.00
MANAGEMENT SCIENCE AND OPERATIONS RESEARCH IN THE USSR AND EASTERN EUROPE. Q.	40.00	15.00

Other Areas

WESTERN EUROPEAN EDUCATION.	30.00	10.00
WESTERN EUROPEAN ECONOMICS. Q.	40.00	15.00
AFRICAN STUDIES IN ECONOMICS. Q.	40.00	15.00
LATIN AMERICAN STUDIES IN ECONOMICS. Q.	40.00	15.00
ASIAN STUDIES IN ECONOMICS. Q.	40.00	15.00
JAPANESE STUDIES IN ECONOMICS. Q.	40.00	15.00

551. REPRINTS FROM THE SOVIET PRESS. 1965 —. BW. $15.00. Compass Publications, Inc., P. O. Box 69, Cooper Station, New York, N. Y. 10003.

Consists largely of major official Soviet documents: policy speeches, documents on internal economic policy, law, government communiqués, statements highlighting USSR Communist Party congresses and plenum meetings, etc. The translations are not cut or slanted in editing. They are designed to give the American student of Soviet affairs the exact source material or the original translated into English and seldom offered uncut anywhere except in the *New York Times*. (Publisher's statement.)

Preliminary translations are furnished by the Novosti Press Agency (APN), Moscow.

552. SOVIET DOCUMENTS. Myron E. Sharpe, ed. 1963–1965. W. Crosscurrents Press, Inc., 156 Fifth Ave., New York, N. Y. Formerly *Current Soviet Documents.*

Diplomatic exchanges, speeches, editorials, special reports, party decisions, statistics, international affairs, internal criticisms, government, nuclear disarmament, space, culture, etc. Official, unabridged texts of important Soviet documents. Quarterly index.

For other periodicals consisting of translations of Soviet Russian and other East European material see: *Current Digest of the Soviet Press* (125); *Ostprobleme* (337); and *Soviet Geography* (194).

Atlas (242) is a journal based entirely on translation of foreign material from many countries, and *Current* (466) is based in part on translations.

Journals which publish summaries rather than translations of foreign source material are: *Maghreb Digest* (317), a survey of French and Arabic periodicals of the Maghreb; and *Mizan* (184), which covers current Soviet writing on the Middle East and Africa.

INDEXES AND LISTINGS OF TRANSLATIONS

553. LIST OF TRANSLATIONS NOTIFIED BY ETC. M. European Translation Centre, 101 Doelenstraat, Delft, Netherlands.

Lists translations deposited with ETC and those of which notification has been given to ETC, if they are not yet announced in any national bulletin. Gives full references; no index.

554. TRANSLATIONS REGISTER-INDEX (TR-I). 1967 —. SM. $30.00. Special Libraries Association Translation Center, John Crerar Library, 35 W. 33rd St., Chicago, Ill. 60616.

TR-I announces and indexes all translations, including those in the social sciences, currently collected by the Special Libraries Translation Center. Formerly indexed translations were also announced in *Technical Translations* (TT) (546). With the discontinuation of *TT* at the end of 1967 the *Translations Register-Index* has become the single U. S. announcement and indexing publication through which availability of translations can be easily determined. The index cumulates quarterly for all entries to date in a volume. Translations pertaining to the social sciences are listed in the category of Behavioral and Social Sciences.

The Center answers promptly inquiries on the availability of inexpensive copies of translations from the Center and many other sources.

555. WORLD INDEX OF SCIENTIFIC TRANSLATIONS. Q. European Translation Centre, 101 Doelenstraat, Delft, Netherlands.

This journal index lists the world's output of translations. It includes the material announced in the *List of Translations Notified by ETC* (553) and the translations listed in other announcement bulletins in 17 countries of Europe and North America, including the *U. S. Government Research and Development Reports* (44) and the *Translations Register-Index* (554).

The Centre also publishes a monthly *Information on ETC* which furnishes information on existing translation facilities, policy, etc.

Section C. Union Lists of Serials

Serials include periodicals published as monthlies, quarterlies, annuals, or at other regular intervals. They also include nonperiodical serials issued irregularly, perhaps several times a year or sometimes not for a whole year. They are consecutively numbered. Serials are characterized by their diversity and like other publications may be either specialized or interdisciplinary.

Ruth S. Freitag, compiler of the *Union List of Serials: A Bibliography* (581) states:

Serials remain the most important means of rapidly disseminating to the learned community new knowledge in all fields of study . . . . The great profusion of serial publications makes it impossible for even the richest libraries to obtain and keep more than a part of what their readers may require . . . .

The published union list is the most convenient device by which libraries located in a certain area, or specializing in a particular subject, may inform users of the serials which each one can make available. Union lists facilitate interlibrary loans and the procurement of photocopies . . . .

For the purpose of this bibliography, serials are defined in the broadest sense to include newspapers, periodicals, annuals, services, government publications, proceedings of conferences and congresses, the publications of learned societies, and similar continuations. (pp. III, V.)

Some compilers of lists of serials interpret the term serial differently. Users of those works should familiarize themselves with the coverage of the particular list they are using.

Because serials are published frequently and more quickly than books they offer the most current and up-to-date information. Their large and constantly increasing number has resulted in special reference works and directories one of which, *Historical Periodicals* (561), lists about 5,000 serials in the field of history and closely related areas.

Union lists of serials may cover a given subject area, or they may name the periodicals found in the libraries of given countries or regions; they indicate either the serials being currently received or the exact number of volumes or issues of a given periodical found in a specified library. Such lists may include periodicals of all kinds, special types, or those covering countries of origin. Some large libraries publish catalogs of their periodical acquisitions in general and in special categories.

It is easier for the research worker to concentrate his energy, time, and money on the most useful places for research if he knows where certain periodicals can be found in complete or partial sets. Such knowledge also facilitates ordering photocopies of desired material.

556. AMERICA'S EDUCATIONAL PRESS: A Classified List of Educational Publications Issued in the U. S. Together with an International List of Educational Periodicals. 1926 —. B. Educational Press Association of America, Glassboro State College, Glassboro, N. J. 08028.
Published in cooperation with UNESCO.

557. Andriot, John L. *Guide to U. S. Government Serials and Periodicals.* McLean, Va., Documents Index, 1967. 2 vols.

558. BIBLIOGRAPHIE DER DEUTSCHEN ZEITSCHRIFTENLITERATUR: Mit Einschluss von Sammelwerken. 1896—1964. SA. Gautzsch bei Leipzig, German Democratic Republic. Vols. 1—128.
This is Series A of the *Internationale Bibliographie der Zeitschriftenliteratur* (572). Recent volumes cover up to 4,500 periodicals. For details see Winchell, *Guide* (603), p. 148.

559. BIBLIOGRAPHIE DER FREMDSPRACHIGEN ZEITSCHRIFTENLITERATUR. 1925—1964. Dietrich, Gautzsch bei Leipzig, German Democratic Republic. Vols. 1—51.
This is Series B of the *Internationale Bibliographie der Zeitschriftenliteratur* (572). Index of some 1,400 periodicals in major Western languages. Includes French items which, as Winchell points out, are hard to locate otherwise because of the lack of French periodical indexes.

560. *Bibliography of Union Lists of Serials.* D. C. Haskell and Karl Brown, comps. Included in *Union List of Serials in Libraries of the United States and Canada,* 2d edition, New York, 1943, pp. 3053—65.
Superseded by Freitag, *Union List* (581).

561. Boehm, Eric H. and Lalit Adolphus, eds. *Historical Periodicals. An Annotated World List of Historical and Related Publications.* Santa Barbara, Calif.: Clio Press, 1961. 620 pp. LC 59—8783.
An annotated directory, prepared by the staff and collaborators of *Historical Abstracts* (67), of 5,000 serial publications in history and related fields, and general publications "if they contain more than 20 percent historical material or are otherwise recommended as worthy of inclusion" (Editorial statement). Covers anthropology, archives, behavioral sciences, bibliography, cartography, demography, economics, education, ethnology, geography, government publications, international relations, international law, political science, religion, sociology, and other fields. Contains original and English translation of titles and subtitles, references to summaries or tables of contents in languages other than those of the country of publication, an index, cross-references, and a detailed explanation of the scope of the periodical.

Defunct periodicals are included if they stopped publication in 1957 and 1958. Otherwise data are for 1958, partly for 1959. Yearbooks and other publications appearing less often or at irregular intervals are included.

This book is a successor to Pierre Caron and Marc Jayre, *World List of Historical Periodicals and Bibliographies* (564).

562. *British Union-Catalogue of Periodicals: A Record of the Periodicals of the World, from the Seventeenth Century to the Present Day, in British Libraries,* New York: Academic Press; London: Butterworth's Scientific Publishers, 1955–1958. 4 vols.

Lists over 140,000 titles located in some 440 libraries. For details see Winchell, *Guide* (603), p. 143.

563. _____. *Supplement to 1960.* London: Butterworth's Scientific Publishers, 1962. 991 pp.

List of periodicals which started publication, changed title, or ceased publication since 1960. Continuing supplement to the *British Union-Catalogue* (562).

564. Caron, Pierre and Marc Jayre, eds. *World List of Historical Periodicals and Bibliographies.* New York: H. W. Wilson Co., 1939. 391 pp.

List of 3,103 periodicals developed as part of the *International Bibliography of Historical Sciences.* Includes allied subjects. Indexes of editors, subjects, and abbreviations. See also Boehm and Adolphus, *Historical Periodicals* (561).

565. Duignan, Peter and Kenneth M. Glazier. *A Checklist of Serials for African Studies.* (Hoover Institution Bibliographical Series No. XIII.) Stanford, Calif.: Hoover Institution, Stanford University, 1963. 104 pp. LC 63–2109. Based on the libraries of the Hoover Institution and Stanford University.

List of more than 1,400 serial publications: periodicals, newspapers, monographic series, annual reports, yearbooks, government debates, etc.

566. *East and East Central Europe: Periodicals in English and Other Western Languages.* Paul L. Horecky, comp. Washington, D. C.: Library of Congress, Slavic and Central European Division, 1958. 126 pp.

Includes serials published outside the geographic area.

567. Erdelyi, Gabor and Agnes F. Peterson. *German Periodical Publications: A Checklist of German Language Serials and Series Received in the Stanford University Libraries.* (Hoover Institution Bibliographical Series No. XXVII.) Stanford, Calif.: Hoover Institution, Stanford University, 1967. vii, 175 pp. LC 66–28530.

Covers German-language serials as well as those published in other languages within the German-speaking countries of Austria, Germany, and Switzerland. All subjects are included. Major English-language series are included when concerned primarily with history, culture, economics, politics, or technical development of the three countries.

Full bibliographic information. Detailed subject index and list of newspapers.

568. *Government Gazettes: An Annotated List of Gazettes Held in the Dag Hammarskjold Library.* New York: United Nations, 1964. iii, 50 pp.

This is No. 10 of the Dag Hammarskjold Library Bibliographical Series.

The February issue of the *Monthly Catalog* (1196) contains a directory of U. S. Government periodicals and subscription publications.

569. Harris, Chauncy D. "Annotated List of Selected Geographical Serials of the Americas and the Iberian Peninsula," REVISTA GEOGRÁFICA, No. 64, 1 Semestre 1966.

Lists 27 current geographical serials from Latin America, including five from Spain and Portugal, selected for listing on the basis of geographic quality, longevity, regularity, frequency, and recency of publication.

570. Harris, Chauncy D. *Annotated World List of Selected Current Geographical Serials in English: Including an Appendix of Major Serials in Other Languages with Regular Supplementary or Partial Basic Use of English* (Research Paper No. 96), 2d revised and enlarged edition. Chicago: University of Chicago, Department of Geography, 1964. 32 pp. LC 64–8750.

Annotated and selected list of 128 current geographic serials published in English and other languages with supplementary use of English from 43 countries. Annotations indicate scope, content, area of specialization, and scholarly value. Lists key American and British periodicals.

571. Harris, Chauncy D. and Jerome D. Fellmann. *International List of Geographical Serials.* (Research Paper No. 63). Chicago: University of Chicago, Department of Geography, 1960 lix, 189 pp. LC 60–16304.

Bibliographic data on 1,651 current and discontinued serials published in 37 languages in 70 countries. Explanation of entries in English, French, German, and Russian. Index.

572. INTERNATIONALE BIBLIOGRAPHIE DER ZEITSCHRIFTENLITERATUR AUS ALLEN GEBIETEN DES WISSENS. 1963/64 –. SA. Osnabrück, Germany.

A merger and continuation of the *Bibliographie der deutschen Zeitschriftenliteratur* (558) and the *Bibliographie der fremdsprachigen Zeitschriftenliteratur* (559). Published in the German Democratic Republic.

A subject index to periodical literature in all parts of the world covering more than 7,600 periodicals. Author index.

573. *Irregular Serials and Annuals: An International Directory.* Emery Koltay, ed. New York: R. R. Bowker Co., 1967. 668 pp. LC 67–25026.

Data on some 14,000 serials, annuals, continuations, proceedings of national and international conferences, and other publications issued irregularly or less frequently than twice a year. Worldwide in scope. Title and subject indexes. Designed as a companion volume to Ulrich's *International Periodicals Directory* (580).

574. Mott, Frank Luther. *A History of American Magazines.* Cambridge, Mass.: Harvard University Press, 1930–57. 4 vols.

Covers 1741–1905. Numerous bibliographic footnotes. Chronological list of periodicals.

575. NEW SERIAL TITLES: Classed Subject Arrangement. 1955 –. M. Library of Congress, Card Division, Washington, D. C. 20541.

Indicates holdings of the Library of Congress.

576. *New Serial Titles, 1950–1960: Supplement to the Union List of Serials,* 3d edition. Washington, D. C.: Library of Congress, 1961. 2 vols.

List of periodicals started since 1950. Record of holdings in some 700 American and Canadian libraries. The section on "Changes in Serials" notes changes of all serials regardless of date of beginning, including suspensions, resumptions, and cessations.

577. *Periodicals for Latin American Economic Development, Trade and Investment: An Annotated Bibliography.* (Reference Series No. 3). Martin H. Sable, comp. Los Angeles: Center of Latin American Studies, University of California, 1965. v, 72 pp.
Descriptions and bibliographic data for 220 English- and Spanish-language periodicals (published mainly in the Western Hemisphere, with some British, Dutch, Italian, and Spanish publications included).

578. *A Selected Inventory of Periodical Publications: Bibliographies in the Social Sciences.* Paris: UNESCO, 1951. 129 pp. *Supplement,* 1953.
Part 1: the problem of documentation services in the social sciences; Part 2: list of 59 major bibliographic services, with details of publication, subjects covered, special features, time lag, etc. Indexes of titles; countries of publication; languages of publication; types of services, such as abstracts and bibliographies; disciplines; and geographic areas.

579. *Serials for African Studies.* Helen F. Conover, comp. Washington, D. C.: Library of Congress, Africana Section, 1961. 163 pp.
List of some 2,000 serials concerned with all aspects of African life including monographs, yearbooks, and reports as well as periodicals. Some annotations. General index.

580. *Ulrich's International Periodical Directory: A Classified Guide to a Selected List of Current Periodicals, Foreign and Domestic, 1965–66,* 11th edition. Eileen C. Graves, ed. New York: R. R. Bowker Co., 1966. 2 vols. 1110 pp. LC 32–16320.
Volume 2, *Arts, Humanities, Business and Social Sciences,* includes some 16,000 selected titles from 117 countries outside the United States. No annotations. Appendix II of Volume 1 is "Subject Guide to Abstracting and Indexing Services." A "List of Ceased Publications" is included in Volume 2. Entries show publishers, prices, frequency of publication, indexes and cumulative indexes, book reviews, language(s) of publications, etc.
Annuals, monographs, and series are not included. The list of government publications is limited to the "most important and representative" titles. Bibliographies issued in periodicals are listed under General Bibliography, Books and Book Trade, and subject fields. According to the publisher the two volumes cover 30,000 magazines. Marietta Chicorel is the new editor of the *Annual Supplements* and of future editions.
Earlier issues are useful for identifying periodicals no longer published, and for special lists. Winchell's *Guide* (603) calls attention to "A list of Clandestine Periodicals of World War II," by Adrienne Florende Muzzy, in the 5th edition (1947).

581. *Union List of Serials: A Bibliography.* Ruth S. Freitag, Comp. Washington, D. C.: Library of Congress, General Reference and Bibliography Division, 1964. xiii, 150 pp.
Updates Haskell and Brown, *Bibliography of Union Lists of Serials* (560). Includes over 1,200 union lists. Defines serials in the broadest sense of the term.

582. *Union List of Serials in Libraries of the United States and Canada,* 3d edition. Edna Brown Titus, ed. New York: H. W. Wilson Co., 1965. 5 vols.
This edition covers serials published through 1949; those published in 1950 and after are listed in *New Serial Titles* (576).
Includes approximately 156,000 titles in 956 cooperating libraries. For detailed information see Winchell, *Guide* (603) pp. 141–142.

583. *World List of Social Science Periodicals,* 2d revised and enlarged edition. Paris: UNESCO, 1957. 210 pp.

A bibliography including 941 periodicals, published in 1955 in 62 countries, which specialize in one or more of the social sciences. General psychology, history, and geography are not included. No purely bibliographic periodicals. Indexes by title, scholarly institution, subject, and discipline. Entries show editorial scope, frequency of publication, date of first issue, publisher, indexes, pages, subjects covered, and number and length of articles.

584. Zimmermann, Irene. *A Guide to Current Latin American Periodicals: Humanities and Social Sciences.* Gainesville, Fla.: Kallman Publishing Co., 1961. x, 357 pp. Periodicals listed by countries of publication. Annotated.

Section D. Dissertation Indexes
and Abstracts

Information on the contents of graduate theses is useful when one wishes to avoid duplication of research already done or desires to attack the same subject from a different, perhaps supplementary angle. Dissertations constitute a treasure of research data. They are often detailed and provide minute attention to a variety of factors. Such data, conclusions, and insights may prove valuable to a writer engaged in a larger work of synthesis. Dissertations often provide facts and corroborating evidence unknown to most researchers in the field.

A number of scholarly periodicals publish the titles of new dissertations periodically including topics chosen and completed. Examples are the *American Historical Review* (195) *American Political Science Review* (370) and the *Slavic Review* (342). *Austrian History Yearbook* (196). Indexes of scholarly periodicals should be consulted for bibliographic data on dissertations.

External Research (77), published by the External Research Staff of the Department of State includes titles of dissertations in its lists of Studies Currently in Progress and Recently Completed Studies.

Because of changing editorial policies the indexes of pertinent journals should be consulted.

585. AMERICAN DOCTORAL DISSERTATIONS. 1957 —. A. $12.00 domestic, $14.00 foreign; when ordered with either section of *Dissertation Abstracts* (589) $55.00 domestic, $83.00 foreign; when ordered with both sections $85.00 domestic, $113.00 foreign. University Microfilms, 300 N. Zeeb Rd., Ann Arbor, Mich. 48106.

Lists dissertation topics, compiled for the Association of Research Libraries. Includes Canadian dissertations.

586. Berton, Peter and Eugene Wu. *Contemporary China: A Research Guide* (see 712).

Includes a selected list of dissertations and theses on contemporary China accepted by American universities.

587. Canadian Bibliographic Centre. *Canadian Graduate Theses in the Humanities and Social Sciences, 1921–1946.* Ottawa: Printer to the King, 1951. 194 pp.

588. CANADIAN THESES. 1962 –. A. National Library of Canada, 330 Sussex Dr., Ottawa, Canada.

589. DISSERTATION ABSTRACTS: Abstracts of Dissertations and Monographs. 1952 –. M. $75.00 domestic and $100.00 foreign; Section A or Section B only, $45.00 domestic and $70.00 foreign. University Microfilms, 300 N. Zeeb Rd., Ann Arbor, Mich. 48106.
Published in two sections: Section A, Humanities and Social Sciences; Section B, Physical Sciences and Engineering. Includes Canadian dissertations.
Copies of dissertations in full are available either on 35mm positive microfilm or as page-size xerographic reproductions, bound. Both prepared on request.
Formerly *Microfilm Abstracts* (1935–1951, Vols. 1–11). Cumulative author index.
"A new research source of potential value to political scientists is the DATRIX system operated by University Microfilms, a Xerox subsidiary and publisher of *Dissertation Abstracts*. Doctoral dissertations now number 200,000, and it is estimated that the total will exceed half a million by 1978. DATRIX has been designed to simplify the process of searching for relevant dissertations, by building a data base comprising over 126,000 dissertations in all fields. The researcher uses a key word list, or submits what information he has on the dissertation (author, title, subject, institution). Key words permit an open-ended search for works related to the researcher's inquiry. Cost is $5.00 for up to ten titles; additional titles are 10¢ each. For further information, key word lists and order forms write to University Microfilms, Ann Arbor, Michigan 48103." Quoted from *Political Science Newsletter of the American Political Science Association,* Winter 1968, No. 1, p. 27.

590. *Dissertations of the Sixties.* 1964 –. A. University Microfilms, 300 N. Zeeb Rd., Ann Arbor Mich. 48106.

591. DOCTORAL DISSERTATIONS ACCEPTED BY AMERICAN UNIVERSITIES, 1933/34–1954/55. 1934–1956. A. H. W. Wilson Co., 950 University Ave., Bronx, N. Y. 10452.
Compiled for the Association of Research Libraries. Includes Canadian dissertations.

592. Dossick, Jesse John. *Doctoral Research on Russia and the Soviet Union.* New York: New York University Press, 1960. 248 pp.
Some 900 American and Canadian dissertations, and "Aids to Further Research"; British dissertations; also bibliographies of bibliographies of doctoral dissertations. Some 300 additional dissertations furnish related material not confined to Soviet Russia.
See also J. J. Dossick, "Doctoral Dissertations on Russia and the Soviet Union accepted by American, British and Canadian Universities, 1960–1964", *Slavic Review,* December 1964, pp. 797–812.

593. Eells, Walter Crosby. *American Dissertations on Foreign Education, 1884–1958.* Washington, D. C.: Committee on International Relations, National Education Association of the U. S., 1959. 300 pp.

594. INDEX TO AMERICAN DOCTORAL DISSERTATIONS. 1957 –. A. University Microfilms, 300 N. Zeeb Rd., Ann Arbor, Mich. 48106.
Compiled for the Association of Research Libraries Annual cumulative list of dissertation abstracts; see *Dissertation Abstracts* (589). Canadian dissertations are included.

595. Kuehl, Warren F. *Dissertations in History: An Index to Dissertations Completed in History Departments of United States and Canadian Universities, 1873–1960.* Lexington, Ky.: University of Kentucky Press, 1965. 264 pp. LC 65–11832.

A guide to 7,635 titles, arranged alphabetically by author. Subject index.

596. Library of Congress, Catalog Division. *List of American doctoral dissertations printed in 1912–38.* Washington, D. C.: Government Printing Office, 1913–40. 26 vols.

597. LIST OF DOCTORAL DISSERTATIONS IN HISTORY NOW IN PROGRESS OR COMPLETED AT UNIVERSITIES IN THE UNITED STATES. 1909 –. B. American Historical Association (since 1947), 400 A St., S. E., Washington, D. C. 20003.

Arranged by fields of history. Author and subject indexes.

598. MASTERS ABSTRACTS: Abstracts of Selected Masters Theses. 1962 –. Q. $6.00 domestic; $8.00 foreign. University Microfilms, 300 N. Zeeb Rd., Ann Arbor, Mich. 48106.

PART III
BOOKS

CHAPTER 11.

GUIDES TO BIBLIOGRAPHIC REFERENCE WORKS

Bibliographies are indexes or guides to books, articles, pamphlets, and documents on given subjects. They may contain complete or selective listings. Their scope may be limited to a certain time span, geographic area, language, person, or type of source. Some of the bibliographic works listed below are generally useful in the field of international relations and recent history, others provide intensive coverage of special topics.

Section A. General Guides to Reference Works

599. Hoffman, Hester Rosalyn. *The Reader's Adviser: An Annotated Guide to the Best in Print in Literature, Biographies, Dictionaries, Encyclopedias, Bibles, Classics, Drama, Poetry, Fiction, Science, Philosophy, Travel, History,* 10th edition. New York: R. R. Bowker Co., 1964. 1292 pp. LC 57–13277.

According to Winchell, *Guide* (603) this standard work is designed primarily for the bookseller and the librarian.

It is useful in evaluating dictionaries, encyclopedias, and other reference works.

600. Malclès, Louise-Noëlle. *Manuel et bibliographie.* Paris: Presses Universitaires de France, 1963. 328 pp.

Lists bibliographies and other reference materials by fields of inquiry. International coverage. Emphasis on French works. This book is an abridgement of the author's *Les Sources du Travail Bibliographique* (601).

601. Malclès, Louise-Noëlle. *Les Sources du Travail Bibliographique.* Geneva, Switzerland: E. Droz; Lille, France: Giard. 1950–1958. 3 vols.

A standard bibliographic work; includes lists of other reference works. Emphasis on the period since 1940 and on French and European publications. See Winchell, *Guide* (603), pp. 27–28, for a detailed description.

602. Walford, Albert J., ed. *Guide to Reference Material.* London: Library Association, 1959. viii, 543 pp. Supplement, 1963, vii, 370 pp. New edition, Vol. I, 1966, 483 pp. LC 59–16733. (Vols. II and III of the new edition scheduled for 1968–69.) (Distributed in the U. S. by R. R. Bowker Co., New York.)

Guide to reference books and bibliographies, some published in periodicals. Emphasis on current material and British publications. Some American, French, German, and Russian items, particularly bibliographies. Approximately 3,000 items. Full annotations, with many additional references. Long section on social sciences, shorter ones on geography, history, and biography. Author, title, and subject index.

In the new edition, Volume I covers science and technology; Volume II will cover social and historical sciences, philosophy, and religion, and Volume III, general works, languages, literature, and the arts.

603. Winchell, Constance M. *Guide to Reference Books,* 8th edition. Chicago: American Library Association, 1967. xx, 741 pp. LC 66–29240.

This is the standard work on reference books. It includes annuals and other serials, and many scholarly publications in foreign languages. Each section includes a selection of basic reference materials in that field. Sections include Bibliography, Encyclopedias, Periodicals, Newspapers, Government Publications, Dissertations, Social Sciences (with subdivisions), Psychology, Law, Education, Biography, History, and Area Studies. Full annotations. Detailed author, subject indexes; some title entries.

Note: Kept up-to-date by semiannual reports in the January and July issues of the library journal *College and Research Libraries,* in articles by Eugene P. Sheehy entitled "Selected Reference Books of 19 —-19 —." Biennial supplements, also edited by Eugene Sheehy, will be published beginning in 1968.

Section B. Bibliographies of Bibliographies

604. Besterman, Theodore D. N. *A World Bibliography of Bibliographies and Bibliographical Catalogues, Calendars, Abstracts, Digests, Indexes, and the Like,* 4th edition. Lausanne, Switzerland; Societas Bibliographica, 1965. 5 vols. 8425 pp.

Lists only separately published bibliographies, including abstracts. No annotations except occasional footnotes. Lists 117,000 items, covering three centuries, arranged under 16,000 headings and subheadings. Numerous cross-references. The approximate number of entries is given in brackets at end of listings. Covers Library of Congress holdings in bibliography. Volume 5 is a title, author, library, and archive index.

605. BIBLIOGRAPHIE DER REZENSIONEN, 1900–43. Dietrich, Gautzsch bei Leipzig, Germany. 77 vols.

This is Series C of the *Internationale Bibliographie der Zeitschriftenliteratur* (572). It is a comprehensive index for scholarly reviews in several thousand journals, including many British and American publications. German- and non-German-language journals are listed separately. For details see Winchell, *Guide* (603), p. 28.

606. *Bibliographie der versteckten Bibliographien aus deutschsprachigen Büchern und Zeitschriften der Jahre 1930–1953.* (Sonderbibliographien der Deutschen Bücherei, No. 3). Leipzig: Verlag für Buch- und Bibliothekswesen, 1956. 371 pp.

Based on bibliographies of 60 or more titles published as parts of German-language books and periodicals between 1930 and 1953. Some 13,000 titles are listed.

607. Body, Alexander C. *Annotated Bibliography of Bibliographies on Selected Government Publications and Supplementary Guides to the Superintendent of Documents Classification System.* Kalamazoo, Mich.: Western Michigan University, 1967. vii, 181 pp. LC 67–28593. (For sale by Edwards Brothers, Inc., Ann Arbor, Mich., and by the author.)

The book contains the following parts: Bibliography of Bibliographies, almost 300 annotations representing more than half a million entries from governmental and nongovernmental sources, including the social sciences and humanities; List of Abbreviations and Symbols Issued and Used by the Government Agencies, about 700 symbols; Inverted List of Abbreviations and Symbols; List of Government Authors (Departments and Agencies); and Index of Bibliographies.

Supplements will be published periodically to provide additional references and indicate changes in the Superintendent of Documents classification system, lists of symbols, and abbreviations.

608. Collison, Robert L. *Bibliographical Services Throughout the World, 1950–59.* (UNESCO Bibliographical Handbook No. 9.) Paris: UNESCO, 1961. 228 pp.
Part I describes national bibliographies, periodical indexes, lists of official publications, bibliographic publications, bibliographic committees and institutes, etc. Part II reports on the bibliographic activities of international organizations. No index. Kept up to date by UNESCO's *Bibliography, Documentation, Terminology* (8).

609. Collison, Robert L. *Bibliographies, Subject and National: A Guide to Their Contents, Arrangement and Use,* 2d revised edition. New York: Hafner Publishing Co., 1962. 185 pp. LC 63–18.
Annotated survey of some 500 of the world's best bibliographies and catalogs. Subject bibliographies and universal and national bibliographies are covered in separate sections. Index.

610. *Index Bibliographicus,* 4th edition. The Hague: Federation Internationale de Documentation, 1959–64. 2 vols. (2 additional vols. in preparation.)
Volume 2, Social Sciences, provides information on current abstract and bibliographic services. Volumes 3 and 4 will cover the humanities and general bibliographies.

611. Jones, Cecil Knight. *A Bibliography of Latin American Bibliographies* (see 762).
Coverage includes collective biographies.

612. Tanghe, Raymond. *Bibliography of Canadian Bibliographies.* Toronto: University of Toronto Press, 1960. 206 pp.
Published in association with the Bibliographical Society of Canada.

613. _____. *Bibliography of Canadian Bibliographies: Supplement, 1960 & 1961.* Toronto: Bibliographical Society of Canada, 1962. 24 pp.

614. _____. *Bibliography of Canadian Bibliographies: Supplement, 1962 & 1963.* Toronto: Bibliographical Society of Canada, 1964. 27 pp.

Section C. Library Collections
and Research Resources

615. Arnim, Max. *Internationale Personalbibliographie, 1800–1943* (see 925).
A bibliography of bibliographies published in books, periodicals, biographic dictionaries, academic yearbooks, *Festschriften,* etc. International coverage.

616. Ash, Lee. *Subject Collections: A Guide To Special Book Collections and Subject Emphases as Reported by University, College, Public and Special Libraries in the United States,* 2d edition. New York: R. R. Bowker Co., 1961. LC 61–17741.
Some 20,000 entries under some 1 300 subjects. Includes the collections in the Library of Congress.

617. BIBLIOGRAPHIE DER DEUTSCHEN BIBLIOGRAPHIEN: Jahresverzeichnis der selbständig erschienenen und der in deutschsprachigen Büchern und Zeitschriften enthaltenen versteckten Bibliographien. Deutsche Bücherei, ed. 1954 –. A. Verlag für Buch- und Bibliothekswesen, Leipzig, Germany.

List of bibliographies; includes both those published separately and those included in books and periodicals. Beginning with Volume 2 references to unprinted lists of holdings compiled by libraries and documentation centers.

618. *Bibliography of Directories of Sources for Information.* The Hague: International Federation for Documentation, 1960. 22 pp.

619. *A Directory of Information Resources in the United States: Social Sciences.* Washington, D. C.: Library of Congress, National Referral Center for Science and Technology, 1965. 218 pp. LC 65–62583.

A guide to public and private institutions and organizations, including universities and libraries active in the United States in the field of the social sciences. Indicates their subject specialization, information services, publications, and research resources. Includes a full description of the various facilities of the Library of Congress and the National Archives. Useful in spite of incomplete coverage. Subject and organization indexes.

620. Downs, Robert Bingham. *American Library Resources: A Bibliographical Guide.* Chicago: American Library Association, 1951. 428 pp. LC 511–11156.

Presents descriptions of library holdings as given in other bibliographies rather than lists of publications. Covers bibliographies, union lists, surveys of library holdings, checklists, library catalogs, and special collections. Author, subject, and library index.

621. Downs, Robert Bingham. *American Library Resources: A Bibliographical Guide; Supplement, 1950–1961.* Chicago: American Library Association, 1962. 226 pp. LC 61–11156.

Includes 2,818 items covering printed library catalogs, union lists of books and periodicals, descriptions of special collections, surveys of library holdings, calendars or archives, manuscripts, selected library reports, and a number of unpublished bibliographies, chiefly dissertations. Sections include General, Psychology, Social Sciences, Geography and Maps, Biography, and History.

For reports on new collections of papers and manuscripts being established at various libraries throughout the country, including collections of papers of presidents and other men in public life, see *American Historical Review* (195).

622. *Handbook of American Resources for African Studies.* (Hoover Institution Bibliographical Series No. XXIX.) Peter Duignan, ed. Stanford, Calif.: Hoover Institution, Stanford University, 1967. 218 pp. LC 66–20901.

623. Kruzas, Anthony T. *Directory of Special Libraries and Information Centers.* Detroit, Mich.: Gale Research Co., 1967. 1048 pp. LC 62–15815.

Information on more than 1,600 subjects in over 13,000 special libraries, information centers, and documentation centers in the United States and Canada, including units operated by business, government agencies, educational institutions, professional societies, cultural organizations, etc. Indicates collection statistics and special subject collections. Nineteen appendixes describe the holdings of information centers not included in the main part of the volume, such as U. S. Information Agency libraries and U. S. Army Map Service depositories.

Compiled with the assistance of an advisory committee appointed by the Special Libraries Association.

624. Lewanski, Richard C. *A Bibliography of Library Directories; Library Science*

Dictionaries. (Bibliography and Reference Series No. 4.) Santa Barbara, Calif.: American Bibliographical Center-Clio Press, 1967. 49 pp. LC 67−20728.

A guide to library directories which indicate their collections and research resources. Some 600 entries.

The bibliography of library science dictionaries describes existing aids for reading library literature in 35 foreign languages. The subject index serves as a key to the listed terminological dictionaries in 20 fields related to librarianship.

625. National Historical Publications Commission. *A Guide to Archives and Manuscripts in the United States.* Philip M. Hamer, ed. New Haven: Yale University Press, 1961. 775 pp. LC 61−6878.

Guide to over 1,300 depositories and 20,000 collections of personal papers and archival groups.

626. NEW RESEARCH CENTERS: An Up-Dating Service for *Research Centers Directory.* Archie M. Palmer and Anthony T. Kruzas, eds. 1965 −. Q. $25.00. Gale Research Co., Book Tower, Detroit, Mich. 48226.

Approximately 200 listings per issue. Cumulative index in each issue. See *Research Centers Directory* (628).

627. QUARTERLY JOURNAL OF THE LIBRARY OF CONGRESS. Sarah L. Wallace, ed. 1943 −. Q. $2.50 including the annual report. Superintendent of Documents, Washington, D. C. 20402.

Formerly *Library of Congress Quarterly Journal of Acquisitions.* Includes reports on recent acquisitions of the Manuscript Division of the Library of Congress. It also describes the contents of special collections acquired earlier. Supplement to the *Annual Report of the Librarian of Congress* is included with a subscription.

628. *Research Centers Directory: A Guide to University-Sponsored and Other Nonprofit Research Organizations Established on a Permanent Basis and Carrying on Continuing Research Programs,* 2d edition. Archie M. Palmer and Anthony T. Kruzas, eds. Detroit, Mich.: Gale Research Co., 1965. 666 pp. LC 60−14807.

This is a revised edition of Gale's *Directory of University Research Bureaus and Institutes* (1960). Lists over 3,000 entries under Government and Public Affairs, Regional and Area Studies, Social Sciences, Humanities, and Religion. Indexes. Updated quarterly by *New Research Centers* (626).

629. *Research Centers on the Developing Areas.* Margaret M. Rhoades, comp. Washington, D. C.: Bureau of Intelligence and Research, Department of State, 1964. 131 pp.

Prepared for the Agency for International Development. Identifies and describes 140 research centers and projects and refers to some 800 recently completed studies and continuing projects. Center descriptions mention 840 senior or principal researchers and their disciplines or departments where known.

630. Totok, Wilhelm, Rolf Weitzel, and Karl-Heinz Weimann. *Handbuch der bibliographischen Nachschlagewerke,* 3d revised edition. Frankfurt am Main: V. Klostermann, 1966. 362 pp.

Primary emphasis on bibliographies but also lists encyclopedias, biographic dictionaries, and leading periodicals. Section 1 covers general bibliography, including bibliographies of bibliographies, national bibliographies, library catalogs, etc. Section 2 covers specialized bibliographies in subject fields such as history, political science, economics, geography, and sociology. Many annotations. Principally West European and U. S. publications. Index.

631. Widmann, Hans. *Bibliographien zum deutschen Schrifttum der Jahre 1939–1950*. Tübingen: Max Niemeyer Verlag, 1951. 284 pp.
List of international bibliographies; bibliographies of books published in German; and regional, personal, and subject matter bibliographies.

Section D. Bibliographies for Selected Subject Areas

SOCIAL SCIENCES

632. *The ABS Guide to Recent Publications in the Social and Behavioral Sciences*. Beverly Hills, Calif.: The American Behavioral Scientist, A Division of Sage Publications, Inc., 1965. xxi, 781 pp. LC 65–17168.
A selective, annotated, interdisciplinary bibliography of 6,664 books, articles, pamphlets, and government reports published between 1957 and December 1964. Also includes several hundred items published previously which illustrate methodology in the social sciences.
The *ABS Guide* covers over 360 journals and reviews, including almost 100 published abroad. The annotations indicate the author's approach to the subject matter, the methodology involved, and the major findings.
Indexes to cited periodicals and books, proper names, and topical and methodological subjects.
Annual supplement, *Recent Publications in the Social and Behavioral Sciences* (642) cites publications since December 1964. In effect, the *ABS Guide* and its supplements serve as a cumulative index to *New Studies: A Guide to Recent Publications in the Social and Behavioral Sciences,* which appears both as a monthly feature in *American Behavioral Scientist* (22) and as a separate periodical (38).

633. *Bibliographie Courant d'Articles de Périodiques Postérieurs à 1944 sur les Problèmes Politiques, Économiques et Sociaux* (Index to Post-1944 Periodical Articles on Political, Economic and Social Problems). Paris: Fondation Nationale des Sciences Politiques. Boston: G. K. Hall & Co. Scheduled for publication in 1968.
Estimated 304,000 cards reproduced in 17 volumes.

634. *Bibliographies Françaises de Sciences Sociales*. Paris: Fondation Nationale des Sciences Politiques, 1960–62. Vols. 1–3. (In progress.)
Classified, annotated bibliographies. Author index.

635. Clarke, Jack Alden. *Research Materials in the Social Sciences*. Madison, Wis.: University of Wisconsin Press, 1959. 42 pp.

636. Grandin, A. *Bibliographie Generale des Sciences Juridiques, Politiques, Economiques et Sociales de 1800 à 1925/26*. Paris: Recueil Sirey, 1926. 3 vols. *Supplements,* 1926–50. Recueil Sirey, 1928–1951. 19 vols.
Comprehensive; worldwide coverage.

637. Harmon, Robert Bartlett. *Political Science: A Bibliographical Guide to the Literature*. New York: Scarecrow Press, 1965.

638. Holland, Henry Marvin. *A Checklist of Paperback Books and Reprints in Political Science*. Washington, D.C.: American Political Science Association, 1962. 47 pp.

639. Library of Congress, General Reference and Bibliography Division. *A Guide to the Study of the United States of America: Representative Books Reflecting the Development of American Life and Thought.* Donald H. Mugridge and Blanche P. McCrum, comps.; under the direction of Roy B. Basler. Washington, D. C.: Government Printing Office, 1960. 1193 pp. LC 60–60009.

Annotations of 6,487 titles, with frequent citations and evaluations of related works not included among the numbered entries. Includes chapters on Geography, General History, Diplomatic History and Foreign Relations, Military History and the Armed Forces, Education, Economic Life, Constitution and Government, Law and Justice, Politics, Parties, Elections, and other topics. Index of authors, subjects, and titles.

640. *London Bibliography of the Social Sciences.* (London School of Economics, Studies in economics and political science: Bibliographies, No. 8.) B. M. Headicar and E. Fuller, comps. London: London School of Economics, 1931–32. 4 vols. Supplements, Vols. 5–11, 1934–60.

Comprehensive; books, pamphlets, documents in several languages. Many cross-references. Worldwide scope. Author indexes only in Volumes 4, 5, and 6.

641. *A Reader's Guide to the Social Sciences.* Bert F. Hoselitz, ed. Glencoe, Ill., Free Press, 1959. 256 pp. (New edition in preparation.)

Chapters on The Social Sciences in the Last Two Hundred Years, History (both by Hoselitz), Geography (Norton S. Ginsburg), Political Science (Heinz Eulau), Economics (Hoselitz), Sociology (Peter M. Blau and Joan W. Moore), Anthropology (Gail Kelly), and Psychology (Walter R. Reitman).

This volume grew out of a research project for the Graduate Library School of the University of Chicago.

In the words of the editor, the book presents a general introduction to the literature of the social sciences that deals with the differences in the literary output in the major disciplines and the nature of available tools—books, journals, pamphlets, and reference works—that are consulted and used by social scientists in their research and teaching. The *Guide* serves not only librarians and the general reader but also the social scientists in one discipline who wish to obtain a general overview of the literature of a sister discipline. Attention has been paid to including not only works incorporating substantive contributions but also those discussing methodological questions (Preface). The Chapter on Political Science includes a section on International Politics.

642. *Recent Publications in the Social and Behavioral Sciences. 1966* and *1967 ABS Guide Supplement.* The American Behavioral Scientist, A Division of Sage Publications, Inc., 1966, 1967. 224 pp. each. LC 65–17168.

Indexed compilations of approximately 1,000 annotated bibliographic citations each year. First issue covered late 1964 and 1965 publications; second issue covered late 1965 and 1966 publications. Can be used independently or to supplement *The ABS Guide to Recent Publications in the Social and Behavioral Sciences* (632).

643. White, Carl M., and Associates. *Sources of Information in the Social Sciences: A Guide to the Literature.* Totowa, N. J.: Bedminster Press, 1964. xiii, 498 pp. LC 63–13892.

Chapters on The Literature of Social Science (Carl M. White), History (James P. Shenton), Economics and Business Administration (Bert F. Hoselitz), Sociology (Hans L. Zetterberg), Anthropology (Felix M. Keesing), Psychology (Robert I.

Watson), Education (William W. Brickman), and Political Science (Heinz Eulau), with lists of reference works and important monographs for each discipline by Thompson M. Little and Carl M. White, and for Economics and Education by Leatrice Kemp.

The Preface states that certain fields are included which do not fall entirely within the social sciences but that it is simpler to include them in full rather than in part. For each subject and its subdivisions a specialist in the discipline or subject field presents a bibliography of basic monographs, followed by reference works, also annotated. Specialized works are included, especially when they represent types of sources considered important for reference purposes. Cross-references. Author and title index. Works mentioned in the annotations are not indexed even when they are important.

Professor Eulau's chapter on Political Science is an excellent introduction to the character and the bibliography of the various subdivisions of that discipline. It includes a section on international politics and organizations which skillfully sketches the change from the earlier institutional and legal approach to the behavioral method developed during the last generation.

While the book was written for graduate students in library science, it is indispensable for students of political science and the other social sciences and areas covered.

GEOGRAPHY

644. Church, Martha, Robert E. Hughes, and Wilbur Zelinsky. *A Basic Geographic Library: A Selected and Annotated Book List for American Colleges.* Washington, D. C.: Commission on College Geography, Association of American Geographers, 1966. xi, 153 pp. LC 66–19595.

A standard list of some 1,300 books, including atlases and serials on all aspects of geography, arranged in four principal sections: I. General Works and Aids; II. Geographical Methods; III. Thematic Geography; and IV. Regional Geography. Bibliographies listed in each major section. Intended primarily for undergraduate students. Preference is given to English-language publications and English translations of foreign-language works, but important books in French, German, Italian, Russian, and Spanish are included. Brief descriptive annotations. Index of authors, editors, and translators.

645. Library of Congress, Reference Department. *Soviet Geography: A Bibliography.* Nicholas R. Rodionoff, ed. Washington, D. C. 1951. 668 pp.

646. Peltier, Louis C. *Bibliography of Military Geography.* Washington, D. C.: Military Geography Committee, Association of American Geographers, 1962. 76 pp.

Emphasis on books and articles in English, French, and German. Other languages also covered.

647. Wright, John K., and Elizabeth T. Platt. *Aids to Geographical Research: Bibliographies, Periodicals, Atlases, Gazetteers and Other Reference Books,* 2d revised edition. New York: Columbia University Press, 1947. xii, 331 pp. LC 47–30449.

Selective annotative bibliography. Stress on American geography but items in many languages. Author, title, and subject index.

648. Zelinsky, Wilbur. *A Bibliographic Guide to Population Geography.* (Department of Geography Research Paper No. 80.) Chicago: University of Chicago, 1962. xxxi, 257 pp. LC 62–21381.

List of 2,588 items in 20 languages published since 1850. Cross-references. Author index.

HISTORY

649. Beers, Henry Putney. *Bibliographies in American History: Guide to Materials for Research,* revised edition. New York: H. W. Wilson Co., 1942. 487 pp. Reprinted Pageant Books, 1959. LC 42–23899.
Classified list of over 11,000 bibliographies, published separately or in other works. All aspects of history. Items in various languages and countries of publication. Chapter 3 lists bibliographies of all U. S. Government publications. Author and subject index.

650. Bemis, Samuel Flagg, and Grace Gardner Griffin. *Guide to the Diplomatic History of the United States, 1775–1921.* Washington, D. C.: Government Printing Office, 1935. 979 pp. LC 35–26001. Reprinted by Peter Smith, Gloucester, Mass., 1959.
Comprehensive guide to printed works and manuscript sources. Part I, Bibliography, lists 5,811 items, with comment. Chapters arranged topically and chronologically. Part II, Remarks on the Sources, analyzes printed state papers and manuscript sources. Cross-references. Indexes to collections of personal papers and authors.
Valuable as a guide to international relations as a whole as well as to American diplomatic history. References to books and articles in many languages.

651. Boehm, Inge P., and Alexander S. Birkos, eds. *Reference Works: History and Related Fields, With Research News on the Social Sciences and Humanities.* (Bibliography and Reference Series No. 6.) Santa Barbara, Calif.: American Bibliographical Center–Clio Press, 1967. 58 pp. LC 67–20730.
Bibliographic and reference news in the social sciences and humanities, with emphasis on history, published originally in the Bibliographical News sections of *Historical Abstracts* (67), 1955 to 1964, inclusive. References primarily to published works, research in progress, and activities of institutions. No geographic or chronological limitations. Index of personal names, subject matter, titles of publications, and names of institutions. (From the Introduction.) Next edition planned for 1965 to 1969.

652. Bullock, Alan, and A. J. P. Taylor. *A Select List of Books on European History, 1815-1914.* 2d edition. Oxford: Clarendon Press, 1957. 79 pp.
Edited for the Oxford Recent History Group. Secondary works only.

653. Coulter, Edith M., and Melanie Gerstenfeld. *Historical Bibliographies: A Systematic and Annotated Guide.* Berkeley, Calif.: University of California Press, 1935. 206 pp.
Guide to retrospective and current bibliographies for all countries. Recommends periodicals for keeping bibliographies up-to-date. Entries mostly in English, French, and German. Lists some reviews.

654. Dahlmann, Friedrich Christoph. *Quellenkunde der deutschen Geschichte: Bibliographie der Quellen und der Literatur zur deutschen Geschichte,* 10th edition. Hermann Heimpel and Herbert Geuss, Max-Planck-Institut für Geschichte, eds. Stuttgart, Germany: A. Hiersemann, 1965 –. (In progress: to be 6 vols.)
A new edition of the standard bibliography for German history. Covers to the end of World War II, with some items published through 1960. The publisher expects three times more entries than the 9th edition, and more non-German writings. The 9th edition will remain a useful source for items dropped in the new edition.

655. Frewer, Louis Benson. *Bibliography of Historical Writings Published in Great Britain and the Empire, 1940–1945.* Oxford: B. Blackwell, 1947. 346 pp.
Edited for the British National Committee of the International Committee of Historical Sciences. Conforms to the International Bibliography of Social Sciences.

656. *Guide to Historical Literature.* George M. Dutcher, et al., eds. New York: Macmillan Co., 1931. Reprinted by the National Bibliophile Service, New York, 1949.
Annotated guide to bibliographies, periodicals, and government publications. Arranged by geographic areas and countries, and by periods and historical movements. Worldwide coverage.
Superseded by Howe, *Guide to Historical Literature* (657).

657. *Guide to Historical Literature.* George F. Howe, et al., eds. New York: Macmillan Co., 1961. xxxv, 962 pp. LC 61–7602.
Sponsored by the American Historical Association. Successor to Dutcher, *Guide to Historical Literature* (656).
The new *Guide* has greater coverage of non-European countries. Some 20,000 items in 35 major sections. Brief annotations. Books selected by section editors who are recognized specialists. Each section lists bibliographies and documents as well as general and specialized histories. No items dated later than 1957. Limited author and subject index.

658. *Harvard Guide to American History.* Oscar Handlin, Arthur Meier Schlesinger, Samuel Eliot Morison, Frederick Merk, Arthur Meier Schlesinger, Jr., and Paul Herman Buck, eds. Cambridge, Mass.: Belknap Press of Harvard University Press, 1954. xxiv, 689 pp. LC 53-5066.
Succeeds and revises, but does not supersede, Edward Channing, Albert B. Hart, and Frederick J. Turner, *Guide to the Study and Reading of American History* (Boston: Ginn and Co., revised edition, 1912). Follows the same main outline. Chapters 1–5 consist of essays dealing with research methods and aids, sources, and materials of American history. Chapters 6–30 provide detailed lists of publications up to the end of 1952, by historical period, including general and special works, sources, maps, and bibliographies which follow summaries on historical topics. Author, editor, and title index. A highly selective guide with little critical or explanatory comment.

659. Herre, Franz, and Hellmuth Auerbach. *Bibliographie zur Zeitgeschichte und zum zweiten Weltkrieg für die Jahre 1945–50.* Munich: Institut für Zeitgeschichte. 254 pp.

660. *The Historiography of the British Empire–Commonwealth: Trends, Interpretations, and Resources.* Robin W. Winks, ed. Durham, N. C.: Duke University Press, 1966. xiv, 596 pp.
Twenty-one historiographic essays written by regional authorities provide critical assessments of the existing literature. Emphasis on studies of the period since World War II. The volume is intended to serve as a bibliography and guide. Section on Commonwealth Literature: Developments and Prospects.

661. Holtzmann, Walther, and Gerhard Ritter. *Die deutsche Geschichtswissenschaft im zweiten Weltkrieg: Bibliographie des historischen Schrifttums deutscher Autoren 1939–1945.* Marburg, Germany: Simons Verlag, 1951. 149 pp.; 512 pp. Published for the Verband der Historiker Deutschlands and Monumenta Germaniae Historica.

Part 2: Medieval and modern history. Author index. German historical writings during World War II, not indexed elsewhere.

662. *International Bibliography of Historical Articles in Festschriften and Miscellanies, 1880–1939.* Paris: Armond Colin, 1955. 433 pp.
Edited by the Comité International des Sciences Historiques. Index of persons, historical events, authors, etc.

663. Lee, Guy A. *Guide to Studies of the Historical Division.* Bonn-Mehlem: Office of the U. S. High Commission for Germany, 1953.
Lists over thirty historical monographs on the organization of the U. S. High Commission (HICOG); on political, cultural, and economic affairs of Germany, including Berlin; and on American programs for information exchange, culture, and special projects. Explanatory comments on each volume, full table of contents for most volumes, and security classification, if any.

664. Miller, Robert W. *United States Policy Toward Germany, 1945–1955. U. S. Government Documents on Germany.* Frankfurt am Main, 1956.
This is No. 12 of *Aktuelle Bibliographien des Europa–Archiv* (248). Annotated documents.

665. Milne, Alexander T. WRITINGS ON BRITISH HISTORY. London: Jonathan Cape. 137–. A.
A classified bibliography for the period from about 400 A.D. to 1914, published annually since 1934 (753). The period 1940–1945 is covered in two volumes published in 1960 (754).

666. Muller, C. F. *A Select Bibliography of South African History.* Pretoria, South Africa: University of South Africa, 1966. 215 pp.
Some 2,500 titles, mostly scholarly books published worldwide; includes articles and unpublished material. References to other bibliographies and atlases. Author and subject index.

667. Ragatz, Lowell Joseph. *A Bibliography of Articles, Descriptive, Historical and Scientific, on Colonies and Other Dependent Territories, Appearing in American Geographical and Kindred Journals,* 2d edition. Compiled in part by Janet Evans Ragatz. Washington, D. C.: Educational Research Bureau, 1951. 2 vols.

668. Ragatz, Lowell J. *A Bibliography for the Study of European History, 1815–1939.* Ann Arbor, Mich.: University Microfilms, Inc., 1963.
Bibliography of some 10,000 items, classified by countries and topics. Biographical sections for each country.

669. _____. *Supplements.* Ann Arbor, Mich.: Edwards Brothers, 1943, 1945, 1957.

670. Weinberg, Gerhard L. *Guide to Captured German Documents.* (Human Resources Research Institute Research Memorandum, Vol. 1, No. 2.) Maxwell Air Force Base, Ala.: Human Resources Research Institute, 1952. 90 pp.
Parts 1 and 2 list books and articles which include German documentary material. Part 3 lists files of captured documents in various depositories, such as the Library of Congress, the National Archives, the Hoover Institution at Stanford. Annotated. Index.

671. _____. *Supplement.* Washington, D. C.: National Archives, 1959. 69 pp.

672. Wiener Library, London. *After Hitler: Germany, 1945–1963.* London: Vallentine, Mitchell, 1963. 265 pp.
List of some 2,700 books and pamphlets on post-Hitler Germany. Sections on Germany under occupation, the Berlin problem, the new Germany, the German Federal Republic, the German Democratic Republic, Jews in postwar Germany, etc.

673. WRITINGS ON AMERICAN HISTORY. 1902 –. A. (irr.). Editors, publishers, and subtitles vary. At present: James R. Masterson, ed. National Historical Publications Commission, Washington, D. C. ca. 50 vols.
Since 1951 published as part of the *Annual Report* of the American Historical Association.
Classified list of books and articles on American history, broadly interpreted, and published worldwide; and of books published in this country, Europe, Latin America, and the Pacific Islands. Canada, the West Indies, and Latin America are not covered since 1936 (for the latter see the *Handbook of Latin American Studies* (760) except for their diplomatic relations with the United States). The Philippine Islands from 1898 to 1946 are covered. Sections on Bibliography, Economic History, Military History, and Political History (including Foreign Relations) are included but Sections have not always been the same. Many annotations. References to book reviews in volumes published prior to 1947; lists review articles. Bibliographies and bibliographic footnotes are indicated. List of over 600 periodicals cited. Author, title, places, and subject index.

674. _____. *Index, 1902–1940.* Washington, D. C.: American Historical Association, 1956. 1115 pp.
Includes references and subject classifications not found in the separate volume indexes.

675. Wynar, Lubomyr R. *History: A Selective and Annotated Guide.* (Social Science General Reference Series No. 4.) Boulder, Colo.: Social Sciences Library, University of Colorado Libraries, 1963. xi, 347 pp.
Sections on General Reference Sources, General Historical References, History by Countries, Regions, Continents. Appendix. Index.

POLITICAL SCIENCE AND INTERNATIONAL RELATIONS

676. *Bibliographies on International Relations and World Affairs: An Annotated Directory.* Eric H. Boehm, ed. Santa Barbara, Calif. American Bibliographical Center-Clio Press, 1965. ii, 33 pp. LC 65–25555.
This study was commissioned by the Carnegie Endowment for International Peace and published for the American Bibliographical Center.
An annotated bibliography of periodical and serial bibliographic sources published in English and other Western languages. At least 10 percent of the entries are concerned with international relations. Lists major English-language journals which contain book reviews, the "Top Twenty" bibliographies with international relations content (on the basis of quantity of titles), and a number of library accession lists. Analysis of publications covered. Index.

677. Burchfield, Laverne. *Student's Guide to Materials in Political Science.* New York: Holt, Rinehart & Winston, 1935. 426 pp.
Guide to important source materials, bibliographies, and general reference works.

International in scope. Many annotations. Section on International Relations still useful for older materials.

678. *Foreign Affairs Bibliography: A Selected and Annotated List of Books on International Relations. 1919–32; 1932–42; 1942–52; and 1952–62.* William L. Langer and Hamilton F. Armstrong, vol. 1; Robert G. Woolbert, vol. 2; Henry L. Roberts, vols. 3 and 4, eds. New York: Harper & Row, vols. 1, 2, and 3; New York: R. R. Bowker Co., vol. 4. Reprints, New York: Russell and Russell, 1960. LC 60–11311. Published for the Council on Foreign Relations.

Selected interdisciplinary list of American and foreign books on all aspects of international relations, in English and major West European languages. Three major sections: General International Relations, The World since 1914, and The World by Regions. Subdivided by subject and area. Limited references to government documents; see section on source material in *Foreign Affairs* (249). Cross-references. Author and title index.

This bibliography is based on, and kept up-to-date by, the annotated book notes appearing quarterly in *Foreign Affairs* (249), but the decennial volumes contain several thousand additional titles.

679. Harvard University, Law School Library. *Index to Multilateral Treaties: A Chronological List of Multiparty International Agreements from the Sixteenth Century through 1963, with Citations to their Text.* Vaclov Mostecky, ed. Cambridge, Mass., 1965. 301 pp.

Index to multilateral treaties, including agreements between international organizations. Supplements the U. S. Department of State *Catalogue of Treaties, 1814–1918,* published in 1919. The citations indicate the sources for the complete text of the treaties. The subject and regional guide serves as a general index.

680. Library of Congress, General Reference and Bibliography Division. *A Guide to Bibliographic Tools for Research in Foreign Affairs.* 2d edition, with supplement. Helen F. Conover, comp. Washington, D. C., 1958. 145 pp.; 15 pp. LC 56–60049.

A selective, annotated bibliography of 351 main entries, including bibliographies, bibliographic serials, journals, encyclopedias, dictionaries, manuals, indexes, directories, yearbooks, and other publications. Many additional titles are referenced in the annotations. Three main sections: 1) General Reference Sources; 2) Sources for International Studies (Reference Tools); and 3) Specialized Sources (for Regional Studies and the U. N.) Author, title, and subject index.

681. *International Affairs.* Princeton, N. J.: The Universal Reference System, 1965. 1240 pp. LC 65–19793.

"This is the first volume in a series of ten heavily indexed bibliographies in political science, government, and public policy, forming part of the Universal Reference System (URS), a computerized reference retrieval system designed and developed under the direction of Professor Alfred de Grazia of New York University, formerly Founder and Editor of the *American Behavioral Scientist* (22). A second edition of this volume, together with nine volumes in other subfields, will be published this year (1967).

Some 3,000 items from all social science and behavioral fields. Foreign coverage included. Each entry is indexed an average of sixteen times. Every time an index term occurs, it is accompanied by all other index descriptors of the item and by its annotation so as to avoid excessive searching. Entries cover primarily the period from 1962 to 1965, but also include items referring to World War I and to classic studies such as Grotius' *Law of War and Peace.*

The user has to thoroughly familiarize himself with a page of instructions (p. xiv). Regular users are also advised to become familiar with the Grazian classification system (pp. xv–xix) for describing materials in the social and behavioral sciences.

The type is printed by computer. Supplements and revisions have been provided quarterly since August 1967.

The URS itself is designed to provide a computerized information retrieval system covering references to books, periodicals, and other forms of documents ordinarily listed separately and diffusely. The plan is to make documents thoroughly retrievable through an exhaustive indexing system and by supplying a complete bibliographic citation, as well as an annotated description, of items pinpointed by the index. (Publisher's statement.)

The ten subject fields to be covered in the series are: International Affairs; Legislative Process, Representation and Decision Making; Bibliography of Bibliographies in Political Science, Government and Public Policy; Administrative Management: Public and Private Bureaucracy; Current Events and Problems of Modern Society; Public Opinion, Mass Behavior and Political Psychology; Law, Jurisprudence, and Judicial Process; Economic Regulation, Business, and Government; Public Policy and Management of Science; and Comparative Government and Cultures.

682. Meyriat, Jean. *French Bibliographical Digest: Political Science (1950–1958).* New York: The Cultural Center of the French Embassy. 138 pp.

Lists 603 items of selected books with brief annotations and articles, classified under nine subject headings including International Relations, Comparative Government, and Area Studies. Includes lectures delivered at universities and available only in mimeographed form. Interdisciplinary. The introductions to chapters constitute a general commentary on all the articles. List of political science periodicals. Index of authors.

"The *French Bibliographical Digest* is intended primarily to make the contributions of French scholars better known in the United States. Libraries, university departments, and scholars will be placed on the mailing list and will receive different issues without charge if they specify the subjects in which they are interested by writing to the Cultural Services Center of the French Embassy, 972 Fifth Avenue, New York, N. Y. 10021." (From the introductory note to the book.)

683. Plischke, Elmer. *American Diplomacy: A Bibliography of Biographies, Autobiographies, and Commentaries.* College Park, Md.: University of Maryland, College of Business and Public Administration, Bureau of Governmental Research, 1957. 27 pp.

Covers biographies, autobiographies, memoirs, commentaries, and collections of essays and letters by and about statesmen, ambassadors and ministers, members of the diplomatic and consular services, and other persons connected with American foreign relations since the turn of the century, including presidents and presidential candidates. Only items by or about Americans. Brief annotations. Index of persons.

684. Plischke, Elmer. *American Foreign Relations: A Bibliography of Official Sources.* College Park, Md.: University of Maryland, College of Business and Public Administration, Bureau of Governmental Research, 1955. viii, 71 pp.

A selective guide to published official source materials—collections, compilations, series, and special reports—and bibliographies.

One-third of the books consist of references to and brief annotations of unofficial publications: bibliographies in diplomatic history and foreign relations, American history, and international relations; and collections of documents and readings in international relations, international law cases and materials, and treaties.

685. Wynar, Lubomyr R., assisted by Linda Fystrom. *Guide to Reference Material in Political Science. A Selective Bibliography,* Vol. 1. Denver, Colo.: Colorado Bibliographic Institute, 1966. 318 pp.

Includes sections on Social Science General Reference Sources, Political Science General Reference Sources, Political Theory, and Ideology.

Volume 2 is to include international relations, government documents, etc.

686. Zawodny, J. K. *Guide to the Study of International Relations.* San Francisco: Chandler, 1966. xiii, 150 pp. LC 65–16765.

Classified lists of bibliographic and biographic publications, scholarly journals, atlases, archives, collections of national libraries, collections and libraries with holdings in international relations, dictionaries, dissertation lists, collections and guides to the use of documents, encyclopedias, guides to films, newspapers, etc.

Some 500 entries, annotated, except for journals. Some 80 annotations are quotes from Conover (701) and Walford (602) published in 1958 and 1959, respectively, which are partly out-of-date. Several listed journals have been dead for years; others are not published in the places indicated.

PSYCHOLOGY

687. Daniel, Robert Strongman, and Chauncey McKinley Louttit. *Professional Problems in Psychology.* New York: Prentice-Hall, 1953. 46 pp. LC 53–11289.

Part I serves as an introduction to psychology. Part II deals with literature in psychology, including reference works and bibliographies. Appendixes include an annotated classified list of 306 reference books and a list of 331 psychological journals.

688. Louttit, Chauncey M. *Handbook of Psychological Literature.* Bloomington, Ind.: Principia Press, 1932. 273 pp.

Superseded by Daniel and Louttit, *Professional Problems* (687), but still valuable for its appended bibliography of 1,000 journals in psychology and related fields and its list of psychological serial publications.

EDUCATION

689. Alexander, Carter, and Arvid J. Burke, *How to Locate Educational Information and Data: An Aid to Quick Utilization of the Literature of Education,* 4th revised edition. New York: Bureau of Publications, Teachers College, Columbia University, 1958. 419 pp. LC 58–10058.

Coverage includes the use and evaluation of references, books, government publications, biographic data, statistics, etc. Index to subjects, forms of material, titles, authors, editors, and compilers.

690. Crabbs, Richard F., and Frank W. Holmquist. *United States Higher Education and World Affairs: A Partially Annotated Bibliography.* New York: Frederick A. Praeger, 1967. LC 66–21775.

Prepared under the auspices of the University Committee on International Affairs of Indiana University.

More than 800 items relating to curricula, educational exchange, institutional relationships, and resource materials. Field coverage includes: the international content of undergraduate and teacher education curricula; area studies; training for international service; aspects and history of educational exchange; American students, teachers, and scholars abroad; foreign students in the United States; training foreign specialists in the United States; alumni, returnees, and program evaluation; U. S. Government policy; higher education and international development; and sections on handbooks, guides, reference works, and bibliographies. Index.

691. *International Guide to Educational Documentation, 1955–1960.* Paris: UNESCO, 1963. 700 pp.
"The first section, devoted to international collaboration, contains an annotated list of international sources, a list of the principal international organizations issuing education documents, and a listing of works on foreign education. The rest of the book, and its major part, consists of a series of national chapters which follow a common pattern: an opening reference to a national documentation center on education where one exists; reference works, legislative, and policy documentation; administration of educational systems; structure and organization of educational establishments; educational studies and research; textbooks and instructional materials; education associations; educational journals; statistics; biography; libraries and museums." (Annotation from UNESCO Bulletin for Libraries, 1964, No. 1, p. 37.)

LAW

692. Andrews, Joseph L., Arthur A. Carpenter, Julius J. Marke, and William B. Stern. *The Law in the United States of America: A Selective Bibliographical Guide.* New York: New York University Press, 1965. vii, 100 pp. LC 64–22264.
Sponsored by the International Association of Law Libraries.
A selective bibliography of American law and subject guide. Sections on Primary and Allied Materials (on Constitutions, Law under the Constitutions, Legislative Law, Legislative Intent, Administrative Regulations, The Law of Court Decisions, Locating Decisions, Encyclopedias, Loose-Leaf Services, and Textbooks, Treatises, Casebooks, and Legal Periodicals); and Text and Secondary Sources (including Atomic Energy, Aviation Law, Comparative Law, Constitutional Law and History, Dictionaries, Encyclopedias of Law, Immigration, International Law and Relations including treaties, Legal Research, Periodicals and Indexes Thereto, Study of Law, and Reference Materials). Brief but precise annotations.

693. Price, Miles O., and Harry Bitner. *Effective Legal Research.* New York: Prentice-Hall, 1955; revised student edition, Boston: Little, Brown and Co., 1962. xx, 496 pp. LC 62–19705.
A guide to the tools of the legal profession written for law students but useful to others. The bibliographic appendixes of the parent edition have been omitted but numerous bibliographic references are found throughout the book.
Includes chapters on Treaties and Other International Acts of the United States, Digests, Legal Encyclopedias, Legal Periodicals, and Dictionaries; Words and Phrases, Maxims.

Section E. Bibliographies for Geographic Areas and Groups of Countries
(See also section on National Libraries and Union Lists.)

AFRICA

694. *The African World: A Survey of Social Research.* Robert A. Lystad, ed. New York: Frederick A. Praeger, 1965. 575 pp. LC 65–10753.

Essays by American, European, and African scholars summarizing recent and important earlier studies. Bibliographies, tables, and maps.

695. Bridgman, Jon, and David Clarke. *German Africa: A Select Annotated Bibliography.* (Hoover Institution Bibliographical Series, No. XIX.) Stanford, Calif.: Hoover Institution, Stanford University 1964. ix, 120 pp. LC 64–7917.
Nearly 1,000 publications and documents pertaining to former German colonies: German East Africa, German Southwest Africa, Togo, and Cameroon. Includes a set of microfilm copies of the confidential prints of the British Foreign Office and Colonial Office dealing with African affairs since 1870.

696. Department of the Army. *Africa: Problems and Prospects; a Bibliographic Survey.* (DA Pam. 550–5.) Washington, D.C. x 226 pp.
Some 900 items arranged under: I. The Military Posture of African States; II. Regional Aspects; III. Africa: The Exploding Continent; IV. Africa's Self-Determination and the World; V. The Ideological Spectrum: The Quest for the Right Direction; VI. The Patterns of Sovereignty and the Domestic Picture; and VII. Source Materials for Research and Reference (including bibliographies published in books and periodicals). There are 16 appendixes consisting of maps and tables in support of the bibliography. The annotated entries for books and articles represent different points of view.

697. Duignan, Peter, and Kenneth M. Glazier. *A Checklist of Serials for African Studies* (see 565).

698. Glazier, Kenneth M. *Africa South of the Sahara: A Select and Annotated Bibliography, 1958–1963.* (Hoover Institution Bibliographical Series, No. XVI.) Stanford, Calif.: Hoover Institution, Stanford University, 1964. 65 pp. LC 64–20983.
Contains 150 annotated titles, in English only. References and quotations from book reviews.

699. *Guide to South African Reference Books,* 4th revised edition. Reuben Musiker, comp. Capetown: A. A. Balkema, 1965. 110 pp.
Lists almost 500 current reference books on South Africa. New sections on South West Africa and the High Commission Territories (Basutoland, Bechuanaland, and Swaziland).

700. Hanna, Wilson John, and Judith Lynne Hanna. *Politics in Black Africa: A Selective Bibliography of Relevant Periodical Literature.* East Lansing, Mich.: African Studies Center, in cooperation with the Office of International Programs, Michigan State University, 1964. vii, 139 pp. LC 64–64995.
Classified bibliography of 1,283 references to articles in English and French on African political systems in periodical literature found at Michigan State University. Index of names.

701. Library of Congress, African Section. *Africa South of the Sahara: A Selected Annotated List of Writings.* Helen F. Conover, comp. Washington, D.C., 1963. 354 pp.
Important, comprehensive guide to source material. Replaces two earlier Library of Congress bibliographies, prepared by Miss Conover, *Introduction to Africa* (703) and *Africa South of the Sahara.* 1951–1956, 1957.
There are 2,173 numbered entries, chiefly books, documents, and serials, with

annotations indicating the scope and character of each work. Almost 1,000 additional titles are referred to in auxiliary notes. References cover Africa south of the Sahara in its widest sense, omitting only the Mediterranean littoral—Morocco, Algeria, Tunisia, Libya, Egypt, and the Spanish Sahara. Includes sources in languages other than English.

First section: general writings on Africa listed under some 30 headings and subheadings stressing the social, economic, and political sciences. Subsequent sections are arranged by country and region. A 40-page author and subject index.

702. Library of Congress, Division of Bibliography. *North and Northeast Africa: A Selected Annotated List of Writings.* Helen F. Conover, comp. Washington, D.C., 1957. 282 pp.

703. Library of Congress, European Affairs Division. *Introduction to Africa: A Selective Guide to Background Reading.* Helen F. Conover, comp. Washington, D.C., 1952. 237 pp. LC 52–60007.

For general orientation. Some 1,000 annotated references, most in English, and written primarily by Europeans whose countries have been connected with Africa. There was very little in English at the time of publication for the French and Belgian colonies, and even less for the Spanish and Portuguese possessions. The editor states that the extensive annotations are written to explain issues rather than books, and to relate individual writings to a basic understanding of each country. Followed by Miss Conover's *Africa South of the Sahara* (701) and *North and Northeast Africa* (702).

704. Munger, Edwin S. *Bibliography of the Geography of Sub-Saharan Africa.* New York: American Universities Field Staff, Inc., 1955. 32 pp.

705. Rydings, H. A. *The Bibliographies of West Africa.* Ibadan, Nigeria: Ibadan University Press, 1961. 36 pp. LC 62–53438.

Published for the West African Library Association.

List of 50 annotated bibliographies.

706. *Select Annotated Bibliography of Tropical Africa.* Daryll Forde, comp. New York: Twentieth Century Fund, 1956. 481 pp.

Published for the International Africa Institute. Seven sections including Geography, Ethnography, Sociology and Linguistics; Administration and Government; Economics; Education; Missions; and Health.

Designed to meet the needs of the general inquirer. Special attention has been given, both in the selection and the annotations, to the more important studies of African problems published in the major countries in various languages and to provide some indication of their scope and significance. The bibliographies, official publications, and periodicals cited will guide the reader to sources for more specialized study. (Introduction.) No indexes.

707. South African Public Library. *A Bibliography of African Bibliographies, Covering Territories South of the Sahara*, 4th edition. (Grey Bibliographies No. 7.) *Cape Town, 1961. 79 pp.*

Classified bibliography of 1,300 sources, covering all aspects of Africa. Over one-third are concerned with the social sciences. Includes bibliographies in periodicals and monographs as well as separate items. Supplemented by the *Quarterly Bulletin of the South African Library.* Author and subject index.

708. *A Select Bibliography: Asia, Africa, Eastern Europe, Latin America* (see 733).

ARCTIC AND ANTARCTICA

709. Hanessian, John, Jr. *A Select Bibliography of the Polar Regions.* New York: American Universities Field Staff, Inc., 1962. 28 pp.

710. Hayton, Robert D. *National Interests in Antarctica: An Annotated Bibliography.* Washington, D.C.: Government Printing Office, 1960. 137 pp. LC 60–60967. Compiled in 1959 for the U. S. Antarctic projects officer.
Material on international law, foreign policy, economic exploitation, strategic significance, world politics, explorations, and expeditions affecting national claims (potential and declared), and analogous rivalries and considerations in the Arctic. (Introduction.)

ASIA

711. *An Annotated Guide to Modern China.* New York: National Committee on United States-China Relations, 1967. 27 pp.
Professor Robert A. Scalapino of the University of California (Berkeley) is chairman of this nonpartisan educational group which includes representatives of many different occupations and points of view.
A selected, annotated guide covering topics of major importance ranging from domestic conditions to foreign policy and American-Chinese relations. Includes books providing background information for lay readers.
The *Guide* states that periodicals and publications printed in Communist China are available from: China Books and Periodicals, 2929 24th Street, San Francisco, California 94110, and Orientalia, Inc., 11 East 12th Street, New York, New York 10003. Similar publications from the Nationalist Government may be obtained from the Chinese Information Service, 100 West 32d Street, New York, New York 10001.

712. Berton, Peter, and Eugene Wu. *Contemporary China: A Research Guide.* (Hoover Institution Bibliographical Series No. XXXI.) Stanford, Calif.: Hoover Institution, Stanford University, 1967. 695 pp. LC 67–14235.
Bibliographic and reference works, selected documentary materials (covering such areas as law, politics, and government; foreign relations; economics; and education and culture), and selected serial publications–mostly in the social sciences and humanities.
The materials incorporated in the *Guide* concern almost exclusively post-1949 mainland China and post-1945 Taiwan, from publications from the mainland, Taiwan, Hong Kong, Japan, the United States, Great Britain, the Soviet Union, and other countries. Each chapter and subsection is preceded by an introduction placing its reference material in proper context; they contain a wealth of additional information and cross-references. Entries are annotated in detail and contain both descriptive and evaluative comment.
The two appendixes include publications devoted to the resources of research libraries and institutions in the United States and abroad, and a selected list of dissertations and theses on contemporary China accepted by American Universities. Author, title, and subject indexes.
The bulk of the material contained in the *Guide* is available in the major East Asian libraries in the United States. (Abbreviated publisher's statement.)

713. *Bibliography of China.* New Haven, Conn.: HRAF, 1956. 132 pp.
Prepared by Stanford University for the Human Relations Area Files (HRAF).
Classified bibliography. Full annotations.

714. *Bibliography of Social Science Periodicals and Monograph Series.* (Foreign Social Science Bibliographies, Series P–92.) Washington, D.C.: Bureau of the Census, 1961–1965.

A series of 22 bibliographies of social science periodicals, monograph series, and monographs published in Communist bloc countries and countries using so-called difficult languages. The series covers the period from 1950 to date of publication. Sections on Book Reviews and Book Notes.

Entries are arranged under 15 disciplines. Brief annotations. Indexes of subjects, titles, authors, and issuing agents.

The series is restricted to holdings of the Library of Congress but does not cover all of them. Covers Albania, Bulgaria, China (Mainland), China (Republic), Czechoslovakia, Denmark, Finland, German Democratic Republic, Greece, Hong Kong, Hungary, Iceland, Japan, Korea (North), Korea (Republic), Norway, Poland, Rumania, Sweden, Turkey, USSR, and Yugoslavia.

715. Borton, Hugh, et al. *A Selected List of Books and Articles on Japan in English, French and German,* revised and enlarged edition. Cambridge, Mass.: Harvard University Press for the Harvard-Yenching Institute, 1954. xiv, 272 pp. LC 53–5055.

Annotated bibliography of 1,781 titles in the social sciences and humanities, published up to 1952. Bibliographies, reference works, and periodicals. Index of authors, titles, and subjects.

716. *Contemporary China.* Richard Sorich, ed. New York: American Council of Learned Societies and Social Science Research Council, 1961, 99 pp. LC 61–4979.

A list of reports on China published by the United States Joint Publications Research Service from 1957 through June 1960. Bibliographic citations, list of serial publications, and index, including category list.

717. Eggan, Fred, et al. *Selected Bibliography of the Philippines.* New Haven, Conn.: HRAF Press, 1956. vi, 138 pp. (Distributed by Taplinger Publishing Co., New York.)

A Human Relations Area Files publication.

718. Embree, John Fee, and Lillian Ota Dotson. *Bibliography of the Peoples and Cultures of Mainland South East Asia.* New Haven, Conn.: Yale University Press, 1950. xxxiii, 821 pp. LC 50–1498.

Extensive bibliography of books and articles in Western languages. Malaya not included in the geographic area covered. Some annotations. Many references to book reviews in scholarly journals. Detailed table of contents; no indexes.

719. Embree, John Fee. *Books on Southeast Asia: A Select Bibliography,* 4th edition revised by Bruno Lasker. New York: American Institute of Pacific Relations, 1956. 50 pp.

Emphasis on history, politics, economics, and social factors.

720. Hay, Stephen N., and Margaret H. Case. *Southeast Asian History: A Bibliographic Guide.* New York: Frederick A. Praeger, 1962. vii, 138 pp. LC 62–20439.

Annotated bibliography of over 600 general bibliographies and books, reference works, articles, and dissertations. Stress on recent publications. References to book reviews. Author and subject indexes.

721. Hucker, Charles O. *China: A Critical Bibliography.* Tucson, Ariz.: University of Arizona Press, 1962, 125 pp. LC 62–10624.

Sections on history, intellectual patterns, politics, society, and economics. A selected and annotated list of books, articles, and parts of books relating to traditional and modern China. Author index.

722. *Institute of Pacific Relations Publications on the Pacific 1925–1952.* New York: IPR, 1953. 117 pp.

A catalog of the publications of the National Councils and the International Secretariat of IPR. Author index.

723. *Introduction to the Civilization of India; South Asia: An Introductory Bibliography.* Maureen L. P. Patterson and Ronald B. Inden, eds. Chicago: University of Chicago Press, 1962. 412 pp.

Some 4,300 works, mostly in English, on India, Pakistan, Ceylon, and Nepal. Author and title index.

724. Kennedy, Ray. *Bibliography of Indonesian Peoples and Cultures,* 2d edition. (Revised and edited by T. W. Maretzki and H. Th. Fisher.) New Haven, Conn.: Human Relations Area Files, 1962. xxii, 207 pp. LC 62–20539.

Stress on anthropology and sociology; includes materials on geography, colonial administration, education, economics, and history. No index.

725. Leeson, Ida. *A Bibliography of Bibliographies of the South Pacific.* New York: Oxford University Press, 1954. x, 61 pp. LC 55–3192.

Brief annotations. Author and subject index.

726. Library of Congress, Orientalia Division. *Southeast Asia: An Annotated Bibliography of Selected Reference Sources in Western Languages,* revised edition. Cecil Hobbs, comp. Washington, D.C., 1964. 180 pp.

A bibliography of 535 books, published mostly between 1952 and 1963. Annotations. Indicates bibliographies, maps, illustrations, statistical tables, and documents contained in the references.

727. Library of Congress, Reference Department. *Introduction to Asia: A Selective Guide to Background Reading.* L. K. Quan, comp. Washington, D.C., 1955. 214 pp. LC 54–60018.

Annotated list of 811 works, mostly in English. Covers the Asian continent, including the Near and Middle East, but excluding Asiatic Russia. Intended for the general reader rather than the specialist.

728. Mahar, J. Michael. *India: A Critical Bibliography.* Tucson, Ariz.: University of Arizona Press, 1964. 199 pp. LC 62–17992.

729. Mason, John Brown, and H. Carroll Parish. *Thailand Bibliography.* (Bibliographic Series No. 4.) Gainesville, Fla.: University of Florida Libraries, Department of Reference and Bibliography, 1958. vii, 247 pp. LC 58–9842.

The first comprehensive bibliography devoted solely to the Kingdom of Thailand (Siam). Over 2,300 references to books, articles, and documents in nine Western languages; many annotated. Guide to specialized publications and documents in history, government, politics, international relations, public administration, economics, geography, sociology, education, etc. Section on bibliographies. List of English-language newspapers and periodicals published in Thailand.

730. Pelzer, Karl J. *Selected Bibliography on the Geography of Southeast Asia.* New Haven, Conn.: Yale University, Southeast Asia Studies, 1949–56. 3 vols.

Published by arrangement with Human Relations Area Files.
Reference guide to the physical, cultural, economic, and political geography of
Southeast Asia. Books and articles. Volume 1 covers Southeast Asia in general,
Volume 2 the Philippines, and Volume 3 Malaya. No index.

731. Sharma, Jagdish Saran. *Indian National Congress: A Descriptive Bibliography
of India's Struggle for Freedom.* (National bibliographies, No. 3.) Delhi: S. Chand,
1959. 816 pp.

732. Silberman, Bernard S. *Japan and Korea: A Critical Bibliography.* Tucson,
Ariz.: University of Arizona Press, 1962. 120 pp. LC 62—11821.
Western-language material, primarily in English. Covers the social sciences and
humanities.

733. *A Select Bibliography: Asia, Africa, Eastern Europe, Latin America.* Talbot
Phillips, ed. New York: American Universities Field Staff, Inc., 1960. ix, 533 pp. LC
60—10482.
Lists some 6,000 books and journals in Western languages, mostly English, for
college students and the general reader. Covers culture, economics, history, philosophy, and religion. Collateral readings on geography. The more important books are
indicated by the letters A and B and are annotated. Index of authors and titles.

734. _____. *Supplements.* Published in 1961, 1963, and 1965; 75, 66, and 82
pp., respectively.
Add some 1,500 titles.

735. Trager, Frank N., et al. *Annotated Bibliography of Burma,* 2d edition. New
Haven, Conn.: HRAF Press, 1956. viii, 230 pp. (Distributed by Taplinger Publishing
Co., New York.)
A Human Relations Area Files publication.

736. Wilber, Donald N. *Annotated Bibliography of Afghanistan,* 2d edition. New
Haven, Conn.: HRAF Press, 1962. ix, 259 pp. (Distributed by Taplinger Publishing
Co., New York.)
A Human Relations Area Files publication. Classified list of over 1,200 books and
articles in Western and other languages. Author index.

737. Wilson, Patrick. *South Asia: A Selected Bibliography on India, Pakistan,
Ceylon.* New York: American Institute of International Relations, 1957. 41 pp.
Books, bibliographies, reference works, and primary source material. Covers his-
tory, geography, economics, population, etc.

738. Yuan, Tung-Li. *Economic and Social Development of Modern China. A Bibli-
ographical Guide.* New Haven, Conn.: HRAF Press, 1956. (Distributed by Taplinger,
Publishing Co., New York.) Part I, vii, 130 pp.; Part II, v, 87 pp. (in one vol.).
A Human Relations Area Files publication.

AUSTRALIA

739. Ferguson, John Alexander. *Bibliography of Australia.* Sydney and London:
Angus and Robertson, 1941—1963. Vols. 1—5. (In progress.)

COMMONWEALTH OF NATIONS

740. Carnell, Francis. *The Politics of the New States: A Select Annotated Bibliography with Special Reference to the Commonwealth.* London: Oxford University Press, 1961. xviii, 171 pp. LC 62–213.
Published for the Institute of Commonwealth Studies. Lists 1,599 items, including books, articles, and documents. Brief annotations.

741. Horne, A. J. *The Commonwealth To-day: A Select Bibliography on the Commonwealth and its Constituent Countries.* London: Library Association, 1965. 107 pp.
List of 720 books published in recent years on the Commonwealth (Great Britain not included). Titles by subject, continent, and country. Index.

EUROPE (See also Soviet Russia and Eastern Europe)

742. *Berlin Booklist.* Bonn: Inter Nationes, 1963. 15 pp. Available free on request.
Contents range from fiction to documentation.

743. *Bibliography of Social Science Periodicals and Monograph Series* (see 714).
This series includes publications in Communist countries and countries using so-called difficult languages. Covers Albania, Czechoslovakia, Bulgaria, Denmark, Finland, German Democratic Republic, Greece, Hungary, Iceland, Norway, Poland, Rumania, Sweden, Turkey, USSR, and Yugoslovia.

744. *Dokumentationen über Deutschland: Auswahl amtlicher und von amtlicher Seite geförderter Publikationen,* 2d revised edition. Helmut Arndt and Edith Teige, eds. Bonn: Inter Nationes, 1964. 198 pp.
This book is available free upon request from Inter Nationes. Listed items may be obtained from the issuing German Government agency.
Selected list of official German Government publications and private and semi-official publications supported or promoted by the Government. Published in German and 46 other languages for distribution abroad by German embassies and consulates.
Lists books, pamphlets, and periodicals dealing with Germany in general, Berlin, East Germany, history, politics, defense, economics, finance, transportation, social welfare, education, science, and culture.
See also *Schrifttum über Deutschland* (755).

745. *General Bibliography on Europe.* Raymond Kennedy, comp. New Haven, Conn.: Human Relations Area Files. 85 pp.
Lists works covering history of European nations to 1939. Variety of topics, with stress on cultural development. No annotations. Not limited to English-language publications.

746. Halász de Beky, I. L. *A Bibliography of the Hungarian Revolution.* Toronto: University of Toronto Press, 1956. 179 pp.
Published under the auspices of the Canadian Institute of International Affairs.

747. *Introduction to Europe: A Selective Guide to Background Reading.* Washington, D.C.: Library of Congress, 1950. 201 pp.
Annotated items on general surveys and reference books, historical background, recent history (including articles), and European culture.

748. _____. *Supplement, 1950–1955.* 181 pp.

749. Mönnig, Richard. *Amerika und England im deutschen, österreichischen und schweizerischen Schrifttum der Jahre 1945–1949; eine Bibliographie.* Stuttgart, Germany: Kohlhammer, 1951. 259 pp.

German, Austrian, and Swiss publications on the literature, history, etc., of the United States and England. Includes translations of English and American works, books by English and American authors published in those countries, and German dissertations. Full annotations. Index of authors. Original titles indicated in each case.

750. Mönnig, Richard. *Bibliography of Paperbound Books Translated From The German and of Works on Germany.* Bonn: Inter Nationes, 1967. 91 pp.

A list of 682 American and British paperbacks translated from German and 151 written by British or American authors on German topics.

751. Mönnig, Richard. *Deutschland und die Deutschen im englisch-sprachigen Schrifttum 1948–1966.* 2d edition. Göttingen, Germany: Vandenhoek und Ruprecht, 1967.

Some 12,000 translations from German into English and English or American books on Germany.

752. Robinson, Richard D. *Developments Respecting Turkey: A Summary of Events and Statistics with Bibliographic Notes.* New York: American Universities Field Staff, Inc., 1954–1957. 841 pp.

753. Royal Historical Society, London. WRITINGS ON BRITISH HISTORY, *1934–1939.* London: J. Cape, 1937–1953.

An annual bibliography of books and articles on British history. The appendix contains a selective list of publications since 1914.

754. _____. WRITINGS ON BRITISH HISTORY, *1940–1945.* London: J. Cape, 1960. 2 vols.

755. *Schrifttum über Deutschland, 1918–1963: Ausgewählte Bibliographie zur Politik und Zeitgeschichte,* 2d edition. Bonn, Inter Nationes, 1964. 292 pp.

Compiled by the Research Institute of the German Society for Foreign Affairs (Forschungsinstitut der Deutschen Gesellschaft für Auswärtige Politik) in Bonn. Prepared primarily for use by German diplomats, consuls, and public affairs officials stationed abroad, but useful for students interested in German history since 1918. Limited to works published since 1946 which offer new interpretations of German history. Tables of contents are reproduced in full or in part. Index of authors and editors.

Part I deals with German publications and Part II with non-German publications. No evaluations except for footnotes to more than a dozen non-German publications which received special notice or resulted in controversies.

756. *A Select Bibliography: Asia, Africa, Eastern Europe, Latin America* (see 733).

LATIN AMERICA

757. Bayitch, Stojan A. *Latin America: A Bibliographical Guide to Economy, History, Law, Politics and Society. Inter-American Legal Studies, No. 6.* Coral Gables, Fla.: University of Miami Press, 1961. xv, 335 pp. LC 60–53473.

Bibliography of 10,000 books and articles in English intended as a research guide for the general reader. Emphasis on law and related topics; international law and foreign relations excluded. Dependent territories within the hemisphere are not covered.

Part I lists bibliographies, reference works, important periodicals and other serials, and books on comparative methods of studying various fields. Part II provides general information on Latin America, followed by information on topics such as culture, economics, and history under separate headings. Part III refers to background material on Indian and European origins of present day Latin America. Part IV classifies items by subjects (e.g., armed forces, elections) related to Latin America generally. Part V relates to specific countries. Indexes for subjects and countries.

758. *Current Caribbean Bibliography.* Port-of-Spain, Trinidad; Caribbean Commission, Central Secreteriat, 1951–57. 7 vols.

List of publications issued in the various Carribbean territories.

759. *A Guide to Latin American Studies.* (Reference Series No. 4). Martin H. Sable, comp. Los Angeles: Center of Latin American Studies, University of California, 1967. 2 vols.; ca. 900 pp.

Over 5,000 descriptions of definitive text and reference books, periodicals and periodical articles, pamphlets, government documents, theses and conference proceedings.

Items from the humanities; and natural, applied, and social sciences. Published in English (about 50 percent), French, German, Portuguese, and Spanish. Annotations are in English. Finding instructions are given in reference book annotations. The work covers the spectrum of Latin-American civilization in general, and of each nation. Most items were published after 1950.

Includes Latin-American Studies as a field of higher education, International Cultural Relations and Scholarly Intercommunication, and U. S. and International Financial and Technical Assistance (Publisher's statement).

A similar bibliography of some 15,000 titles covering the period 1948 to 1964 is scheduled for early publication.

760. HANDBOOK OF LATIN AMERICAN STUDIES. Gainesville, Fla.: University of Florida Press, 1936 –.

Annotated bibliography; comprehensive subject coverage. Also contains articles. Published annually until 1964, the *Handbook* is now divided into two sections published in alternate years: 1) social sciences, and 2) humanities (including history).

761. Humphreys, Robin Arthur. *Latin American History: A Guide to the Literature in English.* London: Oxford University Press, 1958. 197 pp.

Published for the Royal Institute of International Affairs. Annotated guide to books and articles.

762. Jones, Cecil Knight. *A Bibliography of Latin American Bibliographies,* 2d edition, revised with the assistance of James A. Granier. Washington, D.C.: Government Printing Office, 1942. 311 pp.

This is Library of Congress Latin American series No. 2. A basic list of 3,106 bibliographies, collective bibliographies, various reference works, etc. Books and articles. Author, title, subject index.

Supplemented by the "Bibliographies, lists and indexes" subsections of the *Handbook of Latin American Studies* (760).

763. Library Association, London. *Latin America: An Introduction to Modern Books in English concerning the Countries of Latin America,* 2d edition. London: The Association, 1966. 41 pp.
A list of 329 books in English on Latin-American countries, prepared by the Hispanic and Luso-Brazilian Councils. Emphasis on books dealing with economic and social conditions.

764. *Master Directory for Latin America.* (Reference Series No. 2.) Martin H. Sable, comp. Los Angeles: Center of Latin American Studies, University of California, 1965. xxi, 438 pp.
Contains ten subdirectories listing names and latest addresses of Latin-American, U. S., and West European institutions and organizations concerned with Latin-American agriculture, business (industry, finance, research), education, government, international cooperation, publishing, labor cooperatives, religion, social service, and social and professional associations.
The preface contains a survey of Latin-American studies programs in U. S. colleges and universities (1953–1965). Detailed table of contents and index include many hard-to-find items, such as Latin-American free ports and free-trade zones, Cuban-exile organizations, Spanish-language newspapers and radio stations in the United States, and worldwide coverage of Latin-American studies research centers. List of sources for special information, such as library and museum collections, scholarships and fellowships, and market research data.

765. *Social Science Research on Latin America: Report and Papers of a Seminar on Latin American Studies in the United States held at Stanford, Calif., July 8–August 23, 1963.* Charles Wagley, ed. New York: Columbia University Press, 1964. 338 pp. LC 65–11971.
Report on research on Latin America in anthropology, economics, geography, history, political science, and sociology. A number of European and Latin-American publications are included. Excellent bibliographic material.

MIDDLE EAST AND NORTH AFRICA

766. Bolton, Alexander Rollo Collin. *Soviet Middle East Studies: An Analysis and Bibliography.* Oxford: Distributed for the Royal Institute of International Affairs by the Oxford University Press, 1959.
Annotations of books and articles.

767. Dar-al Katub al Misriyah. *Bibliographical Lists of the Arab World.* Cairo: National Library Press, 1960 – (in progress).
Covers the Arab countries. Lists 19th- and 20th-century books published in several languages.

768. Dar-al Katub al Misriyah. *A Bibliography of Works About Arab Nationalism.* Cairo: National Library Press, 1959. 74 pp.

769. Dar-al Katub al Misriyah. *A Bibliography of Works Dealing with the Arab Struggle for Freedom and Unity.* Cairo: National Library Press, 1959. 150 pp.
Lists of books in English, French, and Arabic.

770. Library of Congress, Orientalia Division. *The Arabian Peninsula: A Selected, Annotated List of Periodicals, Books, and Articles in English.* Washington, D.C., 1951. 111 pp.

Some 700 titles in English dealing with geography, ethnology, economics, and politics.

771. Patai, Raphael. *Jordan, Lebanon and Syria.* (Behavior Science Bibliographies.) New Haven, Conn.: Human Relations Area Files Press, 1957. (Distributed by Taplinger Publishing Co., New York.) 289 pp.
Annotations of books and articles.

772. Sauvaget, Jean. *Introduction to the History of the Muslim East: A Bibliographic Guide,* revised edition by Claude Cahen. Berkeley, Calif.: University of California Press, 1965. xx, 252 pp. LC 64–25271.
English translation of Sauvaget's guide. Bibliographic aids in Muslim history, including primary and secondary sources.

773. *A Selected and Annotated Bibliography of Books and Periodicals in Western Languages Dealing with the Near and Middle East with Special Emphasis on Medieval and Modern Times.* Richard Ettinghausen, ed. Washington, D.C.: Middle East Institute, 1954. 137 pp.
Published under the auspices of the American Council of Learned Societies, Committee on Near East Studies.
Classified list of 2,059 of the best recent books in Western languages, periodicals, and maps intended for general use. Covers the social sciences, law, and education. Some 750 items on the contemporary Near East.

774. UNESCO, Middle East Science Cooperation Office. *Middle East Social Science Bibliography: Books and Articles on the Social Sciences Published in Arab Countries of the Middle East in 1955–1960.* Cairo, 1960. 152 pp.
Classified list of some 1,200 items in both Western languages and Arabic.

SOVIET RUSSIA AND EASTERN EUROPE

775. Byrnes, Robert F. *Bibliography of American Publications on East Central Europe, 1945–1957.* (Slavic and East European Series, Vol. 12.) Bloomington, Ind.: Indiana University Publications, 1958. 213 pp.
List of books and articles published by Americans in the United States and some other countries.

776. Clemens, Walter C., Jr. *Soviet Disarmament Policy 1917–1963: An Annotated Bibliography.* (Hoover Institution Bibliographical Series No. XXII.) Stanford, Calif.: Hoover Institution, Stanford University, 1965. 175 pp.

777. Hammond, Thomas T. *Soviet Foreign Relations and World Communism.* Princeton, N.J.: Princeton University Press, 1965, 1240 pp.
A selected, annotated bibliography of 7,000 books in 30 languages. Soviet political and economic relations with all countries since 1917, Communist movements in all regions and countries, Soviet foreign policy, and internal developments in other Communist countries. Three main parts: Soviet Foreign Relations by Chronological Periods; Soviet Foreign Relations and Communism by Regions and Countries; and Special Topics.

778. Maichel, Karol. *Guide to Russian Reference Books.* (Hoover Institution Bibliographical Series, Nos. X and XVIII.) J. G. S. Simmons, ed. Stanford, Calif.:

Hoover Institution, Stanford University. Volume I: 1962, 92 pp., LC 62–14067. Volume II: 1964, 297 pp., LC 62–14067.

Volume I covers general bibliographies and reference books. Volume II covers history, auxiliary historical sciences, ethnography, and geography. The work lists and annotates bibliographies, encyclopedias, atlases, handbooks, biographies, dictionaries, dissertations, abstracts, indexes, chronologies, etc.

These are the first two volumes to a comprehensive 6-volume guide. Volumes 3 to 5 will be devoted to the social sciences, religion, philosophy, the humanities, science, technology, and medicine. The last volume will include supplementary materials and a cumulative index covering all six volumes.

779. *Russia and the Soviet Union: A Bibliographic Guide to Western-Language Publications.* Paul L. Horecky, ed. Chicago: University of Chicago Press, 1965. xxiv, 473 pp. LC 65–12041.

Some 2,000 entries; annotated. Index.

780. Slusser, Robert M., and J. F. Triska. *Calendar of Soviet Treaties, 1917–1957.* Stanford, Calif.: Hoover Institution, Stanford University, 1959.

Chronological list of treaties and international agreements concluded by the Soviet Union. Summaries, references to the full text, and bibliographic references. Index by countries.

MISCELLANEOUS

781. *The Atlantic Community: An Introductory Bibliography.* D. Blaber, ed. Leyden, Netherlands: A. W. Sythoff, 1961. 2 vols. 600 pp. LC 62–39959.

Prepared by the Conference on Atlantic Community, Bruges.

The bibliography is limited almost entirely to books and articles published since 1945 in the United Kindgom, the United States, France, Germany, Austria, Switzerland, and Italy which constitute a basic reading list on: 1) the historical development, common characteristics, and internal problems of the Atlantic Community of nations (not necessarily limited to members of NATO); 2) the organizational structure of international cooperation within the Community, with emphasis on progress achieved in the political and economic fields; and 3) the relations of the Atlantic Community with the Communist and the underdeveloped and uncommitted worlds (Foreword). Subject index and index of contributors.

782. Department of State, External Research Staff. *Game Theory and its Application to the Social Sciences: A Bibliography.* (External Research Paper No. 145.) Washington, D.C., 1964. 12 pp.

783. Kenworthy, Leonard S. *Free and Inexpensive Materials on World Affairs.* New York: Bureau of Publications, Teachers College, Columbia University, 1963. 83 pp.

Section F. Bibliographies for Selected Topics

COMMUNICATIONS

784. Blum, Eleanor. *Reference Books in the Mass Media.* Urbana, Ill.: University of Illinois Press, 1962. vi, 192 pp. LC 62–62509.

Annotated list of books on publishing, broadcasting, film, the press, and advertising for nonspecialists. General books on media audiences and characteristics.

785. *CINFAC (Cultural Information Analysis Center) Bibliographic Review.* (Supplement No. 10.) Nancy Currier, et al., comps. Washington, D. C: Center for Research in Social Systems, American University, 1966. 160 pp.

786. Lasswell, Harold D., et al. *Propaganda and Promotional Activities: An Annotated Bibliography.* Minneapolis, Minn.: University of Minnesota Press, 1935. 450 pp.
  Four essays on the science of mass communications and a selective, annotated bibliography of 2,558 books and articles published between 1934 and 1943, plus some earlier titles. Interdisciplinary. Author and subject index. Some 150 titles are starred as outstanding.
  See continuation publications (788, 789).

787. Library of Congress, Reference Department, European Affairs Division. *Freedom of Information: A Selective Report on Recent Writing.* Washington, D. C., 1949. 153 pp.

788. Smith, Bruce L., Harold D. Lasswell, and Ralph D. Casey. *Propaganda, Communication and Public Opinion: A Comprehensive Reference Guide.* Princeton, N. J.: Princeton University Press, 1946. vii, 435 pp. LC 46–1329.
  Continuation of Harold D. Lasswell, *Propaganda and Promotional Activities; An Annotated Bibliography* (786).
  Four essays on "the science of mass communications" and a selective, annotated bibliography of 2,558 books and articles published between 1934 and 1943, plus some earlier titles. Interdisciplinary. Author and subject index. Some 150 titles are starred as outstanding.

789. Smith, Bruce L., and Chitra M. Smith. *International Communication and Political Opinion: A Guide to the Literature.* Princeton, N. J.: Princeton University Press, 1956. 325 pp.
  Continuation of Smith, Lasswell, and Casey *Propaganda, Communication and Public Opinion* (788).
  Stress on political aspects of international propaganda and promotional activities. Some 2,500 entries in German, French, and English are classified under seven major headings and many subheadings. Covers books, articles, government documents, and some unpublished material. Author and subject index.

COMMUNISM

790. *Books on Communism: A Bibliography.* Robert Nigel Carew Hunt, ed. London: Ampersand, Ltd.; New York: Oxford University Press, 1959, x,333 pp. LC 60–234.
  Selective, classified bibliography with brief annotations on some 1,500 books on communism published in English between 1945 and 1957. Includes translations and revised editions of earlier works.
  Three major sections: 1) Studies of Communism in General and in the USSR; 2) Communism in Other Countries; and 3) Official Documents and Publications (United States and Great Britain). Index of authors and titles.

791. *Communism in Latin America: A Bibliography; The Post-War Years (1945–1960).* (Reference Series No. 1.) Ludwig Laverhass, Jr., comp. Los Angeles: Center of Latin American Studies, University of California, 1962. xv, 78 pp.

792. Delaney, Robert Finlay. *Literature of Communism in America: A Selected Reference Guide.* Washington, D. C.: Catholic University of America Press, 1962. xii, 433 pp. LC 62–6923.
Some 1,700 entries, especially for the years 1919–1961.

793. Kolarz, Walter, ed. *Books on Communism, A Bibliography,* 2d edition. New York: Oxford University Press, 1963. viii, 568 pp. LC 64–5233.
Annotated bibliography of books in English on communism on the national and international scene. Arranged by subject and by countries.

794. Pundeff, Marin. *Recent Publications on Communism: A Bibliography of Non-Periodical Literature, 1957–1962.* Los Angeles: Research Institute on Communist Strategy and Propaganda, School of International Relations, University of Southern California, 1962. iv, 66 pp.
No annotations.

CONFLICT RESOLUTION, DISARMAMENT AND PEACE

795. *Bibliography on Counterinsurgency, Unconventional Warfare, and Psychological Operations.* (Supplement No. 9.) Nancy Currier, et al., comps. Washington, D. C.: Center for Research in Social Systems, American University, 1966. 132 pp.

796. *Bibliography of the International Court of Justice, 1964–1965.* Documents Department to the International Court of Justice.
Bibliography of works and documents related to the Court. Until 1964–1965 it was included in the *Yearbook* of the ICJ (1112).

797. Clemens, Walter C., Jr. *Soviet Disarmament Policy 1917–1963.* (see 776.)

798. Department of Defense. *Disarmament: A Bibliographic Record, 1916–1960.* Harry Moskowitz and Jack Roberts, comps. Washington, D. C., 1960. 66 pp.
Prepared in the Office of the Special Assistant to the Joint Chiefs of Staff of Disarmament Affairs.

799. _____. *U. S. Security, Arms Control, and Disarmament, 1960–1961.* Harry Moskowitz and Jack Roberts, comps. Washington, D. C., 1961. 144 pp.

800. _____. *U. S. Security, Arms Control, and Disarmament, 1961–1965.* Harry Moskowitz and Jack Roberts, comps. Washington, D. C., 1965. vii, 140 pp.
Annotations of 750 items selected from several thousand books, magazine articles, and documents on the subject; some of these from unfriendly sources (Analyst's note).

801. Department of State, U. S. Disarmament Administration. *A Basic Bibliography. Disarmament, Arms Control and National Security.* (Department of State Publication 7193.) Washington, D. C.: Government Printing Office, 1961. 29 pp.
Books and other publications by authors with widely divergent views.

802. *A Brief Bibliography: Arms Control and Disarmament* (U. S. Arms Control and Disarmament Agency Publication 22.) Washington, D. C.: Government Printing Office, 1964. v, 33 pp.
An annotated bibliography of books and other publications by authors with widely differing views and limited to titles generally available through library facilities.

Updates *A Basic Bibliography: Disarmament, Arms Control and National Security* (801).

803. *Disarmament: A Select Bibliography, 1962–1964.* (United Nations Document ST/LIB/15.) New York: United Nations, Secretariat, 1965. 95 pp.
A list of books and periodical articles on various aspects of disarmament selected primarily from the holdings of the Dag Hammarskjold Library.

804. *The Nature of Conflict: Studies on the Sociological Aspects of International Relations.* (Tensions and Technology Series.) Paris: UNESCO, 1957. 314 pp.
Sponsored by the International Sociological Association. A comprehensive survey and evaluation of research by sociologists and social psychologists into the nature, conditions, and implications of human conflict and particularly the conflict between nations. Consists of four essays surveying current knowledge with references to a bibliography of 1,160 items arranged under four major headings: 1) Sociology and Psycho-sociology of Intergroup Conflicts; 2) International Relations; 3) Racial Conflicts; and 4) Industrial and Agrarian Conflicts. Covers books, articles, and reports in various languages, generally published since 1945. Many full annotations. No index. White, *Sources* (643).

805. *Reconciliation Library: Catalogue 1962–1963.* London: The International Fellowship of Reconciliation, 1963. 56 pp.
List of the first 1,000 volumes, mostly in English, of the Reconciliation Library (the Fellowship is a pacifist organization with a religious emphasis). Philosophy and theology in relation to peace, inter-Church relations, East-West relations, race relations, non-Christian religions, and peace organizations.

806. *Read Your Way to World Understanding. A Selected Annotated Reading Guide to Books About the United Nations.* New York: Scarecrow Press, 1963. 320 pp.
Published for the American Association for the United Nations.
Three parts: 1) the United Nations, the family of nations dedicated to world peace; 2) the United Nations works in a changing world; and 3) Resources for individual and group participation program materials, resources, and services to promote international understanding and interpret United Nations concepts. Each book has been graded and reviewed with recommendations for its particular contribution.

807. *World Communism: A Selected Annotated Bibliography prepared by the Legislative Reference Service, Library of Congress, at the request of the Subcommittee to Investigate the Administration of the Internal Security Act and Other Internal Security Laws of the Committee on the Judiciary, United States Senate.* (United States Senate, 88th Congress, 2d Session, Document No. 69. Washington, D. C.: Government Printing Office, 1964. 394 pp.

DEVELOPING AREAS

808. Alexander-Frutschi, Marian Crites. *Human Resources and Economic Growth: An International Annotated Bibliography on the Role of Education and Training in Economic and Social Development.* Menlo Park, Calif.: Stanford Research Institute, 1963. 398 pp. LC 63–3013.
Prepared for the International Development Center of the Stanford Research Institute. A classified and annotated list of 1,150 books, articles, and reports. Five sec-

tions on education; one section on geographic areas and countries. Author and organization index.

809. *Public Administration: A Select List of Books and Periodicals.* London: Longmans, 1964. 120 pp.
Classified list of 1,548 titles covering the Commonwealth of Nations, primarily by British authors. Name and title index. No annotations.

810. *The Economics of "Under-Developed" Areas: An Annotated Reading List of Books, Articles, and Official Publications,* 2d enlarged edition. Arthur Hazlewood, comp. London: Oxford University Press, 1959. xii, 156 pp. LC 59–1650.
Published for the Institute of Commonwealth Studies.
An annotated list of 1,027 books, articles, and official publications published in English since 1930. Classified in 12 sections. Index of authors, editors, and places.

811. Hayes, Samuel P. *Evaluating Development Projects.* Paris: UNESCO, 1966. 116 pp. (Sale through International Publications, Inc., New York.)
This manual on evaluating development projects contains a bibliography of 49 items on the methods of collecting and analyzing data. Contains an additional list of 25 examples of experience in the scientific collection of data outside Europe and North America.

812. Heady, Ferrell, and Sybil L. Stokes. *Comparative Public Administration: A Selective Annotated Bibliography,* 2d edition. Ann Arbor, Mich.: University of Michigan Press, 1960. 98 pp.
Annotated list of some 950 books and articles. Includes developing countries.

813. *The Economics of Development: An Annotated List of Books and Articles Published 1958–1962.* Arthur Hazlewood, comp. London: Oxford University Press, 1964. 104 pp.
Published for the Institute of Commonwealth Studies. Continuation of *The Economics of "Under-Developed" Areas* (810). 732 entries. Index by author and place.

814. International Committee for Social Sciences Documentation. *International Cooperation and Programs of Economic and Social Development: An Annotated Bibliography.* (Reports and Papers in the Social Sciences, No. 151.) Paris: UNESCO, 1962. 107 pp.
A select, classified bibliography of 1,141 books, documents, and articles dealing with the definition, formulation, and execution of programs of international cooperation. Arranged under four headings; 1) General Appraisal of the Assistance Programs; 2) Bilateral Assistance Programs; 3) Multilateral Assistance Programs of the United Nations and its Specialized Agencies; 4) Regional Assistance Programs.

815. Katz, Saul M., and Frank McGowan. *A Selected List of U. S. Readings on Development.* Washington, D. C.: Government Printing Office, 1963. xvii, 363 pp.
Prepared for the United Nations Conference on the Application of Science and Technology for the Benefit of the Less Developed Areas by the Agency for International Development.
A list of 1,195 selected books, periodical articles, and Government reports by American authors or others closely associated with American institutions. In general, United Nations publications are excluded. Most items published since 1950. Brief annotations. Selection based on the needs and interests of educated, nonspecialized persons in developing countries, such as government officials and national leaders, who are engaged in development activities. Readings range from the planning experi-

ences of the TVA and Puerto Rico to the production and marketing policies of large American industries and the role of American universities in research and education in the service of human welfare. Includes many contrasting views. Index.

816. Mukherjee, Ajit Kamar. *Annotated Guide to Reference Materials in the Human Sciences.* New York: Asia Publishing House, 1963. 267 pp.
Bibliographic guide to some 1,200 bibliographies, abstracts, dictionaries, encyclopedias, and standard works on anthropology, sociology, and social psychology. Author and subject indexes.

817. *Public Administration: A Basic List of Selected Books in English.* I. D. Shelley, comp. Paris: UNESCO, 1965. 21 pp.
Selection of 100 items for use in institutes of public administration in developing countries. Includes a section on Comparative Government. Aside from the more general entries, most of the studies relate to the executive process of government. Some books deal with legislative supervision and control of administration.

818. *Public Administration: A Select Bibliography.* London: Department of Technical Cooperation (name changed in 1964 to Ministry of Overseas Development), 1963.
Lists 982 books, pamphlets, and articles dealing with various aspects of public administration in developed as well as developing countries, published primarily in Great Britain, the Commonwealth countries, and the United States. Special section on Africa. Compiled primarily to assist the new Institute of Public Administration in Africa. Very helpful chapters on 29 Bibliographies. Worldwide list of 38 Public Administration Periodicals. Index.

819. _____. *First Supplement,* 1964.

820. ReQua, Eloise G., and Jane Statham. *The Developing Nations: A Guide to Information Sources Concerning Their Economic, Political, Technical and Social Problems.* Detroit, Mich.: Gale Research Co., 1965. 339 pp. LC 65–17576.
Annotated bibliography of books, documents issued by governments and international organizations, and articles published during the past decade in English on economic development and assistance, technical assistance, international private investment, trade and development, social and political development, economic development in specific regions, general reference sources, and bibliographies on underdeveloped areas. Lists pertinent directories, periodicals, agencies, and institutions administering development and the addresses of publishers and periodicals cited.
This interdisciplinary bibliography is concerned with regions and areas rather than specific countries and lends itself at times to interregional comparison. Section 10, Bibliographies on Underdeveloped Areas, is indispensable to professors and students.
The Editors are the Director and Associate Director, respectively, of the Library of International Relations in Chicago, publisher of the *International Information Service.*

821. Spitz, Alan A., and Edward W. Weidner. *Development Administration. An Annotated Bibliography.* Honolulu: East-West Center Press, 1963. xi, 116 pp. LC 63–15837.
A selective bibliography of widely scattered periodical literature in the field of development administration, a subfield of public administration. Articles are in English and include those published between 1945 and 1960, inclusively. Subject headings cover the social, economic, and political problems of development; the several units and areas of government; major features of administrative systems; and the major functions of government. (Preface.) Full annotations. Index.

822. Viet, Jean. *Assistance to Underdeveloped Countries: An Annotated Bibliography.* (International Committee for Social Sciences Documentation, Reports and Papers in the Social Sciences, No. 8.) Paris: UNESCO, 1957. 83 pp.

823. Wish, John R. *Economic Development in Latin America: An Annotated Bibliography.* New York: Frederick A. Praeger, 1966. 160 pp. LC 65—21105.

EUROPEAN INTEGRATION

824. *Bibliography on the Economic and Political Integration of Europe.* Andrew Szabo and Walter H. Posner, comps. San Diego, Calif.: San Diego State College Library, 1965. 47 pp.

825. *A Selected Bibliography on European Integration.* Washington, D. C.: European Community Information Service, 1961. 32 pp.

826. Zellentin, Gerda, and Elizabeth Y. DeKoster. *Bibliographie zur europäischen Integration,* 2d revised edition. Cologne: Bildungswerk Europäische Politik, 1965. 209 pp.
Includes bibliographies, reference works, and periodicals. Annotated.

NATIONALISM

827. Deutsch, Karl W. *An Interdisciplinary Bibliography on Nationalism, 1935—1953.* Cambridge, Mass.: Technology Press of M.I.T., 1956. 165 pp. LC 57—138.
Follow up to Koppel S. Pinson, *A Bibliographical Introduction to Nationalism* (828).
Deutsch's selective, classified bibliography lists monographs and articles in major European languages. Some short annotations. Section 14 lists data by geographic areas. Other sections deal with major surveys and bibliographies; special works on nationalism or by fields, such as history, political science, and philosophy. Author index.

828. Pinson, Koppel S. *A Bibliographical Introduction to Nationalism.* New York: Columbia University Press, 1935. 71 pp.
A selective, classified, and annotated bibliography of 431 items published in English. Two sections: 1) Theoretical and Analytical Studies; 2) Historical and Regional Studies. Monographs and articles. Index of names.
Continued by Karl W. Deutsch, *An Interdisciplinary Bibliography on Nationalism, 1935—1953* (827).

MISCELLANEOUS

829. Eldridge, Hope T. *The Materials of Demography: A Selected and Annotated Bibliography.* New York: International Union for the Scientific Study of Population and the Population Association of America, 1959. 222 pp.
Over 400 English-language items on significant works in the field of population analysis. Compiled for teachers of demography. Author index.

830. Mangalam, J. J. *Human Migration: A Guide to Migration Literature in English, 1955—1962.* Lexington, Ky.: University of Kentucky Press, 1966. 224 pp.

CHAPTER 12.

BIOGRAPHICAL REFERENCE PUBLICATIONS

Biographical information reflects history in the making. It points out the stages in the development of statesmen and other public figures and helps to explain their actions, outlook, and aims. It also records the rise and fall of political, economic, and social movements through the stories of their leaders and antagonists.

Biographical data list the books and other professional achievements of a scholar by which his contribution to the understanding of international relations and history can be judged. They list the positions held by high government officials and the posts of leading newspapers' reporters. Lists of publications help the researcher find book reviews which help establish the scholarly competence of writers. The cross-fire of critical reviewers with divergent views and interpretations helps establish the validity of facts and the pertinency of conclusions.

At times, knowledge of the personal, educational, or professional experience of a writer or columnist helps bring into relief an obvious or camouflaged slant, and assists the reader in assaying the objectivity of a book, article, or statement. Often, it is important to be familiar with the background of less prominent persons because they, too, have their audience and following.

In addition, acquaintance with the life and work of a writer, statesman, or stormy petrel adds human interest to the study of world affairs and repays for some of the drudgery that is the student's lot at times.

Section A. United States

CONGRESS

831. U. S. Congress. *Biographical Directory of the American Congress, 1774–1961.* (H. Doc. 442.) Washington, D. C.: Government Printing Office, 1961. 1863 pp. LC 62–60469.
More than 10,400 biographies of Senators and Representatives since 1774 and officers of the executive branch of the Government since 1789.

832. _____. CONGRESSIONAL DIRECTORY. 1809 –. One edition for each session of Congress. Government Printing Office, Washington, D. C. 20402. LC 6–35330.
Short biographies of the Members of the Senate and the House; committee memberships; names of administrative assistants; foreign diplomats; members of the press, radio, and television galleries, etc.

DEPARTMENT OF STATE

833 Department of State. BIOGRAPHIC REGISTER, 1869 –. A. Irr. LC 9–22072.
Education and career sketches of Foreign Service officers and higher grade officials and employees of the Department of State, including the U. S. Mission to the United Nations, embassies abroad, Agency for International Development, Peace Corps,

U. S. Arms Control and Disarmament Agency, U. S. Information Agency, and the Foreign Agricultural Service of the Department of Agriculture.

In former years this publication included a description of the organization of the Department (useful for historical and comparative purposes) and of the functions of the various units and lists of foreign diplomatic and consular representatives stationed in the United States (now published in the *Diplomatic List* and the *Foreign Consular Officers in the United States* (834). Published at irregular intervals, generally each year, since 1869. Formerly titled *Register of the Department of State*. See Bemis and Griffin, *Guide to the Diplomatic History of the United States* (650) for details, pp. 746, 825–826.

834. _____. DIPLOMATIC LIST. 1893 –. Q. LC 10–16292.

Prepared by the Office of Protocol. A periodic list of foreign diplomatic representatives stationed in Washington, given in order of precedence, with addresses. Unofficially known as the "Blue Book" of diplomatic society. First issued 1887 under the name *Foreign Legations in the U. S.*

835. _____. FOREIGN SERVICE LIST. 1929 –. Q. LC 10–16369.

Prepared by the Division of Publishing and Reproduction Services. Lists field staffs at all foreign posts of the Department of State, the U. S. Information Agency, the Agency for International Development, Peace Corps, and the Department of Agriculture. Shows posts of assignment, category, and classification.

Published first about 1828 under the title of *List of Ministers, Consuls, and Other Diplomatic Agents of the United States in Foreign Countries,* this publication has been published under different names and at varying intervals. Published quarterly since 1955.

836. _____. KEY OFFICERS AT FOREIGN SERVICE POSTS: Guide for Businessmen. Q. LC 64–61222.

A directory, prepared as an aid to Americans with business interests abroad, listing key officers of embassies and consulates general with whom American businessmen would most likely have contact.

Of use to students with corresponding interests; includes economic data and other descriptive information.

837. _____. *The Secretaries of State: Portraits and Biographical Sketches.* (Department of State Publication 6402.) Richard S. Patterson, comp. Washington, D. C., 1950. 124 pp.

LIBRARY OF CONGRESS

838. U. S. Library of Congress, General Reference and Bibliography Division, Reference Department. *Biographical Sources for the United States.* Jane Kline, comp. Washington, D. C., 1961. LC 61–60065.

An annotated bibliography "presented as a guide to current biographical information about living Americans, especially those who have made notable contributions to the arts and the professions, to business and corporate enterprise, and to military and civilian affairs. The collective biographies herein listed date principally from 1945 to 1960. . . ." The time limit explains the nonlisting of a number of bibliographic reference works which are still useful. The book lists a few works outside its particular scope which were deemed indispensable reference tools.

The bibliography is arranged in three main sections: General; Regions and States; and Special and Professional Groups. The first section includes general biographical dictionaries devoted wholly to Americans, as well as international dictionaries or directories in which living Americans are represented in substantial numbers. The second section includes both regional and local biographies and the third reference works listing persons in business, government, and the professions. The biographies vary in number of listed persons from less than 100 to more than 250,000. The data may be brief notices or short articles and chapters.

This guide describes and annotates the latest available edition or issue of more than 160 reference publications and provides the Library of Congress call number. The list is not complete, even for the limited period covered.

The appendix contains an index of authors, subjects, and titles.

PRIVATE PUBLICATIONS

839. American Council of Learned Societies. *Dictionary of American Biography.* Editors: Vols. 1–3, Allen Johnson; Vols. 4–7, Allen Johnson and Dumas Malone; Vols. 8–20, Dumas Malone; Vol. 21 and Index to Vols. 1–20, Harris E. Starr; Vol. 22, Robert L. Schuyler and Edward T. James. New York: Charles Scribner's Sons, 1921–1958.

Scholarly and authoritative American national biography, comparable to the British *Dictionary of National Biography* (897), with 14,870 scholarly biographical articles, with appended bibliographic notes, on deceased persons who made some significant contribution to American life and culture. The sketches vary in length from half a page to 18 pages.

Volume 21, Supplement 1, adds names which failed to be included in the earlier volumes and brings the *Dictionary* up to December 31, 1935. Volume 22, Supplement 2, brings the work to December 31, 1940.

The index is in six sections, including an alphabetic list of biographies, and an analytical index which includes "distinctive topics about which there are definite statements and discussions" (Publisher's statement). The indexes are compiled by the publisher and not by the authors of the *Dictionary.*

840. BIOGRAPHY INDEX: A Quarterly Index to Biographical Material in Books and Magazines. 1946 –. Q; A and 3–yr. cums. H. W. Wilson Co., 950 University Ave., Bronx, N. Y. 10452.

References to biographical material in some 1,500 periodicals indexed in other Wilson indexes, current works of collective biography, books containing incidental biographical material, works of individual biography and autobiography (all in English), and selected obituaries of national and international interest published in the *New York Times.* Refers to living and deceased persons, of current or historical importance. Bibliographies and portraits are indicated when they appear in the indexed material. All listed persons are Americans unless otherwise stated. Indexed by names and by professions or occupations.

841. *Concise Dictionary of American Biography.* Joseph G. E. Hopkins, ed. New York: Charles Scribner's Sons, 1964. 1273 pp. LC 64–10623.

Summaries of articles in the *Dictionary of American Biography* (839). Some revisions, based on recent scholarship. Covers 14,870 Americans who died prior to 1941.

842. CONTEMPORARY AUTHORS: A Bio-Bibliographic Guide to Current Authors and Their Works. James M. Ethridge and Barbara Kopala, eds. 1962 –. SA. $25.00. Gale Research Co., Book Tower, Detroit, Mich. 48226. LC 62–52046.

Covers some 4,000 writers each year whose works appear in English, including

writers in the social sciences. Entries provide personal and career information and full bibliographies of writings in book form. International coverage.
Cumulative index in second volume of each year. Includes about 20,000 authors through Volume 19–20.

843. CURRENT BIOGRAPHY: Who's News and Why. 1940 –. M. $7.00. H. W. Wilson Co., 950 University Ave., Bronx, N. Y. 10452.
Articles on the life and work of prominent people, including non-Americans, based on information in newspapers, magazines, books, and the biographies themselves. References at the end of each article, usually also a photograph. References to the *New York Times* obituaries for deceased persons previously listed. Occasionally a revised biography is published several years after the first one.
Annual cumulation (see 844).

844. CURRENT BIOGRAPHY YEARBOOK. A. H. W. Wilson Co., 950 University Ave., Bronx, N. Y. 10452.
Annual cumulation of *Current Biography* (843). Lists 300 to 350 sketches, revised and brought up-to-date. Each issue contains a cumulative index for the current year and each annual volume for the previous ten years.

845. Dargan, Marion. *Guide to American Biography.* Albuquerque, N. M.: University of New Mexico Press, 1949–52. 2 vols. LC 49–48559.
Entries for some 560 outstanding persons. Lists original sources, biographies, collective biography material, etc. Arranged chronologically and geographically.

846. *Index to Profile Sketches in New Yorker Magazine.* Thomas S. Shaw, ed. Boston, F. W. Faxon, 1940. LC 47–450.
Articles indexed by subject, occupation of the biographee, and author of the sketch. Covers the first fifteen volumes of the *New Yorker,* 1925 to February 19, 1940. Later profiles can be located through the *Readers' Guide to Periodical Literature* (3).

847. Kaplan, Louis, et al. *A Bibliography of American Autobiographies.* Madison, Wis.: University of Wisconsin Press, 1961. 372 pp. LC 61–5499.
Bibliographic notes on 6,377 autobiographies published before 1945 by native or adopted Americans. Details on authors. Arranged by subject; subdivided by occupation, national origin of authors, locale, and association with important historical events.

848. *New York Times Index* (see 1237).
Annual list of obituaries which indicates when a person died and which brings his biographical data up-to-date. Editorial writers and columnists in various newspapers may furnish additional factual information and especially interpretative and evaluative comments on the same date or within a week's time. (The following Sunday edition may have feature articles.) A comparison of editorial comment in several papers is often enlightening.
In regard to living persons the same *Index* leads to easily accessible information on achievements and activities which brought those people to public notice. Again, editorial writers and columnists comment on appointments to public office, promotions, resignations, retirements, proposals for reforms, speeches, achievements, and other claims to public attention.
There are also indexes to other newspapers (see the section on the Press) and to periodicals.

849. O'Neill, Edward Hayes, *Biography by Americans, 1658–1936: A Subject Bibliography*. Philadelphia, Pa.: University of Pennsylvania Press, 1939. 465 pp. LC 39–30813.

850. Phelps, Robert H., ed. *Men in the News: Biographical Sketches from the New York Times. Men and Women Who Made Headlines in 1959*. Philadelphia, Pa.: J. B. Lippincott Co., 1959. LC 59–7787.
A biographical dictionary of men and women who made news, consisting of personality sketches published in the *New York Times* series "Man in the News." International scope. The articles feature a "human" approach to these persons as well as accurate biographical descriptions.

851. Slocum, Robert B. *Biographical Dictionaries and Related Works: A Bibliography*. Detroit, Mich.: Gale Research Co., 1967. 691 pp. LC 67–27789.
Lists some 4,500 "who's who" publications and other collections of biographical information published since 1500 in 108 countries. Includes biobibliographies, historical and specialized dictionaries, government and legislative manuals containing substantial biographical information, bibliographies of individual and collective biographies, biographical indexes, selected portrait catalogs, etc.
Three main sections: Universal Biography; National or Area Biography (including the emerging nations of Africa); and Biography by Vocation. Comprehensive author, title, and subject indexes.

852. *Twentieth Century Authors: A Biographical Dictionary of Modern Literature*. Stanley J. Kumitz and Howard Haycraft, eds. New York: H. W. Wilson Co., 1942. 1577 pp. LC 43–51003.
Supersedes *Living Authors* (1931) and *Authors Today and Yesterday* (1933), edited by Stanley J. Kumitz and Vineta Colby.
Biographies and bibliographies of contemporary writers, mostly American. Many photographs. Includes persons in history, biography, social sciences, and other fields.

853. _____. *First Supplement*. New York: H. W. Wilson, Co., 1955. 1123 pp.
Adds 700 new sketches, obituaries of deceased persons listed in the original work, and some updated biographies.

854. *Webster's Biographical Dictionary: A Dictionary of Names of Noteworthy Persons, with Pronunciations and Concise Biographies*. Springfield, Mass.: G. & C. Merriam Co., 1962. 1734 pp.
Some 40,000 names, including living persons. Worldwide coverage.

WHO'S WHO AROUND THE GLOBE

Editor's note: The "who's who" type of biographical dictionary was started in England and has proliferated most in this country. Similar dictionaries are now being published in many countries in various languages, although most of them are in English. The following list is selective; additional titles can be found by consulting Winchell, *Guide* (603) and Walford, *Guide* (602). Biographical data and sketches are found in other works. Some of these are listed in the section on General Encyclopedias, Dictionaries, Handbooks and Yearbooks and in Appendix 2, New and Ceased Publications.

855. *The Marquis Who's Who Series.* Published by Marquis Who's Who, Inc., Marquis Publications Bldg., 210 E. Ohio St., Chicago, Ill. 60611. The publications in this series are listed separately below.

Who's Who in America: A Biographical Dictionary of Notable Living Men and Women, Vol. 34. 1966–67. 2492 pp. LC 4–16934.

Concise biographies of 62,000 living men and women selected for inclusion on the basis of their prominence or distinction in various fields of endeavor. Some are automatically included when they hold certain positions or high offices. Sketches are based on information furnished in response to a questionnaire. Representatives to the United Nations, ambassadors accredited to this country, and some other non-Americans are included. Published since 1899. The addenda at the back of each volume should be checked for "Latest Listings and Sketch Additions." For names of persons dropped for reasons other than death see "Noncurrent Listings" in the *Indices and Necrology* in editions up to 1958. This standard dictionary of contemporary and historical biography is published in various editions, usually biennially, by the same company.

Who Was Who Series

Who Was Who in America, Historical Volume, 1607–1896. revised edition. 1967. 670 pp. LC 43–3789.

Over 13,000 listings covering the period from Jamestown Colony to 1896. See below for listings for 1897 on.

Who Was Who in America, Vol. 1, 1897–1942. 1943. 1396 pp. LC 43–3789.

25,000 listings. Dates of death and places of interment appended to deceased *Who's Who* biographies.

Who Was Who in America, Vol. 2, 1943–1950. 1950. 614 pp. LC 43–3789.

8,400 listings. Dates of death and places of interment appended to deceased *Who's Who* biographies.

Who Was Who in America, Vol. 3, 1951–1960. 1963. 959 pp. LC 43–3789.

12,828 listings. Dates of death and places of interment appended to deceased *Who's Who* biographies for the past decade.

Regional Who's Who Series

Who's Who in the East. 1968/69. 1200 pp. LC 43–18522.

16,200 listings for the Northeastern and Middle Atlantic States and Eastern Canada. Published since 1943.

Who's Who in the Midwest. 1967/68. 1117 pp. LC 50–289.

17,100 listings for the Central and Midwestern States and Midwestern Canada. Published since 1949.

Who's Who in the South and Southwest. 1967/68. 1095 pp. LC 50–58231.

15,400 listings. Published since 1950.

Who's Who in the West. 1967/68. 1002 pp. LC 49–48186.

14,400 listings, including Western Canada. Published since 1949.

Other Series

Who's Who of American Women, 5th edition. 1968/69. 1200 pp. LC 58–13264.

21,000 listings, including Canadian women. Published since 1958.

Who's Who in Science. (Publication scheduled tentatively for late 1968.)
Is expected to contain some 30,000 listings, including persons in psychology, sociology, anthropology, and economics. No other social scientists are indicated in the publisher's release.

Section B. Continents and Regions

AFRICA

856. Segal, Ronald. *Political Africa: A Who's Who of Personalities and Parties.* London: Stevens and Sons, 1961. 475 pp. LC 61—16754.

AUSTRALIA

857. *Australian Dictionary of Biography,* Vol. 1. Melbourne: Melbourne University Press, 1966. (In progress; probably 12 vols.)
Vol. 1 covers 1788—1850, A through H.

858. Serle, Percival, *Dictionary of Australian Biography.* Sydney: Angus and Robertson, 1949. 2 vols. LC 49—6289.
Patterned after Great Britain's *Dictionary of National Biography* (897).

859. *Who's Who in Australia,* 16th edition. Melbourne: Herald and Weekly Times, 1959.

EUROPE

860. *Who's Who in Europe, 1964— 65.* Brussels: Editions de Jeniks. 2680 pp.
Covers some 25 countries, all in Western Europe, except for Turkey. Includes small countries not covered elsewhere, e.g., Andorra and San Marino.

LATIN AMERICA

861. Jones, Cecil Knight. *A Bibliography of Latin American Bibliographies* (see 762).
A list of collective biographies.

862. CHIEFS OF STATE AND CABINET MINISTERS OF THE AMERICAN REPUBLICS. Q Pan American Union, Washington, D. C.

863. *Directory of Statistical Personnel in the American Nations.* 5th edition. Washington, D. C.: Pan American Union, 1955. 194 pp.
Biographical sketches.

864. Organizations of American States. *Directory.* Washington, D. C.: Pan American Union.
Quarterly list of the delegations of the member states.

865. *Who's Who in Latin America: A Biographical Dictionary of Notable Living Men and Women of Latin America,* 3d edition. Ronald Hilton, ed. Stanford, Calif.: Stanford University Press, 1946—51. 7 vols.
Some 8,000 entries.

Arranged by region on the basis of residence, not nationality. Earlier editions (1935, 1940) were smaller and published in single volumes.

MIDDLE EAST AND NORTH AFRICA

866. *Middle East and North Africa* (see 1004).
Contains bibliographies for this area.

867. *Who's Who in U.A.R. and the Near East: The Greatest Biographical Work in the Middle and Near East.* Cairo, 1959. LC 45–33763.
An annual which has ceased publication. See Winchell, *Guide* (603), p. 185, for titles of earlier editions.

Section C. Countries

AUSTRIA

868. *Who's Who in Austria: A Biographical Dictionary Containing About 4000 Biographies of Prominent Personalities from and in Austria.* Stephen Taylor, ed. Zurich: Central European Times Publishing Co., 1954. LC A 55–4612.
Published every two years since 1954.

BELGIUM & LUXEMBOURG

869. *Who's Who in Belgium and the Grand Duchy of Luxembourg,* 2d edition. F. Michielsen and Stephen S. Taylor, eds. Brussels and New York: Intercontinental Book and Publishing Co., 1962. 1343 pp.

BRAZIL

870. *Quem é Quem no Brasil: Biografias Contemporaneas,* Vol. 4. São Paulo: Soc. Brasileira de Expansao Commercial, 1955. 740 pp.

CANADA

871. *Canadian Diaries and Autobiographies.* William Mathews, ed. Berkeley, Calif.: University of California Press, 1950. 136 pp.
A bibliographic guide to autobiographical source materials, published and unpublished.

872. *Canadian Who's Who, Incorporating Canadian Men and Women of the Time.* Toronto: Trans-Canada Press.
Published irregularly, usually biennially, since 1910. A dictionary of some 8,000 concise biographies of notable living men and women.
There is also a semiannual biographical service which adds late entries and corrects original entries.

873. *Dictionary of Canadian Biography: Dictionnaire Bibliographique du Canada.* Alan Wilson and André Vachon, eds. Toronto: University of Toronto Press. Quebec: Les Presses de l'Université Laval, 1966. (In progress.) LC 66–31909.

A multivolume project based on careful research. Each volume will be published in English and French.

Patterned after Great Britain's *Dictionary of National Biography* and the *Dictionary of American Biography*, but devoted primarily to figures of the second rank drawn from many walks of life. It will also include some major figures who have not yet been sufficiently studied. Biographical essays.

Volume 1 covers the period up to 1700, with 594 entries.

874. *Standard Dictionary of Canadian Biography: The Canadian Who Was Who.* Charles G. D. Roberts and Arthur L. Tunnell, eds. Toronto: Trans-Canada Press. Vol. 1: 1875–1933; 1934, 562 pp. Vol. 2: 1933–1937; 1938, xvii, 478 pp.

Outstanding Canadians who died between 1875 and 1937. Documented entries, with bibliographies, signed by the authors. Includes native Canadians who became distinguished elsewhere and foreign-born Canadians. Volume 2 contains the index to entries in Volume 1.

875. Wallace, William Stewart. *The Macmillan Dictionary of Canadian Biography,* 3d edition. London and Toronto: Macmillan Co. New York: St. Martin's Press, Inc., 1963. 822 pp. LC 64–10158.

Concise biographical sketches, with bibliographies.

876. *Who's Who in Canada: An Illustrated Biographical Record of Men and Women of the Time.* B. M. Greene, ed. Toronto: International Press.

Published biennially since 1922.

CHINA

877. Boorman, Howard L. *Biographical Dictionary of Republican China,* Vol. 1. New York: Columbia University Press, 1967. 560 pp. LC 67–12006.

First of a projected five-volume series, covering deceased and living persons prominent during the republican period (1911–1949). Covers some 600 political and military leaders, individuals prominent in diplomacy, business and banking, literature, the arts, scholarship, social reform, education, the press and publishing, science, and religion.

Sponsored by the School of International Affairs of Columbia University and supported by grants from the Ford Foundation. Contributors from the United States, Europe, and Asia.

878. North, Robert C., and Ithiel de Sola Pool. *Kuomintang and Chinese Communist Elites.* Stanford, Calif.: Stanford University Press, 1952. LC 52–3689.

An analysis of Communist leadership.

879. Perleberg, Max. *Who's Who in Modern China (From the Beginning of the Chinese Republic to the End of 1953).* Hong Kong: Ye Olde Printerie, 1954. 428 pp. LC 54–19583.

Some 2,000 biographies.

880. U. S. Department of State, Bureau of Intelligence and Research. *Directory of Chinese Communist Officials.* Washington, D. C.: Government Printing Office, 1960 –.

Formerly *Directory of Party and Government Officials of Communist China.*

List of names only.

881. *Who's Who in Communist China.* Hong Kong: Union Research Institute, 1966. 754 pp. LC 66–4063.
Some 1,200 biographical sketches of major personalities in state, party, military, united front, diplomatic, cultural and artistic, editorial, and scientific affairs in China today. Introduction by Professor A. Doak Bennett, Columbia University.

FRANCE

882. Académie diplomatique internationale. *Dictionnaire diplomatique* (see 1028).
Volume 5 is devoted to biographies of diplomats from the Middle Ages to the present.

883. *Dictionnaire de biographie française.* Paris: Letouzey, 1933–1963. Ten vols. (in progress).
Signed articles; bibliographies. Covers only deceased persons.

884. *Who's Who in France: Dictionnaire Biographique.* Paris: Lafitte. LC 54–17054 Rev.
Published biennially since 1953. Includes Frenchmen in foreign countries and French-speaking persons in Africa.

GERMANY

885. *Allgemeine Deutsche Biographie, 1875–1912.* Duncker & Humblot, Berlin, 56 vols. (Reprint 1967).
Published for the Historical Commission of the Royal Bavarian Academy of Sciences. Long, signed biographical articles, including lists of publications of the persons described and bibliographic references. Includes 26,300 persons who died prior to 1900.
Index in Volume 56.

886. *Biographisches Jahrbuch und deutscher Nekrolog, 1896–1913.* Berlin: Reimer, 1897–1917. 18 vols. (plus index vol.).
Detailed articles, with bibliographies of prominent Germans who died during the previous year. Published annually. Annual index. Cumulated index for volumes 1–10 (1896–1905).

887. *Biographisches Lexikon.* Leipzig, German Democratic Republic: Dietz Verlag, 1965. 164 pp.
Concise biographical sketches of 600 leading statesmen of some 130 states. Includes governmental and political party officials.

888. *Die grossen Deutschen: deutsche Biographie.* Hermann Heimpel, Theodor Heuss, and Benno Reifenberg, eds. Berlin: Propyläen—Verlag bei Ullstein, 1957–58. 5 vols.
Long biographical articles on prominent Germans from 672 A. D.

889. *Neue Deutsche Biographie.* 1953 – (in progress). 20 vols. projected, including final index vol. Duncker & Humblot, Berlin.
Published for the Historical Commission of the Bavarian Academy of Sciences. A complete revision of the *Allgemeine Deutsche Biographie* (885). Primarily short bio-

graphical sketches but some extend to 16 pages. Includes over 8,000 persons who died prior to 1900 who have gained recognition since. One half of the biographies in the older work are considered as still sufficient and are referenced in this work. Coverage includes persons in Austria and the German-speaking part of Switzerland, if connected with the course of German history. Some 1,000 biographical sketches per volume but many other persons are covered in genealogical references so that the total work will include some 50,000 persons.

890. Rössler, Helmut, and Günther Franz. *Biographisches Wörterbuch zur deutschen Geschichte.* Munich: Oldenbourg, 1953.
Includes 2,000 biographies from Roman times to 1933. Companion volume to *Sachwörterbuch zur deutschen Geschichte* (1050).

891. *SBZ-Biographie: ein biographisches Nachschlagebuch über die Sowjetische Besatzungszone Deutschlands.* Bonn: Deutscher Bundes-Verlag, 1964. 406 pp.
Published for the Bundesministerium für gesamtdeutsche Fragen. Biographical sketches of persons in the German Democratic Republic, issued by the Federal Ministry of all-German Affairs in Bonn. 1958 title was *Wer ist Wer in der SBZ?*

892. U. S. Department of State, Division of Biographic Information. *A Guide to the Government, Political Parties, and Organizations of the So-Called "German Democratic Republic."* (Biographic Directory No. 277.) Washington, D. C., 1961. xviii, 62 pp.

893. *Wer ist Wer? Das Deutsche Who's Who,* 15th edition of Degener's *Wer Ist's?* Berlin: Arani Verlagsgesellschaft, 1966. Vol. I: West Germany, West Berlin, 2000 pp. Vol. II: East Germany, East Berlin, 384 pp.
Some 25,000 entries covering West Germans, Austrians, Swiss, and 5,000 East Germans.

894. *Who's Who in Germany: A Biographical Dictionary Containing about 11,000 Biographies of Prominent People in and of Germany and 2,400 Organizations,* 2d edition. Munich: Oldenbourg, 1960. 2 vols. 1618 pp; 140 pp.

GREAT BRITAIN

895. Boase, Frederic. *Modern English Biography, Containing Many Thousand Concise Memoirs of Persons Who Have Died Since 1850, with an Index of the Most Interesting Matter.* Netherton, England: Truro, 1892–1921. 6 vols. Reprinted by Frank Cass, London, 1964.
Especially good for minor names not included in the *Dictionary of National Biography* (897).

896. *Chambers's Biographical Dictionary.* J. O. Thorne, ed. Edinburgh: W. & R. Chambers, Ltd., 1961. New edition, New York: St. Martin's Press, Inc., 1962. 1432 pp.
Important persons of all countries, throughout history. Includes many contemporaries. Bibliographic references. Subject index.

897. *Dictionary of National Biography.* Leslie Stephen and Sidney Lee, eds. London: Smith, Elder, 1908–1909. 22 vols. Reprinted in 1938. LC 8–31671.

898. _____ . 2d–6th *Supplements.* London: Oxford University Press, 1912–1959. 5 vols.

899. _____. *Index and Epitome.* Sir Sidney Lee, ed. London: Smith, Elder, 1903–1913. 2 vols.
Scholarly work. Includes bibliographies. Covers Great Britain and the Colonies.

900. _____. *The Concise Dictionary.* London: Oxford University Press, 1903. 2 vols. 1503 pp. Reprinted 1953–1961. LC 58–26259.
An abridgment of the *Dictionary* (897) and its *Supplements* (898). Corrections and additions are found in the 1953 reprint. This publication serves as both an index and a biographic dictionary.

901. Matthews, William. *British Autobiographies: An Annotated Bibliography of British Autobiographies Published or Written Before 1951.* Berkeley and Los Angeles: University of California Press, 1955. 376 pp. LC 55–13593.

902. *Twentieth Century Dictionary of National Biography.* London: Oxford University Press, 1920–1959. 5 vols.

903. *Who's Who: An Annual Biographical Dictionary.* London: Black; New York: St. Martin's Press, Inc.
Published annually since 1849. Until 1897 it presented only a list of names of titled and official persons. Since, it includes bibliographic sketches.
The pioneer among who's who publications. Principally British, incorporated with *Men and Women of the Time.* See *Who Was Who* (904).

904. *Who Was Who, 1897–1915, 1916–1928, 1929–1940, 1941–1950, 1951–1960.* London: Black, 1929–1961. 5 vols.
A companion to the British *Who's Who* (903).

INDIA

905. Buckland, Charles Edward. *Dictionary of Indian Biography.* London: Sonnenschein, 1906. 494 pp.
Covers some 2,600 Englishmen, Indians, and others connected with India since 1750.

ISRAEL

906. *Who's Who: Israel.* Tel Aviv: Who's Who in the State of Israel Publishing House.
Published annually since 1952.

ITALY

907. *Chi E? Dizionario degli Italiani d'oggi,* 7th edition. Rome: Scarano, 1961. 714 pp.

908. *Who's Who in Italy, 1957–58.* Milano: Intercontinental Book and Publishing, 1958. 1137 pp.
A biographical dictionary containing about 7,000 biographies of prominent people in and of Italy, and 1,400 organizations.

JAPAN

909. *Japan Biographical Encyclopedia and Who's Who.* Tokyo: Japan Biographical Research Department, Rengo Press.
Published three times a year since 1958. Covers all fields, in all periods of history; living and deceased persons.

910. *Who's Who of Contemporary Japan.* Tokyo: Japanese Politics Economy Research Institute, 1963. 466 pp.

NEW ZEALAND

911. *Encyclopedia of New Zealand* (see 1000).
Contains some 900 biographies, including contemporary persons.

912. Scholefield, Guy Hardy. *A Dictionary of New Zealand Biography* (897). Wellington, New Zealand: Department of Internal Affairs, 1940. 2 vols.
Patterned after Great Britain's *Dictionary of National Biography.* Includes bibliography.

913. *Who's Who in New Zealand,* 7th edition. F. A. Simpson, ed. Wellington, New Zealand: Reed, 1961. 307 pp.

PAKISTAN

914. *Biographical Encyclopedia of Pakistan, 1960/61,* 2d edition. Lahore, Pakistan: Biographical Research Institute for International Publishers.

PHILIPPINES

915. Manuel, E. Arsenio. *Dictionary of Philippine Biography.* Quezon City, Philippines: Filipiniana Publishers, 1955 — (in progress).
Includes bibliographies.

SOVIET RUSSIA

916. Osteuropa Institut, Munich. *5000 Sowjetköpfe: Gliederung und Gesicht eines Führungskollektivs.* Cologne: Deutscher Industrie-Verlag, 1959. 862 pp.

917. *Porträts der UdSSR-Prominenz.* Munich: Institut zur Erforschung der UdSSR, 1960–61. Nos. 1–24.
Some 500 biographies.

918. U. S. Department of State, Division of Biographic Information. *Directory of Soviet Officials, 1960/61.* Washington, D. C., 1961. LC 61–60816.
Directory only, no biographical information.

919. *Who's Who in the USSR 1965–66,* 2d edition. New York: Scarecrow Press, 1966. 1189 pp.
Some 5,000 biographies, compiled by the Institute for the Study of the USSR in Munich.

SPAIN

920. *Who's Who in Spain: A Biographical Dictionary Containing About 6000 Biographies of Prominent People in and of Spain and 1400 Organizations.* Barcelona: Intercontinental Book and Publishing Co., 1963. 998 pp.

SWITZERLAND

921. *Who's Who in Switzerland, Including the Principality of Liechtenstein, 1962–63*, 4th edition.

TURKEY

922. *Who's Who in Turkey.* Ankara, Turkey: Oktay, 1961 –.

UNION OF SOUTH AFRICA

923. *Who's Who of Southern Africa: Incorporating South African Who's Who and "Who's Who of the Federation of Rhodesia and Nyasaland, Central and East Africa."* Johannesburg: Wootton & Gibson.
Published annually since 1907.

Section D. International

924. *Almanach de Gotha. annuaire généalogique, diplomatique et statistique.*
Published annually since 1763. Covers the nobility of European countries, includes royal and princely genealogies.

925. Arnim, Max. *Internationale Personalbibliographie, 1800–1943*, 2d edition. Leipzig, Germany: Hiersemann, 1944–52. 2 vols.
Index of bibliographies of books, articles, biographical dictionaries, *Festschriften,* etc. Also useful for biographical references. International coverage, with German personalities predominant. The first volume of the second edition omitted a number of names for political reasons; consult the first edition.

926. _____. *Vol. III, 1944–1959 and Supplements.* Gerhard Bock and Franz Hodes, eds. Stuttgart, Germany: Hiersemann, 1961–63. 659 pp.

927. *A Dictionary of Universal Biography of All Ages and People,* 2d edition. Albert M. Hyamson, ed. New York: E. P. Dutton and Co., 1951. 679 pp. LC 51–14243.
Brief identifications of some 110,000 deceased persons of all countries and generations who died before 1950. Coded references to one or more of the 23 most comprehensive biographical dictionaries and encyclopedias in which fuller biographies can be found.

928. *The International Who's Who, 1965–66,* 29th edition. London: Europa Publications Ltd.
Leading personalities in every country of the world. Covers many countries where no national Who's Who is published.

929. *International Yearbook and Statesman's Who's Who.* London: Burke's Peerage. LC 53–1425.
Published annually since 1953.
Information on international organizations. Sketches of world leaders in government, church, commerce, education, etc.

Section E. Professional Groups and Specialists in the Social Sciences

930. American Economic Association. *Handbook, 1964,* 4th edition. Evanston, Ill.
Issued from time to time as a supplement to, or number of, the *American Economic Review* (367).
Biographical data on some 10,000 members, including education, fields of specialization or major research interest, titles of representative publications, research projects under way, and listings in other biographical directories. Section on Classification of Members by Fields of Specialization.

931. *American Men of Science: A Biographical Directory, 1960–62; Vol. 5, The Social and Behavioral Sciences,* 10th edition. Tempe, Ariz.: Jaques Cattell Press, 1962. 1220 pp. LC 6–7326.
Some 24,000 biographical sketches of men and women in economics, political science, statistics, psychology, geography, and anthropology.
(For historians see the *Directory of American Scholars* (1939)).

932. _____. *Supplements.*
New names, significant changes in affiliations and addresses, obituary notices, etc.

933. American Political Science Association. *Biographical Directory,* 5th edition. Washington, D. C., 1968. LC 46–38 Rev.
Education, career history, present position, publications, and primary fields of interest of some 4,000 political scientists, including a number of non-Americans. Also separate listing of biographies by fields of interest.

934. American Society for Public Administration, Comparative Administration Group. *Revised Membership List.* Bloomington, Ind.: Indiana University, Department of Government, 1964.

935. Association of American Geographers. *1961 Handbook-Directory.* Washington, D. C. 192 pp. LC 56–12884.
The Directory section lists members with personal data, education, chief fields of research and interest, occupation, and home address.

936. _____. *Supplement.* 1964.
Only names and addresses.

937. Bernsdorf, Wilhelm. *Internationales Soziologen Lexikon.* Joseph Maier, ed. for USA. Stuttgart, Germany: Ferdinand Enke Verlag, 1959. 662 pp.
Biographical sketches of some 1,000 sociologists and other social scientists. Bibliographies.

938. *Congressional Staff Directory.* Charles B. Brownson, ed. Washington, D. C.: Congressional Staff Directory. 416 pp. LC 59–13987.
Published annually since 1959. Includes data on Members of Congress, their professional staffs, staff members of committees and subcommittees, and staff of the Library of Congress.

939, *Directory of American Scholars, 1963–64,* 4th edition. Jaques Cattell Press, eds. New York: R. R. Bowker Co., 4 vols. LC 57–9125. Published with the cooperation of the American Council of Learned Societies.
Volume I, *History,* published in 1963, provides some 6,700 brief biographies which include personal data, area of specialization and research, education, positions held, memberships and offices held in professional societies, publications, and mailing address.
For other social scientists see *American Men of Science, Vol. 5. The Social and Behavioral Sciences* (931).

940. *Directory of Organizations and Individuals Professionally Engaged in Governmental Research and Related Activities.* New York: Governmental Research Association, 1935 –.

941. Directory of Statistical Personnel in the American Nations (see 863).
Biographical sketches.

942. Greene, Katrine R. C. *Institutions and Individuals* (see 1075).
Includes references to biographical directories.

943. Kosch, Wilhelm. *Biographisches Staatshandbuch: Lexikon der Politik, Presse und Publizistik.* Berne and Munich: Francke Verlag, 1963. 2 vols. 1220 pp.
Biographical articles on living and deceased Germans, Austrians, and Swiss prominent in politics, the press, and as contributors to periodicals.

944. *Kürschners deutscher Gelehrten-Kalender, 1961,* 9th edition. Berlin: de Gruyter, 1961. 2 vols.
Dictionary of German scholars. Some 17,000 entries. Bibliographies.

945. Library of Congress, Reference Department. *National Directory of Latin Americanists.* Hispanic Foundation, comp. Washington, D. C., 1966. iii, 351 pp. LC 65–61762.
A highly selective list of 1,884 specialists in the social sciences and humanities resident in the United States who qualify by experience and professional training as specialists in the Latin-American field. The first and largest class consists of "area specialists." Bibliographic data include the interests and research of these specialists. The other class consists of political scientists, economists, etc., who are not exclusively Latin Americanists.

946. *National Radio-Television-News Directory: Official Press Guide of the Radio-Newsreel-Television Working Press Association.* New York: Radio-Newsreel-Television Working Press Association.
Published annually since 1954.
Directory and biographical information on staff members of networks, newsreels, news services, stations, press clubs, association members, etc. Includes White House and other federal government personnel; State officials; and United Nations delegation staffs, nonmember observers, and staffs of its specialized agencies.

947. Osterroth, Franz. *Biographisches Lexikon des Sozialismus.* Hannover, Germany: Dietz, 1960 — (in progress).
Biographies of prominent German Socialists, living and dead.

948. United Nations Educational, Scientific and Cultural Organization. *Social Scientists Specializing in African Studies.* The Hague: Mouton, 1963. 375 pp.
Biographies of 2,072 social scientists from Africa and elsewhere. Geographic and subject specialty indexes.

949. *Taylor's Encyclopedia of Government Officials: Federal and State.* Dallas, Tex.: Taylor Publishing Co., 1967.
Published biennially with quarterly supplements.
Names and addresses of the key people responsible for the operation of U. S. Government departments, agencies, and commissions; U. S. ambassadors; U. S. and state senators and representatives; party chairmen and vice chairmen for all states; and all delegates to the 1964 political conventions. Some 20,000 names; 850 pictures. 1964 election statistics.

950. *Who's Who in American Education: A Biographical Dictionary of Eminent Living Educators of the United States and Canada.* Robert C. Cook, ed. Nashville, Tenn.: Who's Who in American Education. LC 29−2351.
Published biennially since 1928.

951. *Who's Who in American Politics.* Paul A. Theis and Edmund L. Henshaw, Jr., eds. New York: R. R. Bowker Co., 1967. xiv, 748 pp.; Addenda 24 pp.
Biographies of more than 12,000 key political figures on the national, state, and local levels including the minority parties.
Mr. Theis is Public Relations Director, Republican Congressional Committee, and Mr. Henshaw is Research Director, Democratic Congressional Committee.

952. *Who's Who in Soviet Social Sciences, Humanities, Art, and Government.* Ina Telberg, comp. New York: Telberg Book Co., 1961. 147 pp. LC 61−16892.
Some 700 sketches based on the latest Soviet sources.

CHAPTER 13.

OTHER REFERENCE WORKS

Section A. General Encyclopedias, Dictionaries, Handbooks and Yearbooks

Encyclopedias have met an insistent demand for knowledge since 77 A. D. when the *Natural History of Pliny the Elder* was first published in Latin. In recent times encyclopedias have been published in various countries and languages—new ones appear periodically. They appear in numerous revised editions and are also kept up-to-date through the publication of yearbooks and supplements.

Encyclopedias and dictionaries (which are a form of encyclopedia) are virtually universal in their coverage of human knowledge. Some treat all subjects while others specialize in subject areas such as political science, history, geography, or religion. Some are prepared by authoritative specialists for scholarly readers, others are intended for beginning students or the general public. Some are erudite and insightful, others lack quality and depth.

Encyclopedias are written to represent particular religious or political points of view. These publications reflect changes in the intellectual, ecumenical, and political climate by offering different facts and viewpoints in successive editions. Encyclopedias frequently reflect the national interest of a particular government or regime. A German work stresses the reunification problem while a French set may emphasize the loss of France's colonial empire. Both may treat the Treaty of Versailles but their facts and interpretations will differ, and both may include a special section on Trotsky while the Soviet Russian volume omits mention of him.

In spite of their differences encyclopedias remain an excellent source of useful information. But the user should consult several encyclopedias, old and new, of several viewpoints to ensure accurate and comprehensive coverage of his subject matter. The user should consult Winchell's *Guide* (603), pp. 81–91; Walford's *Guide* (602), and Hoffman's *Reader's Adviser* (599), p. 28, as well as reviews in the various professional and library journals for authoritative evaluations of encyclopedic works.

953. *Americana Annual: An Encyclopedia of Events.* New York: Americana Corp. LC 23–10041.
Published annually since 1923. Supplements the *Encyclopedia Americana* with developments over the past year. Biographies and a necrology list.

954. *American Yearbook: A Record of Events and Progress.* New York: Nelson. 36 vols. LC 11–1626.
Published annually for the years 1910–1919 and 1925–1950. Includes coverage of international relations. Bibliographies and statistics.

955. *Britannica Book of the Year.* Chicago: Encyclopedia Britannica. LC 38–12082.
Published annually since 1938. Annual surveys and supplements to the *Encyclopaedia Britannica.*

956. *Brockhaus Encyclopaedie in zwanzig Bänden,* 17th revised edition. Wiesbaden, Germany: Brockhaus, 1966 – (in progress).
First edition under a new title; formerly *Brockhaus Konversations-Lexikon: Der Grosse Brockhaus* (957). Provides wider coverage than before. Special attention to bibliographies.

957. *Brockhaus Konversations-Lexikon: Der Grosse Brockhaus,* 16th edition. Wiesbaden, Germany: Brockhaus, 1952–63. 12 vols.; supplement; 2 vols.; atlas.
Standard German encyclopedia. Many articles include bibliographies. Biographies of living persons.

958. *Chamber's Encyclopedia,* new edition. New York and London: Oxford University Press, 1959. 15 vols.
For "the educated layman who has some general grounding in a variety of subjects." Contributions by scholars often with bibliographies. Volume 15 contains maps and indexes, including a classified list of articles, list of contributors, and subject index with many cross-references.

959. *Columbia Encyclopedia In One Volume,* 3d edition. William Bridgwater and Seymour Kurtz, eds. New York: Columbia University Press, 1963. 2388 pp. LC 63–20205.
Concise articles for quick reference. Biographical information. Maps.

960. *Encyclopedia Americana.* New York and Chicago: Encyclopedia Americana. 30 vols. LC 59–6519.
Comprehensive; for the general reader. Updated by *Americana Annual* (953).

961. *Encyclopaedia Britannica: A New Survey of Universal Knowledge.* Chicago: Encyclopaedia Britannica. 24 vols. LC 64–2141.
Many long scholarly contributions by specialists, although the more recent editions of the *Encyclopaedia Britannica* have not reached the standard of excellency which graced the 9th and 11th editions of 1902–1903 and 1911, respectively. The 14th and last edition was dated 1929.
Revisions are published in the *Britannica Book of the Year* (955).

962. _____. *10 Eventful Years: A Record of Events of the Years Preceding, Including and Following World War II, 1937 through 1946.* Prepared under the editorial direction of Walter Yust, editor of *Encyclopaedia Britannica.* Chicago: Encyclopaedia Britannica, 1947. 4 vols.
Useful in addition to the annual *Britannica Book of the Year* (955).

963. *Encyclopédie Française.* Paris: Comité de l'Encyclopédie Française, 1935–1964 (in progress). 20 vols.
Index in each volume; to be followed by a cumulative index for the completed set. Publication plans include a separate volume of bibliography and index of names.
Winchell's *Guide* (603), p. 88, notes that volume 10, *L'état moderne,* was written in the Nazi-influenced days around 1938.

964. *Grand Larousse Encyclopédique en Dix Volumes.* Paris: Librairie Larousse, 1960–1964. 10 vols.
A new work, based on the famous Larousse encyclopedias of the 19th century.

965. *Der grosse Herder, Nachschlagewerk für Wissen und Leben,* 5th revised edition of Herder's *Konversationslexikon.* Freiburg, Germany: Herder, 1953–56. 10 vols.
A standard encyclopedia. Catholic viewpoints.

966. _____. *Supplement.* 1962. 2 vols.

967. *Meyers neues Lexikon.* Leipzig, German Democratic Republic: VEB Bibliographisches Inst., 1961–64 (in progress).
This is, in fact, the ninth edition of an encyclopedia founded in 1840. The unfinished eighth edition was Nazi directed; this edition adheres to the Communist ideology of the German Democratic Republic. Biographies of living and deceased persons. Few bibliographies.

968. Walsh, Padraig S. *Anglo-American General Encyclopedias: A Historical Bibliography.* New York: R. R. Bowker Co., 1968. 300 pp. LC 67–25023.
Traces the evolution of all current titles to their origin.

969. Walsh, Padraig S. *General Encyclopedias in Print: A Comparative Analysis,* 6th. edition. New York: R. R. Bowker Co., 1967. 96 pp. LC 63–24124.

Guide lines for choosing a general-knowledge encyclopedia, covering over 30 non-specialized American encyclopedias. Includes a consensus-of-opinion rating chart showing recommended and nonrecommended encyclopedias and other charts listing encyclopedias by suggested age suitability, methods of arrangement, etc.

970. *Worldmark Encyclopedia of the Nations: A Practical Guide to the Geographic, Historical, Political, Social, and Economic Status of all Nations, Their International Relationships, and the United Nations System.* New York: Worldmark Press, Harper & Row, 1963. 5 vols. LC 63–12056.
Factual information on the United Nations (Vol. 1) and the various countries of the world, arranged by continents. Bibliographies.

Section B. Special Function

ACRONYMS AND FOREIGN-LANGUAGE TECHNICAL TERMS

971. *Acronyms and Initialisms Dictionary: A Guide to Alphabetical Designations, Contractions, Acronyms, Initialisms, and Similar Condensed Appellations,* 2d edition. Detroit, Mich.: Gale Research Co., 1964. LC 64–8724.
A guide to 45,000 alphabetic designations, contractions, and initialisms. Includes political, public affairs, international, military, United Nations, and other terms.

972. Back, Harry, et al. *Dictionary of Politics and Economics* (1029).
Published in English, French, and German.

973. Haensch, Günther. *Dictionary of International Relations and Politics.* Systematic and alphabetic in four foreign languages: German, English/American, French, and Spanish. Amsterdam, London, and New York: Elsevier Publishing Co., 1965. xv, 638 pp. LC 64–8710.
Covers the basic vocabulary of politics, of international law and international cooperation. Notes differences between British and American English and the usage of German, French, and Spanish as spoken in different countries.
Indispensable for the correct use of foreign-language material.

974. *Statistical Vocabulary, Vocabulario estadistico, Vocabulaire Statistique,* 2d edition. Washington, D. C.: Pan American Union, 1960. 83 pp.

ATLASES AND GAZETTEERS

975. *Ambassador World Atlas.* Maplewood, N. J.: Hammond, Inc., 1956. 416 pp. LC Map 56–301.
Includes both physical and political maps.

976. *The Columbia Lippincott Gazetteer of the World.* Leon E. Seltzer, ed. New York: Columbia University Press, 1952. 2148 pp. LC 52–9199.
A basic reference work. Supplemented in 1961 by *Rand McNally World Guide* (981). Edited with the cooperation of the Geographic Research Staff of the Columbia University Press and the American Geographic Society.

977. Fage, John D. *An Atlas of African History.* London: Edward Arnold, 1958. 64 pp. LC Map 59–100.

Historical development from the 4th century on is shown in 62 black and white maps.

978. Ginsburg, Norton Sidney. *Atlas of Economic Development.* (University of Chicago, Department of Geography, Research Paper No. 68.) Chicago: University of Chicago Press, 1961.
Worldwide coverage of economic geography, population, agriculture, commerce and industry, transportation, etc.

979. Hazard, Harry W. *Atlas of Islamic History,* 3d revised edition. Princeton, N. J.: Princeton University Press, 1954. 49 pp.
From 600 A. D. to 1953. Summaries of important historical events facing each map. Conversion table of Christian and Muslim dates. Index of place names.

980. Kerr, Donald G. G. *An Historical Atlas of Canada.* Toronto: T. Nelson, 1960. 120 pp. LC Map 61—5.
Prepared in cooperation with the Canadian Historical Association's Committee on a Historical Atlas of Canada.
Historical maps, contemporary drawings, charts and graphs, and commentary on significant aspects of Canadian exploration, settlement, socioeconomic developments, and international relations.

981. *Rand McNally World Guide.* Chicago: Rand McNally, 1963. 22 pp. LC 53—13329.
Reproduced from *The Columbia Lippincott Gazetteer of the World* (976). Serves as a 1961 supplement to that publication.

982. Shepherd, William Robert. *Historical Atlas,* 9th edition. New York: Barnes and Noble, 1964. 341 pp. LC Map 64—26.
Contains 266 pages of detailed maps showing political and military activities and colonization for the period 1450 B. C. to 1964.

983. *The Times Atlas of the World.* John Bartholomew, ed. Boston: Houghton Mifflin, 1955—1960. 5 vols. LC A 56—8641.
Originally published by The Times Publishing Company, London. Highly rated atlas, with fine cartography. Some 220,000 place names cited in the index. Main roads, airports, pipelines, oil fields, and other features are shown.

984. *The Times Index-Gazetteer of the World.* London: The Times Publishing Co., 1965. 964 pp.
A companion volume to *The Times Atlas of the World* (983). Serves as a location guide to 345,000 geographic features listed in the atlas.

985. Toynbee, Arnold J., and Edward D. Meyers. *Historical Atlas and Gazetteer.* London: Oxford University Press, 1959. 257 pp.
Issued under the auspices of the Royal Institute of International Affairs.

Note: For other atlases and gazetteers serving other and more specialized needs see:
986. Church, Martha, Robert E. Hughes, and Wilbur Zelinsky. *A Basic Geographic Library: A Selected and Annotated Book List for American Colleges* (see 644).

987. Walsh, Padraig S. *General World Atlases in Print.* New York: R. R. Bowker Co., 1966. 66 pp. LC 66—23105.

Description and rating of 35 general world atlases published in the United States, currently in print. Index.
Ratings derived from the recommendations of professionally accepted sources of reference book evaluation (Publisher's statement).

Section C. Continents and Groups of Countries

AFRICA

988. *Africa: A Handbook to the Continent,* revised edition. Collin Legum, ed. New York: Frederick A. Praeger, Inc., 1966. xii, 558 pp. LC 66—12478.
Political, economic, and cultural information for each country or territorial unit. Bibliography. Some biographical sketches. By experts for the general reader.

989. Kitchen, Helen. *A Handbook of African Affairs.* New York: Frederick A. Praeger, Inc., 1964. 311 pp. LC 64—16680.
Published for the African-American Institute. Information on the political structure, population, area, languages, and armies of African countries and territorial units. Includes material on the organization of African unity. Maps.

990. *Meyers Handbuch über Afrika.* Mannheim, Germany: Bibliographisches Institut, 1962. 779 pp.
Sections on geography, ethnology, economy, culture, etc. Information on individual countries and territorial units covering geography, economics, and political facts. Maps and illustrations.

991. Rosenthal, Eric. *Encyclopedia of Southern Africa,* 2d edition. London and New York: Frederick Warne, 1964. 604 pp.
Data include history, biography, and geography of countries and territorial units in southern Africa, including South Africa and Rhodesia. Maps and illustrations.

992. *West Africa Annual, 1964—1965.* L. K. Jakande, ed. Lagos, Nigeria: John West Publications Ltd., 1964. 337 pp.
Information on the economic, geographic, and political structure of all countries of West Africa, preceded by a general survey of the area, dealing with geography, population, mineral and power resources, history, and joint organizations.

993. *The Yearbook and Guide to East Africa.* A. Gordon-Brown, ed. London: Robert Hale Ltd., 1965. 320 pp.
Information on area, population, resources, and other facts. Maps.

994. *The Yearbook and Guide to Southern Africa.* A. Gordon-Brown, ed. London: Robert Hale Ltd., 1965. 703 pp.

ASIA

995. *Asian Annual: The "Eastern World" Handbook.* London: Eastern World. LC 55—18104.
Published annually since 1954. Factual information on Asian countries. Section on non-Asian countries' diplomatic and consular representation in Asia, Asian representatives in non-Asian countries, and their trade.

996. *Communist China,* Hong Kong, Union Research Institute.
Published annually since 1955.

997. National Commission for UNESCO, Japan. *Japan: Its Land, People and Culture,* revised edition. Tokyo: Printing Bureau, Ministry of Finance, 1964. 885 pp. LC 65–71358.
Encyclopedic in scope; covers all aspects of Japanese life together with its geographic, historical, social, economic, and cultural backgrounds, etc. (Preface).

998. *Times of India Directory and Yearbook including Who's Who.* Bombay and London: Bennett, Coleman. LC A 19–14 Rev.
Published annually since 1914. Title varies: was "including *The Indian and Pakistan Yearbook and Who's Who,*" 1949–52/53.
Descriptive and statistical information.

AUSTRALIA AND NEW ZEALAND

999. *Australian Encyclopedia.* East Lansing, Mich.: Michigan State University Press, 1958. 10 vols.
Signed articles on all aspects of Australian history, life, and culture. Detailed index in Volume 10.

1000. *Encyclopedia of New Zealand.* A. H. McLintock, ed. Wellington, New Zealand: R. E. Owen, Government Printer, 1966. 3 vols.
The first encyclopedia with information on the country, people, and resources of New Zealand. The editor is the Parliamentary Historian. Articles by scholars and government officials. Many bibliographies included; some 900 biographies of contemporary persons. Detailed index.

1001. *Modern Encyclopedia of Australia and New Zealand.* Sydney: Horwitz-Grahame, 1964. 1199 pp. LC 65–2387.
Includes biographies of living persons. Also covers Papua-New Guinea.

COMMONWEALTH OF NATIONS

1002. *British Commonwealth Yearbook.* Ronald S. Russel, ed. London: Newman Neame.
Published annually since 1952/53. Earlier titles: 1952/53, *Commonwealth Cooperation; the Empire and Commonwealth Yearbook;* 1953/54–1959/60, *The Empire and Commonwealth Yearbook.*
General information on the various countries and dominions. Statistics.

1003. *Commonwealth Yearbook.* London: Europa Publications 1956–1959. 3 vols.
Published as *The British Commonwealth,* 1956–1958. Articles on Commonwealth countries covering geography, history, economics, government, constitutions, administration, law, churches, education, and the press.

MIDDLE EAST AND NORTH AFRICA

1004. *Middle East and North Africa.* London: Europa Publications. LC 48–3250.
Published annually since 1948. Entitled *Middle East* until 1964–65.
Includes information on economic, historical, political, cultural, and educational organizations; economic, geographic, and historical surveys; and a Who's Who for the area.

1005. *Middle East Record.* Tel Aviv, Israel: Israel Oriental Society, Reuven Shiloah Research Center.
Published annually since 1960. Covers politics and international relations of the nations of the Middle East.

1006. Ronart, Stephan, and Nandy Ronart. *Concise Encyclopedia of Arabic Civilization: The Arab East.* New York: Frederick A. Praeger, Inc., 1960. 589 pp. LC 60–10553.
Information on various aspects of Arabic civilization, including persons and places of the Arab East.

1007. Ronart, Stephan, and Nandy Ronart. *Concise Encyclopedia of Arabic Civilization: The Arab West.* New York: Frederick. A. Praeger, Inc., 1966. 416 pp. LC 66–13401.
Deals with the principal driving forces behind the evolution of the Arab West, or Maghreb (Morocco, Algeria, Tunisia, and Libya). Deals with the cultural, social, economic, and political aspects of the western section of the Arab world including the issues, events, ideas, intellectual achievements, and the actions of those leaders who have shaped its development.

1008. Sharabi, Hisham B. *A Handbook on the Contemporary Middle East: Sectional Introductions with Annotated Bibliographies.* Washington, D. C.: Georgetown University, 1956. 113 pp.
Covers Egypt, the Arabian peninsula, the Fertile Crescent, Iran, and Turkey. Current information; annotated lists of selected books and periodical literature.

SOUTH AMERICA

1009. *Master Directory for Latin America* (see 764).

1010. *South American Handbook: A Yearbook and Guide to the Countries and Resources of South and Central America, Mexico and West Indies.* London: Trade and Travel Publishers. LC 25–514.
Published annually since 1924.

Section D. Countries

CANADA

1011. *Canadian Annual Review.* John T. Saywell, ed. Toronto: University of Toronto Press. LC 61–3380.
Published annually since 1960. This survey annual includes coverage of foreign affairs and defense, the national economy, etc. Partly in French.

GERMANY

1012. Arntz, Helmut. *Germany of Today,* 6th revised edition. Wiesbaden, Germany: Franz Steiner, 1961. 917 pp.
Published by the Presse-und-Informationsamt of the Government of the German Federal Republic.

Statistical and other detailed information on cultural, economic, governmental, political, religious, and social affairs, including summaries on the development of German foreign policy, law, and public opinion.

1013. Arntz, Helmut. *Germany Reports,* 3d edition. Bonn: Press and Information Office of the Federal Government. 1962. 917 pp. LC 63–3833.

Descriptive and statistical information on German Life: economics, population, refugees, *Laender,* Berlin, "The Territory which became the Soviet-occupied Zone in 1945," "The German Eastern Territories under Alien Administration," foreign policy, constitution, public opinion, political parties and elections, military affairs, legislation, youth, culture, radio, film, and television. Chronology. Index. List of charts and diagrams. Maps.

1014. *Handbuch der deutschen Demokratischen Republik.* Berlin, German Democratic Republic: Staatsverlag der Deutschen Demokratischen Republik.

Published annually since 1964 for the Deutsches Institut für Zeitgeschichte. Supersedes *Jahrbuch der Deutschen Demokratischen Republik.* Describes the structure of the government, political parties, other political groups as well as developments in commerce, trade, finance, public health, education, cultural life, and foreign relations. Chronological list of events, 1949–63.

1015. *SBZ von A bis Z: ein Taschen- und Nachschlagebuch über die Sowjetische Besatzungszone Deutschlands.* Bonn: Deutscher Bundes-Verlag.

Published for the Bundesministerium für Gesamtdeutsche Fragen. Published irregularly, but usually annually, since 1953. A handbook of political, economic, cultural, and biographical information on the German Democratic Republic published by the Government of the German Federal Republic.

GREAT BRITAIN

1016. *An Official Handbook, Prepared by the Central Office of Information.* London: H. M. Stationery Office. LC 50–14073.

Published annually since 1948–49. Information on the government, economy, industry, labor, press, etc. Bibliography.

SOVIET RUSSIA

1017. Florinsky, Michael T. *McGraw-Hill Encyclopedia of Russia and the Soviet Union.* New York: McGraw-Hill, 1961. 624 pp. LC 61–18169.

Written by specialists for the general reader. Many bibliographic entries. Covers all aspects of Russia since the Middle Ages.

1018. *Information U.S.S.R.: An Authoritative Encyclopedia About the Union of Soviet Socialist Republics.* Robert Maxwell, ed. New York: Pergamon Press, 1962. 982 pp. LC 62–9879.

The main body of the work (763 pages) is a translation by J. T. McDermott of the *Great Soviet Encyclopedia,* presenting the Soviet point of view.

Section E. Worldwide

1019. *The Annual Register: World Events in 1965.* Ivison Macadam, ed. New York: St. Martin's Press, 1966. 581 pp.

1020. *Facts on File Yearbook.* New York: Facts on File, Inc. LC 42–24704. Annual cumulative volumes, published since 1941. *Facts on File* (528) is a weekly world news digest.

1021. *International Yearbook of Education* (see 1109).

1022. *International Yearbook and Statesman's Who's Who* (see 929). Includes political, statistical, and other information about all countries.

1023. *Länderlexikon.* Hamburg: Verlag Weltarchiv, 1955–60. 3 vols. Long articles on the social, governmental, political, and economic structure of all countries and their geography, agriculture, trade, and industry.

1024. *Political Handbook and Atlas of the World: Parliaments, Parties and Press.* New York: Council on Foreign Relations. LC 28–12165. Published annually since 1927. Political information on every country in the world: composition of governments; programs of political parties and their leaders; leading newspapers and periodicals, their political affiliation, and names of editors; and the organization, functions, and personnel of the United Nations and related international agencies. Maps.

1025. *Statesman's Year-Book: Statistical and Historical Annual of the States of the World.* London and New York: Macmillan Co. LC 4–3776. Published annually since 1864; a standard reference work. Descriptive and statistical information on all countries of the world: government, population, area, religion, education, finance, and diplomatic representatives. Selected bibliographies on statistics and other reference works for each country. Information on the United Nations.

1026. Whitaker, Joseph. *Almanack.* London: Whitaker. Published annually since 1869. Statistics on various countries, especially full data on the Commonwealth.

1027. *World Almanac and Book of Facts.* New York: World Almanac Division, Newspaper Enterprise Association. LC 4–3781. Published annually since 1868. A handbook of useful statistical, historical, political, and other miscellaneous information on the United States and other countries.

Section F. Diplomacy, Economics, Political Science, Social Sciences and World Affairs

1028. Académie Diplomatique Internationale. *Dictionnaire Diplomatique.* Geneva and Paris: Impressions Réunis, 1957. 1268 pp. 6 vols. Published under the direction of A. F. Frangulis. The *Dictionnaire* as a whole offers a review of political and diplomatic history since the end of World War I. Volume 5 provides biographies of diplomats from the Middle Ages to the present. Volume 6 is concerned with the period 1947–1957. Many topics are presented by persons with different points of view. The Suez Canal, for instance, is treated by Christian Pinay, John Foster Dulles, Sir Anthony Eden, and Dimitri Shepilov, and supplemented by a 38-page statement of the Egyptian Government. Numerous bibliographic references and texts of documents.

1029. Back, Harry, Horst Cirullies, and Günter Marquard. *Dictionary of Politics and Economics (Dictionnaire de politique et d'économie) (Wörterbuch für Politik und Wirtschaft).* Berlin: Walter de Gruyter and Co., 1965. 961 pp.

A trilingual dictionary of 14,000 political and economic terms in English, French, and German. For each term there is a brief explanation and definition in one language, with a reference to corresponding terms in the other two languages.

Very useful for research in these two non-English languages since literal, or non-technical translations can lead to misinterpretation and misunderstanding.

1030. Chamberlin, Waldo, and Thomas Hovet. *A Chronology and Fact Book of the United Nations, 1941–1964.* Dobbs Ferry, N. Y.: Oceana, 1954. 95 pp.

A chronological list of important actions, events, meetings, and memberships. Subject index.

1031. *Concise Dictionary of American History.* Wayne Andrews, ed.; Thomas C. Cochran, advisory ed. New York: Charles Scribner's Sons, 1962. 1156 pp. LC 62–9635.

Based on the *Dictionary of American History* (1034). Some of its articles have been reproduced, some omitted, cut, or brought up-to-date. Some 2,200 articles by specialists.

1032. *Congress and the Nation 1945–1964.* Washington, D. C.: Congressional Quarterly, Inc. 2000 pp.

Review of legislation and politics, including foreign policy. Records some 64,000 key votes of Senators and Representatives. Also covers election campaigns for the period-presidential, congressional, and gubernatorial. The appended Directory of Persons and Events provides brief biographical sketches of all Senators and Representatives of this period, committee chairmen since 1947, and all controversial nominations since 1945. Review of 217 major Supreme Court cases.

1033. *CQ Almanac.* Washington, D. C. Congressional Quarterly, Inc.

Published annually since 1945. An account of some 1,600 pages, cross-indexed, of the full year in Congress: Covers politics and lobbying.

1034. *Dictionary of American History,* 2d revised edition. James Truslow Adams, ed. in chief; R. V. Coleman, man. ed. New York: Charles Scribner's Sons, 1942–61. 6 vols. and index.

Signed contributions by specialists. Covers various aspects of history.

1035. *Dictionary of Political Science.* Joseph Dunner, ed. New York: Philosophical Library, 1964. xii, 585 pp. LC 63–15600.

Definition of terms and descriptions of concepts, events, nations, and personalities. Concise biographies.

1036. *A Dictionary of the Social Sciences.* Julius Gould and William L. Kolb, comps. New York: Free Press of Glencoe, Inc., 1964. LC 64–20307.

Prepared under the auspices of UNESCO. A dictionary of terms in the social sciences, providing both current definitions and history.

1037. Elliott, Florence, and Michael Summerskill. *Dictionary of Politics,* 3d edition. London: Penguin, 1961. 372 pp.

Includes terms, places, and living persons.

1038. *Encyclopedia of the Social Sciences.* E. A. R. Seligman, ed. in chief; Alvin Johnson, assoc. ed. New York: Macmillan Co., 1930–35. 15 vols.
Projected and prepared under the auspices of ten learned societies. Covers the social sciences and the social aspects of other fields. International in scope, with emphasis on the English-speaking world and Western Europe. Signed articles by specialists. Bibliographies. Biographical articles of outstanding contributors to the social sciences with lists of the authors' works. Many of the contributions are classics in their field.
See also the *International Encyclopedia of the Social Sciences* (1043).

1039. Gebhardt, Bruno. *Handbuch der deutschen Geschichte* (see 1255).

1040. *Geographisches Jahrbuch.* Hermann Haack, ed. Gotha, Germany: VEB Hermann Haack Geographisch-Kartographische Anstalt. LC 62–3398.
Published irregularly between 1866 and 1956; until World War II, published by the firm of Justus Perthes, Gotha. Comprehensive essays on selected fields of study in geography, with many annotated references. Cumulative table of contents. Author index.
This work is described in detail in Wright and Platt *Aids to Geographical Research* (647), as of pre-1943.

1041. *Handwörterbuch der Sozialwissenschaften.* Stuttgart, Germany: Fischer, 1952–65. 11 vols. Vol. 12 in progress.
Long articles on persons, places, and topics. Extensive bibliographies. Its fourth edition was called *Handwörterbuch der Staatswissenschaften* (1042).

1042. *Handwörterbuch der Staatswissenschaften,* 4th revised edition. Ludwig Elster, Adolf Weber, Fr. Wieser, eds. Jena, Germany: Fischer, 1923–29. 8 vols. and supplement.
A leading political science encyclopedia. Comprehensive. Long, signed articles by scholars. Bibliographies. Biographies of deceased persons.

1043. *International Encyclopedia of the Social Sciences.* David L. Sills, ed. New York: Macmillan and Free Press, 1968. 17 vols.
Covers, in the words of the editor, the "Big Six" sciences of human behavior (anthropology, economics, history, political science, sociology, and psychology) and the "Little Four" (geography, law, psychiatry, and statistics) which deal only in part with behavior.
All essays—by 1,505 contributors from 33 nations (but 80 percent by American)—are signed. They run 5,000 words or fewer.
The editors have included articles on contemporary problems while stressing the methods of social science and projecting lines of future development. This work is much more theoretical than the earlier *Encyclopedia of the Social Sciences* (1038).

1044. Johnson, Thomas H. *The Oxford Companion to American History.* New York: Oxford University Press, 1966. 906 pp.
Summaries of the principal events, persons, and places in American history, including its cultural, economic, and social aspects. Bibliographic references in the longer articles.

1045. Langer, William Leonard. *An Encyclopedia of World History: Ancient, Medieval and Modern, Chronologically Arranged,* revised edition. Boston: Houghton Mifflin Co., 1952. 1243 pp. LC 48–11571.
Political, military, and diplomatic history in outline. Indexes up to and since 1945.

1046. Martin, Michael R., and Gabriel H. Lovett. *Encyclopedia of Latin American History.* New York: Abelard-Schuman, 1956. 392 pp.
Essential information on the political, economic, and cultural development of all Latin-American countries from earliest times to the present. Many biographical entries, including living persons.

1047. Monkhouse, Francis John. *A Dictionary of Geography.* London: Edward Arnold, 1965. 344 pp.
Definitions of some 3,400 terms plus statistical and other information.

1048. Palmer, Alan Warwick. *A Dictionary of Modern History, 1789–1945.* London: Cresset; and Baltimore: Penguin Books, Inc., 1962. 314 pp. LC 63–1446.
Covers the important world events, personalities, places, and ideas of the period. Emphasis on British history and political topics. Economic, social, religious, and scientific developments are also treated.

1049. Plano, Jack C., and Milton Greenberg. *The American Political Dictionary,* 2d edition. New York: Holt, Rinehart & Winston, 1967. 416 pp. LC 62–18757.
Definitions and explanations of 1,100 terms relating to American government, politics, and foreign affairs. Includes pertinent court cases, statutes, and agencies.

1050. Rössler, Helmut, and Günther Franz. *Sachwörterbuch zur deutschen Geschichte.* Munich: Oldenbourg, 1956–1958.
Covers events, institutions, states, peoples, and ideas, including cultural, economic, and political aspects of all periods of German history. Bibliographies.

1051. Sloan, Harold S., and Arnold J. Zurcher. *A Dictionary of Economics,* 4th revised edition. New York: Barnes and Noble, 1964. 371 pp. LC 64–18785.

1052. Smith, Edward Conrad, and Arnold J. Zurcher. *Dictionary of American Politics.* New York: Barnes and Noble, 1955. 437 pp. LC 55–11359. The 1949 edition had the name *New Dictionary of American Politics.*
Concise definitions of some 3,500 terms.

1053. Sperber, Hans, and Travis Trittschuh. *American Political Terms: An Historical Dictionary.* Detroit, Mich.: Wayne State University Press, 1962. 516 pp. LC 11233.
Origins of terms and their various meanings, with reference to sources. Bibliography of the literature upon which the work is based.

1054. *Staatslexikon: Recht, Wirtschaft, Gesellschaft,* 6th revised edition. Freiburg, Germany: Herder, 1957–1963. 8 vols.
Published for the Görres-Gesellschaft. Standard encyclopedia for the social sciences and law. Catholic viewpoints. Bibliographies.

1055. Steinberg, Sigfried Heinrich, et al. *A New Dictionary of British History.* London: Edward Arnold; and New York: St. Martin's Press, 1963. 407 pp. LC 63–19376.
Covers Great Britain and her overseas possessions. No biographies or bibliographies.

1056. *Webster's Geographical Dictionary,* revised edition. Springfield, Mass.: G. & C. Merriam Co., 1963. 1293 pp. LC 59–1405.

1057. *Wörterbuch der Aussenpolitik.* Wolfgang Kerff and Horst Seydewitz, eds. Leipzig, German Democratic Republic: Dietz Verlag, 1966. 752 pp.

Concepts, international relations, treaties and agreements, conferences, problems in international law, and diplomatic practice as seen by Communist editors and contributors.

1058. *Yearbook of World Affairs.* London: Stevens and Sons; and New York: Frederick A. Praeger, Inc. LC 47–29156.
Published annually since 1947 under the auspices of the London Institute of World Affairs. Survey articles.

1059. Zadrozny, John Thomas. *Dictionary of Social Science.* Washington, D. C.: Public Affairs Press, 1959. 367 pp. LC 58–13401.

Section G. Directories of American and International Organizations

1060. *Annuaire européen; European Yearbook.* The Hague: Nijhoff.
Published annually since 1955 under the auspices of the Council of Europe. Aims to promote the scientific study of European organizations and their work. Covers their constitutions and functions. Includes the Council of Europe, the European Coal and Steel Community, and other organizations. Documents, articles, and bibliographies.

1061. *Annual International Congress Calendar.* Brussels: Union of International Associations.
Published annually since 1961. Lists schedules for current and future international meetings with additional pertinent information.

1062. Asia Society, Inc. *American Institutions and Organizations Interested in Asia: A Reference Directory,* 2d edition. Ward Morehouse, ed. New York: Taplinger Publishing Co., 1961. 581 pp. LC 61–11435.
Descriptive list of almost 1,000 American institutions and nonprofit organizations with interest in Asia. Summaries of activities by country and type of program. Index of organizations, their departments, and programs. List of Asian diplomatic, consular, and information offices, and list of United States information offices in Asia.

1063. Collison, Robert L. *Bibliographical Services Throughout the World, 1950–59* (see 608).
Includes a section on Bibliographical Activities of International Organizations, pp. 167–228.

1064. Council on Foreign Relations. *American Agencies Interested in International Affairs,* 5th edition. Donald Wasson, comp. New York: Frederick A. Praeger, Inc., 1964. 200 pp. LC 64–22497.
Information on 293 private organizations active in research programs in international affairs. Includes some international organizations with a strong American interest. Subject and personnel index.

1065. *1964 Directory of American Firms Operating in Foreign Countries,* 5th edition Juvenal L. Angel, comp. New York: World Trade Academy Press, 1964. 187 pp.

1066. *Directory of Non-Governmental Organisations Offering Assistance in the Developing Countries.* Rome: Centre for Labour and Social Studies, 1964 –.
Covers both educational and research organizations.

1067. *Directory of Organizations and Individuals Professionally Engaged in Governmental Research and Related Activities.* New York: Governmental Research Association, 1935 –.

1068. *Directory of Periodicals Published by International Organizations,* 2d edition. Burssels: Union of International Associations, 1959. 241 pp.
The term "periodicals" is broadly interpreted. Covers 1,340 publications of supranational and intergovernmental organizations, and international nongovernmental organizations. Includes information on initial date of publication, frequency, and size with additional descriptive comments.

1069. *Encyclopedia of Associations,* 5th edition. Detroit, Mich.: Gale Research Co., 1968. 1330 pp. LC 68–17314.
List of over 12,000 associations representing interests in foreign relations, civil rights, national politics, communications, etc. Provides name and address of each organization, its chief official and title, founding date, number of members, size of staff, number of state and local chapters, description of membership and activities, list of special committees, and publications. Alphabetic listing of names of association executives with organization and title.

1070. _____. *New Associations.*
Loose-leaf supplement to the *Encyclopedia of Associations* (1069) published approximately every four months between editions of the *Encyclopedia.* Index cumulated in each issue.

1071. *Europa Yearbook,* 1959 –. London: Europa Publications, Ltd. LC 59–2942.
Published earlier with the titles *Europa year-book* (1926–1929); *Europa* (incorporated with *Europa year-book,* 1930–1937); *Orbis: Encyclopedia of Extra-European Countries* (1938–1945); *Europa: The Encyclopedia of Europe* (1946–1959); These volumes covered international organizations, including the United Nations and its specialized agencies, world politics, texts of documents, and information on various European countries. *Orbis* (1938–1945) contained information on countries outside of Europe, i.e., surveys and directories of political, industrial, financial, cultural, educational, and scientific organizations. See Winchell, *Guide* (603) for additional information.
Beginning with 1959 there are bound annual volumes instead of the former loose-leaf series: two volumes per year beginning in 1960; Volume 1, International Organizations: Europe; and Volume 2, Africa, the Americas, Asia, Australasia.
Since 1963 information on educational and learned societies and institutions has been omitted and transferred to *The World of Learning* (1098).

1072. European Communities, Information Service. *Guide des Communautés Européennes.* Brussels and Luxembourg: Marché commun, Euratom, C.E.C.A., 1962. 179 pp.

1073. *Foundation Directory,* 2d edition. New York: Russell Sage Foundation, 1964. 1000 pp. LC 60–13807.
Detailed information on some 6,000 foundations.

1074. Garrigue, Katharine. *Citizens in World Affairs: A Directory of Non-Governmental Organizations.* New York: Foreign Policy Association, 1953.
A directory of 434 organizations active in the field of international relations. Data on each organization.

1075. Greene, Katrine R. C. *Institutions and Individuals: An Annotated List of Directories Useful in International Administration.* Chicago: Public Administration Clearing House, 1953. 59 pp.
List of 215 biographical, institutional, and organizational directories.

1076. *Handbook of International Organizations in the Americas.* Ruth D. Masters, et al, comps. Washington, D. C. (now New York): Carnegie Endowment for International Peace, 1945. 453 pp.
Information on 109 organizations, including brief bibliographic notes.

1077. *Handbuch der Internationalen Organisationen.* Gert Höhne and Harald Rose, eds. Leipzig, German Democratic Republic: Dietz Verlag, 1967 (announced). About 800 pp.
Information on the most important international public, political, and societal private organizations, including peace and labor organizations. Descriptions of their goals, activities, historical development, membership, structure, important publications, and a brief evaluation as seen from the East German Communist point of view.

1078. *American Agencies Interested in International Affairs* (see 1064).

1079. *International Congresses and Conferences, 1840–1937: A Union List of Their Publications Available in Libraries of the United States and Canada.* Winifred Gregory, ed. New York: H. W. Wilson Co., 1938. 229 pp.
Lists holdings in more than 100 libraries. Does not include diplomatic conferences, nor those held under the auspices of the League of Nations.

1080. *International Organizations.* Amsterdam: J. H. de Bussy, 1960. 99 pp.
Information on some 75 economic, social, and scientific organizations of special interest to Western Europe.

1081. *International Regional Organizations: Constitutional Foundations.* Ruth Catherine Lawson, ed. New York: Frederick A. Praeger, Inc., 1962. 387 pp. LC 62–13746.
Texts of treaties, charters, and other constitutional documents basic to regional organizations, such as OAS, SEATO, and NATO. Introductory notes.

1082. Library of Congress, International Organization Section. *International Scientific Organizations: A Guide to Their Library, Documentation, and Information Services.* Prepared under the direction of Kathrine O. Murra. Washington, D. C.: Government Printing Office, 1962. 794 pp.
The term "science" is broadly interpreted to include technology, agriculture, and medicine. Detailed information on the structure and functions of the societies, and a list of their publications. List of acronyms.

1083. Ljunnggren, Florence, and Charles L. Geddes. *An International Directory of Institutes and Societies Interested in the Middle East.* Amsterdam: Djambatan, 1962. 159 pp. LC 63–36286.

1084. *Minerva: Jahrbuch der gelehrten Welt.* Berlin: de Gruyter.
Published irregularly, but formerly annually, covering the periods
1891/92–1913/14; 1920–38; 1952–56. Information on universities, colleges, libraries, archives, publications, and learned societies. Volume I, published in 1952,
covers Europe; Volume II covers countries outside Europe.

1085. *Minerva-Handbücher.* Berlin: de Gruyter.
Supplement to *Minerva* (1084), published since 1927.

1086. Pan American Union, Division of Conferences and Organizations. *Orga-
nismos especializados Interamericanos y otros vinculados a la O.E.A.* Washington,
D. C.: Pan American Union, 1958. 214 pp.
A mimeographed supplement was published in 1960.

1087. Peaslee, Amos Jenkins. *International Governmental Organizations: Constitutional Documents,* 2d revised edition. The Hague: Nijhoff, 1961. 2 vols.
LC 62–32304.
Constitutional documents of some 100 public international organizations. Brief
notes on history and constitutional developments. Bibliographies.

1088. Union of International Associations. *Petit Repertoire des organisations Internationales.* Brussels: The Union, 1965. 160 pp.
A list, in French, of international, worldwide, regional, intergovernmental, and
nongovernmental organizations, with their addresses and names in English.

1089. Speeckaert, Georges P. *International Institutions and International Organizations: A Select Bibliography.* Brussels: Union of International Associations, 1956.
116 pp.
Published with assistance from UNESCO and in collaboration with the International Federation for Documentation.
Almost 800 items dealing with the operating methods of international organizations, their legal status, the relations between intergovernmental and nongovernmental organizations. No references to international politics, economics, and law
(Introduction).

1090. Speeckaert, Georges P. *Select Bibliography on International Organization,
1885–1964.* Brussels: Union of International Associations, 1965. 150 pp.
The first part lists 350 publications dealing with international organization in gen-
eral. Four sections: 1) History of International Relations; 2) Theory and General
Study; 3) Legal Status, Immunities, Administration, Civil Service; 4) Yearbooks,
Directories, Periodicals, Bibliographies. The second part has 730 titles relating to 214
different international organizations.
Entries are listed according to the organization's French title.

1091. UNESCO. *Review List of Nongovernmental Organizations Admitted to Consultative Status and Evaluation of their Relations with UNESCO.* Paris, 1958.
423 pp.
Reports on 128 nongovernmental organizations, describing their membership, purpose, structure, main activities, and publications.

1092. _____. Social Science Clearing House. *Foundations with Social Science
Activities: An International Catalogue.* (Reports and Papers in the Social Sciences
No. 7.) Paris, 1957. 89 pp. LC 58–672.
Information on structure, activities, staff, and other characteristics.

1093. _____. Social Science Clearing House. *International Organizations in the Social Sciences: A Summary Description of the Structure and Activities of Nongovernmental Organizations in Consultative Relationship with UNESCO and Specialized in the Social Sciences,* revised edition. Paris, 1965. LC 61–3171.
Detailed information on 18 nongovernmental organizations. Introduction by Jean Meynaud.

1094. _____. Social Science Clearing House. *Research Councils in the Social Sciences.* (Reports and Papers in the Social Sciences No. 6.) Paris, 1955. 54 pp.
Entries listed by country.

1095. _____. Social Science Clearing House. *Research Councils in the Social Sciences: Addenda 1956.* Paris, 1957.

1096. White, Lyman Cromwell. *International Non-Governmental Organizations: Their Purposes, Methods, and Accomplishments.* New Brunswick, N. J.: Rutgers University Press, 1951. xi, 325 pp. LC 51–10977.
Survey of the activities of major private international organizations from the middle of the nineteenth century to the beginning of World War II. The organizations are concerned with communications, transport, travel, arts and sciences, religion, social welfare, sports, etc. Index.

1097. WORLD LIST OF FUTURE INTERNATIONAL MEETINGS, 1959 –.
M & Q. Reference Department, Library of Congress, Washington, D. C. 20540.
Schedule of meetings for the next three years, with interim information on new meetings and changes. Indexed by place of meeting, sponsor, and subject. Part 2: Social, Cultural, Commercial, Humanistic.

1098. *World of Learning.* London: Europa Publications Ltd.
Published annually since 1947. Lists universities and other institutions of higher learning, learned societies, research institutions, libraries, and museums. Information on UNESCO and international councils and organizations. Until 1963 much of this information was carried in the *Europa Yearbook* (1071).

1099. *Yearbook of International Organizations; Annuaire des organisations Internationales.* Brussels: Union of International Organizations. LC 49–22132.
Published annually 1948–1950 and biennially beginning with 1951–52. Editions are published alternately in English and in French. A comprehensive survey of 1,500 governmental and nongovernmental international organizations. Information on their establishment, purpose, structure, officers, and activities. Subject index.

Section H.   Publications of Public International Organizations

UNITED NATIONS

1100. *Demographic Yearbook.*
Published annually since 1949. Official statistics for over 250 countries and territories on population trends, marriages, divorces, births, deaths, and life expectancy, with technical notes and explanation. Each issue contains bibliography of publica-

tions containing official demographic statistics; the 1955 issue includes a cumulative bibliography of all previous issues.

1101. *Statistical Yearbook.* New York.
Published annually since 1948. Continues the *Statistical Yearbook of the League of Nations,* 1926–1942/44.
Statistical data for more than 250 countries and territories covering a wide range of economic and social subjects, including population, manpower, agriculture, production, consumption, transportation, external trade, national income, finance, social statistics, education, and culture. References to sources. Subject and country indexes.
See *Monthly Bulletin of Statistics* for current data.

1102. *United Nations Judicial Yearbook 1964.* 1965. 337 pp.
Documentary materials of a legal character concerning the United Nations and related intergovernmental organizations covering legal status, legal activities, judicial decisions. Legal documents index. Bibliography.

1103. *Yearbook of International Trade Statistics.* New York.
Published annually since 1950. Carries on the *International Trade Statistics* published by the League of Nations, 1925–1939. Covers over 130 countries and territories, with some statistics going back to 1934. Summaries of trade by large commodity classes and by principal regions and countries.

1104. *Yearbook of National Accounts Statistics.* New York.
Published annually since 1957. Supersedes the semiannual United Nation's publication, *Statistics of National Income and Expenditures* (Statistical papers, Series H), 1952–1957, which, in turn, continued the survey of national income in *National Income Statistics of Various Countries* published by the League of Nations, 1938–1947.

1105. *Yearbook of the International Law Commission.*
Published annually since 1949. Issued in two volumes: Volume I, summary records of the annual sessions of the 21 international law experts who are members of the commission. Volume II, documents relating to the subjects discussed, including the annual report of the Commission to the General Assembly.
Among the subjects dealt with by the Commission are: arbitral procedure, diplomatic immunities, law of the sea, nationality, law of treaties, defining aggression, offenses against the peace and security of mankind, and the rights and duties of states.

1106. *Yearbook of the United Nations.* New York: Columbia University Press.
Published annually since 1946–1947. Chronicles the activities of the United Nations and its specialized agencies during the calendar year. Deals with developments in the political, economic, social, legal, and administrative fields, including the non-self-governing areas. For example, the 1964 issue (published in 1966) dealt with differences among U. N. members about the establishment, conduct, and financing of U. N. peace-keeping operations; the situation in Cyprus; aspects of the disarmament problem; peaceful uses of outer space; the uses of atomic energy; the *apartheid* policies of the Union of South Africa; the representation of China in the United Nations; the situation in Southern Rhodesia; developments concerned with international trade; industrialization; human rights issues; social development activities; U. N. endeavors to speed the granting of independence; and questions concerning

international law. Subjects are treated in detailed essays, with appended documentary references.

1107. *Yearbook on Human Rights.*
Published annually since 1946. Records significant constitutional, legislative, and judicial developments on personal, civil, political, social, and cultural rights throughout the world. It includes: 1) relevant extracts from decisions of national and international courts for 92 states; 2) texts and summaries of basic laws relating to human rights in trust and non-self-governing territories; 3) international agreements. Subject index.

1108. _____. *First Supplementary Volume: Freedom From Arbitrary Arrest, Detention and Exile.* New York, 1959. 249 pp.
For a detailed documented report on U. N. activities in this area see the chapter "Human Rights" in the *Yearbook of the United Nations* (1106).

UNESCO

1109. *International Yearbook of Education.* Paris: UNESCO.
Published annually since 1948; issued jointly by UNESCO and the International Bureau of Education. Succeeded the *Annuaire Internationale de l'Éducation,* 1933–1947.

1110. *UNESCO Statistical Yearbook.* Paris: UNESCO.
Published annually since 1963. Supersedes UNESCO's *Basic Facts and Figures.* Data on population, education, illiteracy, libraries and museums, publications, films, and radio and television.

1111. *World Survey of Education.* Paris: UNESCO.
Published every three years since 1955. Supersedes *World Handbook of Educational Organizations and Statistics.* Volume 1: *Handbook of Educational Organizations and Statistics,* 1955, 943 pp. Volume 2: *Primary Education,* 1958, 1387 pp. Volume 3: *Secondary Education,* 1961, 1482 pp. Volume 4: *Higher Education,* 1966, 1433 pp.
All volumes cover some 200 states and territorial units, including nonmembers of UNESCO. Bibliographies.

INTERNATIONAL COURT OF JUSTICE

1112. *International Court of Justice: Yearbook.* The Hague.
Published annually since 1946–1947. Chapters on the organization of the Court, biographies of the judges, the Court's jurisdiction, documents governing its jurisdiction, the work of the Court during the preceding year, its other activities, summaries of judgments, advisory opinions, orders, administration of the Court, and finances.
Until the 1963–1964 edition the *Yearbook* included the annual *Bibliography of the International Court of Justice,* prepared by the documents section of the Court. Published separately since that time.

CATALOGS OF PUBLICATIONS

Many public international organizations publish annual or biennial catalogs of their publications, and periodically, cumulative catalogs. A number of these organizations are listed below. The most recent catalog and other information regarding their respective publications can be obtained by writing to the desired organization at the address listed below.

General Agreement on Tariffs and Trade (GATT)
GATT Secretariat, Villa le Chêne
Geneva 10, Switzerland.

International Atomic Energy Agency (IAEA)
Kaerntnerring 11
Vienna 1, Austria

International Bank for Reconstruction and Development (IBRD)
1818 H Street, N.W.
Washington, D. C. 20006

International Civil Aviation Organization (ICAO)
International Aviation Building
1080 University Street
Montreal 3, Quebec, Canada

International Development Association (IDA)
1818 H Street, N.W.
Washington, D. C. 20006

International Finance Corporation (IFC)
1818 H. Street, N.W.
Washington, D. C. 20006

International Labour Organisation (ILO)
154 Rue de Lausanné
Geneva, Switzerland

Inter-Governmental Maritime Consultative Organization (IMCO)
Chancery House, Chancery Lane
London, W.C.2, England

International Monetary Fund (IMF)
19th and H Streets, N.W.
Washington, D. C. 20431

International Telecommunication Union (ITU)
Place des Nations
Geneva, Switzerland

Universal Postal Union (UPU)
Schosshaldenstrasse 46
Berne 15, Switzerland

World Health Organization (WHO)
Palais des Nations
Geneva, Switzerland

World Meteorological Organization (WMO)
Avenue Giuseppe Motta
Geneva, Switzerland

The names of specialized agencies of the United Nations, inter-American organizations, and other international organizations in which the United States participates, and their addresses, can be found in the latest issue of the *United States Government Organization Manual* (see Supplemental Information) published by the Office of the

Federal Register, National Archives and Records Service, General Services Administration, Washington, D. C. 20402.

1113. Council of Europe. *Catalogue of the Publications of the Council of Europe.* Publications Section, Council of Europe, Strasbourg, France.

1114. Food and Agriculture Organization. *1945/1960 Catalogue of Publications.* Distribution and Sales Section, FAO, Viale delle Terme Caracalla, Rome, Italy.

1115. International Atomic Energy Agency. *Publications in the Nuclear Sciences.* Division of Scientific and Technical Information, International Atomic Energy Agency, Kärntner Ring 11, A 1010 Vienna I, Austria.

1116. International Court of Justice. *Publications of the International Court of Justice.* Sales Section, United Nations, New York, N. Y. 10017.
The 1967 edition lists all the publications of the International Court from its establishment in 1946 until the end of 1966.

1117. Organization of American States. *Catalog of Publications about the American Republics and Reports on the Strengthening of Our Inter-American Community.* Pan American Union, General Secretariat, Organization of American States, Washington, D. C. 20006.

1118. UNESCO. *Current List of UNESCO Publications.* UNESCO Publications Center, 317 E. 34th St., New York, N. Y. 10016.

1119. _____. *General Catalogue of UNESCO publications and UNESCO Sponsored Publications, 1946–1959.* New York, 1962.

1120. _____. *Supplement 1960–1963.* New York, 1964. 131 pp.
Lists publications issued during these years or which first became available for cataloging during this period, as well as reprints or new editions of works contained in the *General Catalogue;* also a substantial number of publications issued before 1960 which were omitted from the original catalog for various reasons.
UNESCO documents have been excluded. For further details see introductory pages on the "Plan of the Catalogue."

1121. _____. QUARTERLY LIST OF UNESCO PUBLICATIONS. UNESCO Publications Center, 317 E. 34th St., New York, N. Y. 10016.

1122. United Nations. *United Nations Publications 1945–1966: Catalogue of United Nations Publications.* United Nations Publications, United Nations, Room 1059, New York, N. Y. 10017.

1123. World Health Organization. *1947–1964 Catalogue of World Health Organization Publications.* Distribution and Sales, World Health Organization, Palais des Nations, Geneva, Switzerland.

Section I. Miscellaneous

1124. *American Jewish Yearbook.* Philadelphia, Pa.: Jewish Publication Society. Published annually since 1899. Copublished with the American Jewish Committee.

The standard reference annual on Jewish affairs. Comprehensive review of Jewish life and developments affecting Jews the world over. Statistics on the Jewish population, migrations, education, philanthropy, and social services. Obituary notices. Directories of Jewish organizations and periodicals. Bibliographies and other basic reference material.

1125. *Yearbook of the International Socialist Labour Movement.* Julius Braunthal, ed. London: Lincolns-Prager International.

Published annually since 1956–57 under the auspices of the Socialist International and the Asian Socialist Conference.

Information on Socialist and labor parties and international Socialist organizations.

1126. *Zionist Yearbook.* Joseph Litvin, ed. Zionist Federation of Great Britain and Ireland. LC 52–65547.

Published annually since 1951–52. Information about Zionist organizations all over the world. Biographies of Zionist leaders and a Zionist "Who's Who." Detailed information about Israel, including its institutions and diplomatic corps abroad.

PART IV
NATIONAL AND TRADE
BIBLIOGRAPHIES

CHAPTER 14.

NATIONAL LIBRARY AND UNION CATALOGS

National libraries of many countries collect national publications and provide vital reference and research information to interested students, scholars, and researchers. These libraries make their national collections as complete as possible, publish union catalogs which list possessions of other libraries in the country which supplement their own holdings, and issue special catalogs of their own collections. In recent years many national libraries have preserved their collections on magnetic tape or microfilm as well as in original printed form. National libraries do not, of course, limit themselves to publications issued in their respective countries.

These institutions may, or may not, be officially designated a "national library." The Bibliothèque Nationale of Paris and the British Museum have both achieved worldwide acclaim as national libraries but the Library of Congress in the United States has neither the name nor the formal, legal status of a national library—yet it has come to serve that purpose and the quality of its collection as well as its staff are easily the equal of the French and British institutions.

The outstanding catalogs are produced by these three great national libraries and the Deutsche Bibliothek (Frankfurt am Main, German Federal Republic) and the Deutsche Bücherei (Leipzig, German Democratic Republic). Other smaller national libraries maintain collections which are more complete in terms of their own national publications and are indispensable sources for that reason.

Detailed information on the national catalogs of many countries can be found in Walford, *Guide to Reference Material* (602); Winchell, *Guide to Reference Books* (603); White, *Sources of Information in the Social Sciences* (643); and Collison, *Bibliographical Services Throughout the World* (608).

The catalog of the Library of Congress, issued under various names, is outstanding for the excellent quality of the cataloging, the full bibliographic data furnished, and the enormous number of titles it covers. It helps, in addition, to locate items not available even in the library of Congress.

Section A. General

1127. Conover, Helen F. *Current National Bibliographies.* Washington, D. C.: Library of Congress, General Reference and Bibliography Division, 1955. 132 pp.

Lists current national bibliographies worldwide, with references to books, government publications, directories of periodicals and newspapers, pamphlets, serials, etc. Annotated entries. Title index.

1128. Esdaile, Arundell. *National Libraries of the World: Their History, Administration and Public Services,* 2d edition, revised. F. J. Hill, ed. London: Library Association, 1957. 413 pp.

1129. International Committee for Social Science Documentation. *A Study of Current Bibliographies of National Official Publications: A Short Guide and Inventory.* Jean Meyriat, ed. Paris: UNESCO, 1958. 260 pp.

Section B. United States

1130. Library of Congress. *A Catalog of Books Represented by Library of Congress Printed Cards Issued to July 31, 1942.* Ann Arbor, Mich.: Edwards, 1942–1946. 167 vols.

Issued under the auspices of the Association of Research Libraries, this was the first Library of Congress catalog reproduced in book form for wide circulation. It is commonly called the "L.C. Catalog."

Includes some two and a half million author and main-entry catalog listings in the form of photoreproductions of Library of Congress cards, covering books, pamphlets, periodicals, tracts, newspapers, and other material published between 1898 and 1946, with some additional items published earlier.

1131. _____. *Supplement: Cards Issued August 1, 1942–December 31,1947.* Ann Arbor, Mich.: Edwards, 1948. 42 vols.

1132. _____. *Library of Congress Author Catalog: A Cumulative List of Works Represented by Library of Congress Printed Cards, 1948–1952.* Ann Arbor, Mich.: Edwards, 1953. 24 vols.

Published under various titles in different years: *Cumulative Catalog of Library of Congress Printed Cards* (1948); *Library of Congress Author Catalog* (1949–1952); *Library of Congress Catalog: Books–Authors* (1953).

1133. _____. *National Union Catalog: A Cumulative Author List Representing Library of Congress Printed Cards and Titles Reported by 600 Other American Libraries, 1953–1957.* Ann Arbor, Mich.: Edwards, 1958. 28 vols.

1134. _____. *National Union Catalog. . . , 1958–1962.* New York: Rowman and Littlefield, 1963. 54 vols.

Note: Serial titles not printed on L.C. cards are listed in *New Serial Titles* (575).

1135. _____. *The National Union Catalog, 1952–1955; Imprints: An Author List Representing Library of Congress Printed Cards and Titles Reported by Other American Libraries.* Ann Arbor, Mich.: Edwards, 1961. 30 vols.

1136. _____. *Library of Congress Catalog: A Cumulative List of Works Represented by Library of Congress Printed Cards: Books–Subjects, 1950–1954.* Ann Arbor, Mich.: Edwards, 1955. 20 vols.

Complement to the *Author Catalog* (1132).

1137. _____. *Library of Congress Catalog: A Cumulative List of Works Represented by Library of Congress Printed Cards: Books–Subjects, 1955–1959.* Paterson, N. J.: Pageant Books, 1960. 22 vols.

Continued by quarterly and annual cumulations.

1138. NATIONAL UNION CATALOG: A Cumulative Author List. 1963 –. M; Q and A cums. Library of Congress, Card Division, Washington, D. C. 20541.

Note: According to the *New York Times* of March 14, 1967, the English firm Mamsell Information-Publishing, Ltd., has been given a contract by a committee of the American Library Association to print and publish a part of the *National Union Catalog* listing more than 12 million books held in 700 major libraries in this country and Canada, for the period up to 1956, and currently listed on 16 million index cards at the Library of Congress. The project calls for 600 volumes of 704 pages each, published by a new photographic process, with the first volume scheduled for the end of 1968. Since 1956 the Library of Congress has published photographic copies of these cards, 30 or 40 to a page, bound in book form, and issued monthly, quarterly, and annually.

The English firm is a subsidiary of Universal Printers, Ltd., which produced the 263—volume general catalog of printed books of the British Museum through another subsidiary.

Section C. Foreign Countries

AUSTRALIA

1139. AUSTRALIAN NATIONAL BIBLIOGRAPHY. 1961 —. Beginning with 1967 4 x m; M, Q, and A cums. (formerly M). A $13.00. National Library of Australia, Canberra, Australia.

Lists books published in Australia and books dealing with Australian subjects or written by Australian authors.

Also lists pamphlets, maps, prints, and the first issue of each new annual, periodical, or newspaper, as well as Commonwealth and State government publications, including acts and bills.

FRANCE

1140. Bibliothèque Nationale. *Catalogue Général des Livres Imprimés: Auteurs.* Paris: Imprimerie Nationale, 1900—1963. 189 vols. (In progress.)

Important author catalog with cross-references.

GERMANY

1141. *Deutscher Gesamtkatalog.* (Preussische Staatsbibliothek.) Berlin: Preussische Druckerei- und Verlags-Aktiengesellschaft, 1931—39. 14 vols.

Volumes 1—8 were named *Gesamtkatalog der preussischen Bibliotheken.* A union catalog of German and Austrian libraries. According to Winchell, *Guide* (603) p. 9, the catalog contains many works in foreign languages, including English works not listed in the British Museum's *General Catalogue of Printed Books* (1146) and French works not listed in the *Catalogue Générale* (1140) of the Bibliothèque Nationale. Covers books published up to 1930.

1142. DEUTSCHER GESAMTKATALOG: Neue Titel. 1893—1944. W; Q and A cums. Staatsbibliothek, Berlin, Germany.

Supplements the *Deutscher Gesamtkatalog* (1141).

1143. *Berliner Titeldrucke Fünfjahre Katalog, 1930—34, 1935—39.* (Preussische Staatsbibliothek.) Berlin: Staatsbibliothek, 1935—40. 8 vols.

Title varies.

GREAT BRITAIN

1144. British Museum, Department of Printed Books. *Catalogue of Printed Books.* London: W. Clowes, 1881–1900. 95 vols. Reprinted by Edwards Co., Ann Arbor, Mich.: 1946 (59 vols.) and 1950 (10 vols.).

1145. _____. *Supplement.* London: W. Clowes, 1900–1905. 13 vols. Reprinted 1950 (10 vols).
These two publications are primarily author catalogs, with some title and subject entries and cross-references.

1146. *General Catalogue of Printed Books.* London: Trustees of the British Museum, 1931–1954.
This edition of the catalog was discontinued in 1954 with Volume 51 (letters "Dez") because of the high costs. Beginning with 1959 a new edition was begun, with photo-offset lithography, and was finished in 1966 with a total of 263 volumes and some four million entries. It lists all books published in Britain since printing began 500 years ago until the end of 1955 as well as a large number of books published in every other Western nation.

1147. _____. *Additions,* 1963–1965. Letters A–Z. 6 vols. Includes entries added each year to the *General Catalogue* (1146).

1148. _____. *Subject Index of the Modern Works Added to the Library of the British Museum in the Years 1881–1900.* G. K. Fortescu, ed. London: Trustees of the British Museum, 1902–1903, 3 vols. Followed by quinquennial supplements for the years 1901–1950, published in London, 1906–1961, 10 vols.

CHAPTER 15.

NATIONAL AND TRADE BIBLIOGRAPHIES

Section A. United States

1149. AMERICAN BOOK PUBLISHING RECORD (see 534).
Information identical with *Publishers' Weekly* (514). Annual index.

1150. BOOKS IN PRINT: An Author-Title Index to the Publishers' Trade List Annual, 1948 –. A. $19.85. R. R. Bowker Co., 1180 Ave. of the Americas, New York, N. Y. 10036.
Published in October in two volumes. Author and title indexes. Lists all books in print, no matter when published. Over 200,000 titles. Helpful for finding the publisher and price of a book, or the author's name if only the book title is known.

1151. CUMULATIVE BOOK INDEX: A World List of Books in the English Language. 1989 –. M. R. R. Bowker Co., 1180 Ave. of the Americas, New York, N. Y. 10036.

Semiannual and permanent cumulations form supplements to the *United States Catalog* (1157). Includes a selected list of books published in English in other parts of the world. Omits government documents and paperbacks. List of publishers' addresses in each volume.

See Winchell, *Guide* (603), AA343 and AA345, for additional details.

1152. Orton, Robert Merritt. CATALOG OF REPRINTS IN SERIES. 1940 –. A. H. W. Wilson Co., 950 University Ave., Bronx, N. Y. 10452.
Author and title list of reprint editions and list of reprint publishers and series.

1153. PAPERBOUND BOOKS IN PRINT. 1955 –. M. $16.00. R. R. Bowker Co., 1180 Ave. of the Americas, New York, N. Y. 10036.
New titles and titles remaining in print. Annotated previews of forthcoming paperbacks. Index three times each year.

1154. PUBLISHERS' TRADE LIST ANNUAL. 1873 –. A. $14.00. R. R. Bowker Co., 1180 Ave. of the Americas, New York, N. Y. 10036. (1967: 4 vols.)

1155. PUBLISHERS' WEEKLY: The Book Industry Journal (see 514).
Lists of new and forthcoming publications. Editorials, articles, and government publications are omitted.

1156. SUBJECT GUIDE TO BOOKS IN PRINT: An Index to the Publishers' Trade List Annual. 1957 –. A. $18.25. R. R. Bowker Co., 1180 Ave. of the Americas, New York, N. Y. 10036.
Index of over 175,000 books published by 1,600 United States publishers. Some 30,000 subject headings, with 39,000 cross-references. Lists only books now available and forthcoming books.

1157. *United States Catalog: Books in Print,* 4th edition. New York: H. W. Wilson Co., 1928. 3164 pp.

1158. VERTICAL FILE INDEX (see 5).

Section B. Foreign Countries

AUSTRALIA

1159. National Library of Australia. *Australian Bibliography and Bibliographical Services.* Canberra: Australian Advisory Council on Bibliographical Services, 1960. 219 pp.

CANADA

1160. *Canadian Catalogue of Books Published in Canada, about Canada, As Well as Those Written by Canadians, with Imprint 1921–1949.* Toronto: Toronto Public Libraries, 1959. 2 vols.
Up to 1,943 selected government publications were included. Superseded by *Canadiana* (1161).

1161. CANADIANA. 1950 –. M. National Library of Canada, Ottawa, Canada. Supersedes the *Canadian Catalogue of Books* (1160).

FRANCE

1162. BIBLIOGRAPHIE DE LA FRANCE: Journal Général de l'Imprimerie et de la Librairie. 1811–. W. Cercle de la Librairie, 117 bd. Saint-Germain, Paris (6ᵉ) France.
The standard weekly list of publications.

1163. *Librairie Française: Catalogue Général des Ouvrages en Vente.* Paris: Cercle de la Librairie, 1930. 3 vols.
Similar volumes for later years. Compiled from *Bibliographie de la France* (1162). List includes new periodicals.

1164. LES LIVRES DE L'ANNÉE. 1933–. A (except 1939–1945). Cercle de la Librairie, 117 bd. Saint-Germain, Paris (6ᵉ), France.
Cumulations of listings in *Bibliographie de la France* (1162).

1165. *Nouveau Dictionnaire National des Contemporains.* Paris.
Published irregularly since 1962.

GERMANY (POST-WORLD WAR II)

Note: Because of the governmental and ideological division of Germany since 1945 there are now two bibliographic centers in that country: the Deutsche Bücherei (the oldest) in Leipzig, German Democratic Republic, and the Deutsche Bibliothek in Frankfurt am Main, German Federal Republic.
Both centers publish bibliographies which follow similar patterns. Both endeavor to publish all books published on both sides of the divided country and German-language books published in other countries. A few books are listed by one of the centers only.

1166. DEUTSCHE BIBLIOGRAPHIE: Das Deutsche Buch; Auswahl wichtiger Neuerscheinungen. 1950 –. BM. DM 5.40 ($1.35). Buchhändler-Vereinigung, Gr. Hirschgraben 17/19, Frankfurt am Main, Germany.
Edited by the Deutsche Bibliothek. Selective, classified list of important new books.

1167. DEUTSCHE BIBLIOGRAPHIE: Wöchentliches Verzeichnis. 1947 –. W. DM 12.50 per month. Buchhändler-Vereinigung, Gr. Hirschgraben 17/19, Frankfurt am Main, Germany.
Compiled by the Deutsche Bibliothek. Former name (1947–1952) *Bibliographie der deutschen Bibliothek.* List of German-language books published in Germany or elsewhere. Weekly and monthly index.

1168. DEUTSCHE BIBLIOGRAPHIE: Halbjahresverzeichnis. 1951 –. SA. Buchhändler-Vereinigung, Gr. Hirschgraben 17/19, Frankfurt am Main, Germany.
Semiannual cumulation of the weekly edition (1167).

1169. *Deutsche Bibliographie: Bücher und Karten.* Frankfurt am Main: Buchhändler-Vereinigung.
Published every five years since 1952 as the five-year cumulation of the weekly edition (1167). The 1952 edition covered the years 1945–1950.

1170. DEUTSCHE NATIONALBIBLIOGRAPHIE und Bibliographie des im Ausland erschienenen deutschsprachigen Schrifttums. 1931–. VEB Verlag für Buch- und Bibliothekswesen, Leipzig, Germany.

Series A, books in the regular trade, is published weekly (DM 14); Series B, other books, such as dissertations and publications of societies, is published semimonthly (DM 48). Author and title indexes are published quarterly.

1171. *Jahresverzeichnis des Deutschen Schrifttums.* Leipzig: Börsenverein der deutschen Buchhändler.
Annual cumulations of Series A and the more important publications of series B of the *Deutsche Nationalbibliographie* (1170), published since 1948. Author, title, and subject indexes.

1172. *Deutsches Bücherverzeichnis.* Leipzig: VEB Verlag für Buch- und Bibliothekswesen.
Five-year cumulations of titles published in Germany, Austria, Switzerland, and of German-language titles published in other countries since 1911. Includes foreign publications issued in Germany. Covers books, periodicals, maps, and government publications. Title and subject indexes.

GREAT BRITAIN

1173. BRITISH NATIONAL BIBLIOGRAPHY. 1950–. W (Q, A, and 5-year cums.). Price on application. British Museum, London, W.C.1, England.
Compiled at the British Museum. Lists and describes new books and editions, the first issue of a new periodical or periodical with a new title, and most government publications. Author and title index in each issue. Cumulated author, title, and subject index at the end of each month.

1174. _____. *Cumulative Subject Catalogue, 1951–54* (2 vols.), *1955–59* (3 vols.). London: British Museum, 1958–63. (1960–64 in preparation).

1175. _____. *Cumulated Index, 1950–54, 1955–59, 1960–64.* London: British Museum, 1955–65.

1176. ENGLISH CATALOGUE OF BOOKS. 1801–. Irr. Publishers' Circular, 171 High St., Peckenham, Kent, England. Standard English trade list, does not include all new books. See Winchell, *Guide to Reference Works* (603) for details.

1177. BRITISH BOOKS: Incorporating the Publishers' Circular and Booksellers' Record. 1959 –. M. 42s. British Books, 79 Limpsfield Rd., Sanderstead, Surrey, England.
Formerly *Publishers' Circular* (1837–1959). List of new books and articles. Basis for *English Catalogue* (1176). Index.

1178. PAPERBACKS IN PRINT: A Reference Catalogue of Paperbacks in Print and on Sale in Great Britain. 1960 –. SA. Whitaker, London, England.
Includes author and title index.

INDIA

1179. INDIAN NATIONAL BIBLIOGRAPHY: Bibliographical Record of Current Indian Publications Received in the National Library of Calcutta under the Delivery of Books. 1957 –. M. $30.24. Central Reference Library, Ministry of Education, Calcutta 27, India.

LATIN AMERICA

1180. PAN AMERICAN BOOKSHELF. 1938–1948. M. Columbus Memorial Library, Pan American Union, 17th and Constitution Ave., Washington, D. C. 20006. Annual author index.

1181. LEA: Librarians, Editors, Authors. 1949–1950. Pan American Union, 17th and Constitution Ave., Washington, D. C. 20006.
Superseded *Pan American Bookshelf* (1180).

1182. INTER-AMERICAN REVIEW OF BIBLIOGRAPHY.
Supersedes *LEA* (1181). (See 120.)

NEW ZEALAND

1183. CURRENT NATIONAL BIBLIOGRAPHY OF NEW ZEALAND BOOKS AND PAMPHLETS. 1950–1965. A. National Library Centre, National Library Service, Wellington, New Zealand.
An annual list by author, title, and subject of all books and pamphlets published in New Zealand or elsewhere by New Zealanders, or referring to New Zealand. Issued with *Index to New Zealand Periodicals* (1185). Superseded by *New Zealand National Bibliography* (1186).

1184. COPYRIGHT PUBLICATIONS. 1933/34–1965. A. General Assembly Library, Wellington, New Zealand.
An annual list of copyrighted publications (monthly list processed). Includes government publications, new periodicals, and periodicals which have ceased publication. Superseded by *New Zealand National Bibliography* (1186).

1185. INDEX TO NEW ZEALAND PERIODICALS. 1940 –. A. NZ $5.00. National Library of New Zealand, Wellington, New Zealand.
Published from 1950 to 1965 as *Index to New Zealand Periodicals and Current National Bibliography of New Zealand Books and Pamphlets,* the latter section being replaced by *New Zealand National Bibliography* (1186).

1186. NEW ZEALAND NATIONAL BIBLIOGRAPHY. 1967 –. M; A cums. NZ $5.00. National Library of New Zealand, Wellington, New Zealand.
A monthly list with annual cumulation of all books and pamphlets published in New Zealand, or overseas dealing wholly or in part with New Zealand, or by authors normally resident in New Zealand. Arranged by author, title, and subject. Includes government publications, art prints, maps, new periodicals, and periodicals which have ceased publication. Replaces the *Current National Bibliography* (1183) and *Copyright Publications* (1184).

PART V
U.S. GOVERNMENT
PUBLICATIONS

The Government publishes a large number of documents, books, periodicals, pamphlets, and maps. These publications include thousands of items useful to the study of international relations and recent history, American and foreign. Many of them are useful to the scholar and advanced student. Others are written in journalistic style for the general reader.

Government publications appear as separate items, standing by themselves, or as parts of series such as the *Foreign Relations of the United States* which numbers some 250 volumes, with new titles added each year. Many items are distributed free by the issuing agency, others range in price from five cents to twenty-five dollars. Many of these items may be obtained free from Members of Congress who receive a certain number of publications for distribution to their constituents and others. A number of university, college, and public libraries throughout the country are official depositories for many or all U. S. Government publications.

Access to the endless number of government publications is a continuing problem for the researcher. This problem is complicated because many price lists and bibliographic aids list only "available" publications and omit those which are out-of-print but still available in libraries. Many publications, including some Department of State items, are out-of-print after only a year and subsequent reprints may not be identical with the earlier issues.

To compound the confusion the names of many government agencies are changed from time to time as the result of governmental reorganizations—a part of a department or agency may gain independent status and a new designation. For example, most of the so-called public affairs activities of the Department of State were transferred to the newly established U. S. Information Agency in 1953. Other agencies lose their independent status and become part of a permanent agency. For example, the Administration for International Development (AID) and its predecessors, with half a dozen different names, have been in and out of the Department of State. Changes in government structure and nomenclature can be checked in the annual edition of the *U. S. Government Organization Manual* (1193) in the section on Supplemental Information.

Many government publications are identified under a group designation but the name of the series is subject to change. *Foreign Relations of the United States* has been issued under three different names in its hundred-year history. Treaties to which the United States is a party have been published in three different series and they also appear in the *United States Statutes at Large*.

The reference classic in the field of U. S. Government publications was written by the late Dr. Schmeckebier and was first published in 1936. It is indispensable to students in many areas of research, including international relations and recent history although a complete search should cover additional guides and references.

CHAPTER 16.

GUIDES TO GOVERNMENT PUBLICATIONS

1187. Schmeckebier, Laurence F., and Roy B. Eastin. *Government Publications and Their Use,* revised edition. Washington, D. C.: The Brookings Institution, 1961. xi, 476 pp. LC 61—7718.

This is the reference classic in the field of U. S. Government publications. The Foreword of the revised edition lists the valuable features of the book:

> The purpose of this volume is to describe the basic guides to government publications, to indicate the uses and limitations of available indexes, catalogs, and bibliographies, to

explain the systems of numbering and methods of titling, to call attention to certain outstanding compilations or series of publications, and to indicate how the publications may be obtained. Although this book cites many publications by title, it is not a catalogue, a bibliography, or a checklist. It is an aid to the acquisition and utilization of the publications.

The scope of the book can best be indicated by a list of chapter headings: 1) Introduction; 2) Catalogs and Indexes; 3) Bibliographies; 4) Classification; 5) Availability of Publications; 6) Congressional Publications; 7) Federal and State Constitutions; 8) Federal Laws; 9) State Laws; 10) Court Decisions; 11) Administrative Regulations and Departmental Rulings; 12) Presidential Papers; 13) Foreign Affairs (covering Treaties, Executive Agreements, Diplomatic Correspondence, Current Developments in Foreign Relations, Conferences, Arbitrations, Regional Problems, Congressional Publications on Foreign Relations, and Miscellaneous Publications on Foreign Relations); 14) Reports on Operations; 15) Organization and Personnel; 16) Maps; 17) Technical and Other Departmental Publications; 18) Periodicals; 19) Microfascimile Editions of Government Publications. Appendix. List of Depository Libraries. Indexes.

A new edition of this work would constitute a service of international significance to students and scholars.

1188. Boyd, Anne Morris. *United States Government Publications,* 3d edition revised by Rae E. Rips. New York: H. W. Wilson Co., 1949. 627 pp. LC 55–694.

A comprehensive guide to government publications, designed as a textbook for library schools. Discusses the nature, character, and types of the publications; lists executive, congressional, and judicial publications, with annotations for important examples. Bibliographic references at end of each chapter. The chapter on the Department of State is especially useful for documents related to the study of international relations. Includes publications of agencies no longer in existence.

1189. Body, Alexander C. *Annotated Bibliography of Bibliographies on Selected Government Publications and Supplementary Guides to the Superintendent of Documents Classification System* (see 607).

1190. Brown, Everett S. *Manual of Government Publications, United States and Foreign.* New York: Appleton-Century-Crofts, Inc., 1950. (New York: Johnson Reprint Corp., 1964.) ix, 121 pp. LC 50–4788.

Selective guide. Emphasis on the U. S. and British Governments, though governments in continental Europe, Asia, and Latin America are included, as well as the League of Nations and United Nations. Topical arrangement. Extensive and valuable bibliographic footnotes. Chapter I, United States Government, contains an annotated list of guides to public documents published since 1916. See Chapter XVII for General References and Methodology. No index.

CHAPTER 17.

GENERAL GOVERNMENT PUBLICATIONS

1191. *Code of Federal Regulations.* Office of the Federal Register, National Archives and Records Service, 1938.

Annual supplements; complete recodifications every five years.

Central publication of presidential proclamations, executive orders, administrative rules, regulations, and similar documents which have general applicability and the force of law. This is a codification rather than a mere compilation of existing regulations. The *Code* is composed of 50 titles and a general index.

For details see Schmeckebier and Eastin, *Government Publications and Their Use* (1187), pp. 280–282. As noted by these authors, the contents of the *Federal Register* (1192) and *Code of Federal Regulations* are by law prima facie evidence of the text of the original documents and are required to be judicially noticed.

1192. FEDERAL REGISTER. National Archives and Records Service, 1936 –. D. LC 37–2681 rev.

This serial publishes presidential proclamations and executive orders, other presidential documents, and certain congressional documents. The bound volumes were discontinued in 1938 and replaced by the *Code of Federal Regulations* (1191). For details see Schmeckebier and Eastin, *Government Publications and Their Use* (1187), pp. 278–280.

1193. UNITED STATES GOVERNMENT ORGANIZATION MANUAL. 1935 –. A. Office of the Federal Register, National Archives and Records Service, 8th and Pennsylvania Ave., N.W., Washington, D. C. 20408. LC 35–26025.

Appendix B of the section, Supplemental Information, provides a list of Representative Publications of Departments and Agencies of the Federal Government which shows the kind of publications published by specific government departments and agencies, and quasi-official agencies. Complete lists are available from most of the agencies upon request.

Appendix B also includes several price lists of government publications which are available free from the Superintendent of Documents upon request. Of special interest to the study of international relations are: No. 36, Government Periodicals and Subscription Services; No. 50, American History (including World War II); No. 54, Political Science; and No. 65, Foreign Relations of the United States, Publications Relating to Foreign Countries, and the United Nations.

The primary purpose of the *Manual* is to describe the organization and functions of the legislative, judicial, and executive branches of the U. S. Government. It also lists agencies which have been abolished or transferred. For data on the history, organization, and duties of government agencies see also the *Congressional Record* (1198). For detailed descriptions of agency organization in the government and addresses for securing information consult the indexes to the daily issues of the *Federal Register* (1192).

The types of information available in the *Manual,* and *Federal Register,* and the *Congressional Record* help the student and researcher place documents and other official publications in their correct governmental context. They are especially valuable for tracing government activities to specific government agencies, under the various names and structures resulting from government reorganizations.

The section of the *Manual* on Supplemental Information lists Selected Multilateral International Organizations in which the United States participates and Selected Bilateral Organizations of which it is a member, describing their organization, purposes, and activities.

CHAPTER 18.

CHECKLISTS AND CATALOGS OF
GOVERNMENT PUBLICATIONS

1194. *Catalogue of the Public Documents of the 53d to 76th Congresses and all Departments of Government of the United States* for the Period from *March 4, 1893 to December 31, 1941.* Government Printing Office, 1896–1945. 25 vols. LC 6–12151.

Popularly known as the *Document Catalog*, this work began where the Ames *Index* stopped. It was issued in dictionary form, with entries listed under subject matter, individual authors, and governmental authors. According to Schmeckebier and Eastin (1187), p. 23, this catalog was the only one containing a complete list of presidential executive orders, now included in the *Code of Federal Regulations* (1191). Everett S. Brown, *Manual of Government Publications* (1190), p. 24, states that the *Document Catalog* is remarkably accurate and complete, considering the number and complexity of the publications covered.

Because of several years lag in the publication of the *Document Catalog* and its prohibitive cost, this massive publication was discontinued in 1947 when the Superintendent of Documents decided to concentrate on one catalog—an expanded and improved version of the *Monthly Catalog* (1196). Three supplements to the *Monthly Catalog* were issued to cover publications which would have been included in the *Document Catalog* had it been continued.

1195. *Checklist of United States Public Documents, 1789–1909,* 3d revised and enlarged edition. Superintendent of Documents, 1911. 1707 pp. LC 12–35731.

This is the latest general compilation of government documents. Its second, or index volume, was never published.

According to Bemis and Griffin, *Guide to the Diplomatic History of the United States* (650), pp. 819–820, this is the most concise and valuable guide to public documents of the United States. Schmeckebier and Eastin (1187), p. 15, note correctly that the *Checklist* is of greatest value to librarians and students who have considerable familiarity with government publications. See also pp. 12–15, 29–30, 59, and 101–102 of the *Checklist*.

The publications of the Department of State are listed in one group, including the following categories of titles: diplomatic correspondence published in the series *Foreign Relations* (1203); general publications; consular regulations; register of the Department of State; diplomatic and consular service (lists of officers); diplomatic lists (foreign diplomats in Washington); instructions to diplomatic and consular officers; arbitrations and mixed commissions to settle international disputes; international congresses and commissions; treaties; and others.

At first, most public documents were published as congressional documents. Later various departments issued their own publications. The Department of State, for instance, began a series of publications in 1929 (1203). It should be noted that a number of documents have been published both as congressional documents and departmental publications. The *Checklist* is invaluable as a key to congressional documents.

1196. MONTHLY CATALOG OF UNITED STATES GOVERNMENT PUBLICATIONS. 1951 –. M.

Published since 1895 under various names:
Catalogue of Publications Issued by the Government of the United States (1895);

Catalogue of United States Public Documents, Issued Monthly (1895–1905);
Catalogue of United States Public Documents (1906–1907);
Monthly Catalogue ("*Catalog*" beginning July 1933) *United States Public Documents* (1907–1939);
United States Government Publications Monthly Catalog (1940–1950).

Volume 22, 1933–1934, of the Document Catalog (1194) covers various New Deal agencies and their publications which ceased to exist in later years.

1197. SELECTED UNITED STATES GOVERNMENT PUBLICATIONS. 1928 –. BW. Free upon request. Superintendent of Documents, Washington, D. C. 20402.
A leaflet listing titles, with annotations, and prices of government publications of special importance or wide appeal. Includes checklist order form.
It is indispensable between the time of publication of a document and its listing, up to eight weeks later, in the *Monthly Catalog* (1196). The latter is still needed for publications in more specialized fields.

CHAPTER 19.

PUBLICATIONS OF GOVERNMENTAL UNITS

Section A. Congress

GENERAL

1198. CONGRESSIONAL RECORD. 1873 –. D.
Preceded by the *Annals of Congress,* 1789–1824; *Register of Debates,* 1824–1837; and the *Congressional Globe,* 1833–1873. Contains a very useful index. See Schmeckebier and Eastin, *Government Publications and Their Use* (1187), pp. 119–121 and 125–129 for details.

COMMITTEE PUBLICATIONS

The Senate Committee on Foreign Relations and the House of Representatives Committee on Foreign Affairs publish documents dealing with foreign relations. These documents are listed in the following publications.

1199. *Legislative Calendar.* Committee on Foreign Relations, U. S. Senate.

1200. *Legislative Calendar.* Committee on Foreign Affairs, U. S. House of Representatives.
One or more of these *Calendars* are published each session of Congress.
Committee hearings are often an important source of valuable information offered in testimony or through the questioning of witnesses. About half of such hearings and subsequent reports are published. A list of Committee hearings prior to 1909 is given in the *Checklist of United States Public Documents, 1789–1909* (1195), pp. 1532–1652. Current hearings are listed in the *Monthly Catalog* (1196) and the *Public Affairs Information Service: Bulletin* (39).

1201. U. S. Congress, Senate Library. *Cumulative Index of Congressional Committee Hearings (not Confidential in Character) from the 74th Congress through the 85th Congress in the U. S. Senate Library.* F. M. Johnson and R. D. Hupman, comps. Washington, D. C.: Government Printing Office, 1959. 823 pp.

Section B. Department of State

1202. *Foreign Affairs Research: A Directory of Governmental Resources.* (Department of State Publication 8277.) Washington, D. C.: Office of External Research, Bureau of Intelligence and Research, Department of State, 1967. vii, 83 pp. LC 67–61715.

The name of the predecessor publication was *Government Resources Available for Foreign Affairs Research* (1965).

Descriptive listing of government resources accessible to the scholar engaged in social and behavioral science research in foreign areas and the field of international affairs. This booklet explores Government activities related to research that may render substantive and financial assistance to private scholars (Introductory statement.)

The list of government agencies covered includes military as well as civilian departments and agencies.

1203. *Major Publications of the Department of State.* (Department of State Publication 7843.) Washington, D. C.: Historical Office, Bureau of Public Affairs, Department of State, 1966. 17 pp. Free upon request.

Revised and up-to-date editions are published periodically. Section on the Documentary Record of United States Foreign Policy lists publications issued by the Department of State or under other auspices relating to the conduct and organization of United States diplomacy and major postwar meetings and conferences in Europe. Also lists collections of documents relating to Germany and other countries and problems in Europe, the Far East, the American Republics, Africa, the Middle East, South Asia, and Antarctica; arms control, disarmament, nuclear energy, and outer space; United States participation in the United Nations; and foreign economic relations and programs. It also lists various publications containing or related to the captured German Foreign Office documents and the trial records of the International Military Tribunal in Nuremberg and Tokyo.

Describes in pertinent detail the character and scope of such Department of State serial publications as *Foreign Relations of the United States; American Foreign Policy: Current Documents; United States Treaties and Other International Agreements; Treaties in Force; Digest of International Law; Department of State Bulletin; Foreign Service List; Diplomatic List;* and many others.

Section C. U. S. Information Agency

The U. S. Information Agency has conducted sample surveys of foreign attitudes and communication habits in over fifty countries. Trend comparisons extending over several years exist for a number of countries, particularly in Western Europe, Latin America, and the Far East. While the studies of Agency programs and their effectiveness usually remain classified, many of the attitude surveys are declassified periodically. The data from these declassified surveys are available at the Roper Public Opinion Research Center at Williams College, Massachusetts; the Political Data Center at Yale University; and the Survey Research Center at the University of California, Berkeley. (Statement in *Foreign Affairs Research* (1202), p. 63.)

Section D. Joint Publications Research Service

1204. *Catalog of Current Joint Publications Research Service Publications,* revised edition. Washington, D. C.: Joint Publications Research Service, 1965. 16 pp.
The Joint Publications Research Service, a component of the Clearinghouse for Federal Scientific and Technical Information, Department of Commerce, translates, abstracts, and performs foreign-language research for other Federal agencies. Thousands of these reports may be purchased at cost by the public. See *JPRS Reports* (543).

Section E. Office of Education

1205. U. S. Office of Education. *Publications, Office of Education, 1937–1959.* (Bulletin 1960, No. 3). Washington, D. C.: Government Printing Office, 1960. 157 pp.

1206. _____. *Publications of the Office of Education* (Bulletin). Washington, D. C.: Government Printing Office.
Published annually since 1959. Lists currently available publications; annotations. Includes education in foreign countries.

Section F. Library of Congress

1207. *Annual Report of the Librarian of Congress.* A. $2.50. Supt. of Documents, Washington, D. C. (627).
Includes a list of new Library of Congress Publications.

1208. *A Directory of Information Resources in the United States. Federal Government.* Washington, D. C.: Library of Congress, 1967. 419 pp. LC 67–60084.
Information on more than 1,600 information resources, either within the Federal Government or sponsored by it. Description of the areas of interest, holdings, publications, and information services of the various agencies, offices, libraries, committees, commissions, boards, and other organizations.

1209. INFORMATION BULLETIN. 1942 –. W. Library of Congress, Washington, D. C. 20540.
Lists new Library of Congress publications. An appendix, *The Microfilm Clearinghouse Bulletin* is issued irregularly.

1210. *Library of Congress Publications in Print.* Washington, D. C.: Library of Congress. LC 6–35005.
Published annually since 1906. List of Library of Congress publications currently available. Earlier editions of this list should be checked for out-of-print publications now available only in libraries.
This publication does not list works published as congressional documents and administrative memoranda, nor does it include reprints except those from Library of Congress publications. Some of the titles cited are not published by the Library but are included because of their authorship.

A number of bibliographies prepared by the Legislative Reference Service of the Library of Congress for Members and committees of Congress are printed as congressional documents or committee prints. These are ordinarily listed in the *Monthly Catalog of United States Government Publications* (1196). New publications are announced in the *Monthly Catalog*, and in *Price List 83*, Library of Congress (available from the Superintendent of Documents).

Section G. Other U. S. Government Agencies

Various Federal Government agencies publish periodical lists of their publications which may be had upon request. See the latest issue of the *United States Government Organization Manual* (1193) for complete and correct names of the agencies and their addresses.

PART VI
THE PRESS: AMERICAN
AND FOREIGN

CHAPTER 20.

PRESS DIRECTORIES, BIBLIOGRAPHIES AND SURVEYS

1211. *Annuaire de la Presse Française et étrangère et du monde politique: Annuaire Internationale de la Presse.*
Published annually since 1880. Information on the French and foreign press and periodicals. Also statistical, governmental, and political information on France. Names of French officials, members of the Senate and Chamber of Deputies. Indexes French newspapers, foreign newspapers, and names.

1212. *N. W. Ayer and Son's Directory of Newspapers and Periodicals.* Philadelphia, Pa.: N. W. Ayer and Son.
Published annually since 1880. Title varies 1880–1930. Absorbed Rowell's *American Newspaper Directory* (1869–1908; 40 vols.) in 1910.
The standard directory of some 22,500 newspapers and periodicals, including foreign-language publications, in the United States and its possessions, Canada, Bermuda, Cuba, Panama, and the Philippines. Omits certain types of minor publications. Detailed information about each newspaper and periodical, including political affiliation or subject field, date of establishment, circulation figures, and names of editors and publishers.

1213. Bibliothèque Nationale, Départment des Périodiques. *Bibliographie de la press française politique et d'information générale.* 1865–1944. Paris, 1964 –. 4 vols. (scheduled).
Historical and bibliographic data.

1214. _____. *Repertoire de la presse et des publications periodiques françaises, 1960.* Prepared by H. F. Raux. Paris: Éditions de la documentation française, 1961. 1161 pp.

1215. Cannon, Carl L. *Journalism: A Bibliography.* Alta Claflin, comp. New York: Public Library, 1924. Reprinted with additions from the *Bulletin of the New York Public Library,* various issues of 1923, by Gale Research Company, Detroit, Michigan. $13.00. LC 66–25646.

1216. *Die deutsche Presse 1961: Zeitungen und Zeitschriften.* Berlin: Duncker & Humblot, 1961.
Published since 1954 for the Institut für Publizistik der Freien Universität, Berlin. Foreword by Emil Dovifat. Lists, with statistical and other information, 1,636 newspapers, 6,482 periodicals, and 1,164 news agencies and syndicates in both the German Democratic Republic and the German Federal Republic. Indicates political affiliation of the publications. Part I of the volume contains articles with extensive characterizations of the press, periodicals, and news-syndicate agencies in both parts of Germany. Supersedes *Handbuch deutsche Presse, 1951.*

1217. EDITOR AND PUBLISHER: INTERNATIONAL YEARBOOK. 1920 –. A. Editor and Publisher Co., 850 Third Ave., New York, N. Y. 10022.
The annual issue of the weekly periodical *Editor and Publisher* (1218). Lists and provides information on daily and weekly newspapers, syndicates, wire services, and foreign correspondents.

1218. EDITOR AND PUBLISHER–THE FOURTH ESTATE: Spot News and Features about Newspapers, Advertisers and Agencies. 1884 –. W. $6.50. Editor and Publisher Co., 850 Third Ave., New York, N. Y. 10022.
Includes articles on the press in foreign countries and problems of news gathering.

1219. *European Press Today.* Washington, D. C.: Library of Congress, European Affairs Division, 1949. 152 pp.
An annotated guide to some 1,000 newspapers and periodicals.

1220. *Der Leitfaden für Presse und Werbung,* Essen, Germany: Stamm Verlag.
Published annually since 1947. Covers both the German Federal Republic and the German Democratic Republic. Lists over 1,100 daily and weekly newspapers, with an indication of their political, religious, or other orientation, and circulation, except, in most cases, for the GDR. Also lists some 8,000 periodicals and annuals with pertinent information. Additional list of periodicals by category. List of German-language newspapers in foreign countries.

1221. Merrill, John C., Carter R. Bryan, and Marvin Alisky. *The Foreign Press.* Baton Rouge, La.: Louisiana State University Press, 1959. 256 pp. LC 63–16659.
Short introductions to the press in foreign countries. Data on editorial policies of leading papers and their changes over the years. Documented.

1222. *Newspapers on Microfilm,* 5th edition. George A. Schwegmann, comp. Washington, D. C.: Library of Congress, Union Catalog Division, 1967. 487 pp. LC 53–60042.
List of some 16,000 newspapers in American and Canadian libraries. Includes 4,000 foreign newspapers.

1223. Olsen, Kenneth E. *The History Makers: The Press of Europe from its Beginnings Through 1965.* Baton Rouge, La.: Louisiana State University Press, 1966. 471 pp. LC 66–13660.
A history of the press in 24 European countries. Covers current newspapers.

1224. PRESS DIRECTORY OF AUSTRALIA AND NEW ZEALAND. 1914 –. Irr. Country Press, Sydney, N.S.W., Australia.
The 15th edition was published in 1961. Covers newspapers and periodicals.

1225. Price, Warren C. *The Literature of Journalism: An Annotated Bibliography.* Minneapolis: University of Minnesota Press, 1959. xiv, 489 pp. LC 59–13522.
Largely historical and biographical. Sections on public opinion, radio and television, and the foreign press.

1226. Ruth Sloan Associates. *The Press in Africa.* Helen Kitchen, ed. Washington, D. C., 1956. 96 pp.
Covers periodicals and newspapers in each country or territorial unit in Africa. Indicates their orientation.

1227. *Tentative International Bibliography of Works Dealing with Press Problems, 1900–1952.* Paris; UNESCO, 1955.

1228. Wilcox, Dennis L. *English-Language Dailies Abroad: A Guide to Daily Newspapers in Non-English Speaking Countries.* Detroit, Mich.: Gale Research Co., 1967. 243 pp. LC 67–25558.
List of 202 papers published at least five times a week with all or part of the

editorial content in English. Covers 56 countries or geographic areas—106 in Asia, 61 in Africa, 10 in the Middle East, 5 in Central America, 8 in Mediterranean countries, 3 in the Pacific area, 3 in Europe, 3 in South America, and 3 elsewhere. Various types of information, lists owners, news agencies used, the socioeconomic class of readership, and data on policy and editorial content, etc.

Includes a bibliography and a union list of newspapers which are available on microfilm in American libraries. Circulation statistics.

1229. *Willing's European Press Guide.* London: Hutchinson Willing; and New York: R. R. Bowker Co. LC 66—31876.

Published annually since 1966—67. Provides classified lists of daily newspapers, periodicals, and specialized journals published in Western Europe, except Great Britain.

1230. *Willing's Press Guide: British Edition.* London: Hutchinson Willing; and New York: R. R. Bowker Co. LC 53—36485.

Published annually since 1874. Covers British newspapers, over 4,000 periodicals, and some 1,500 annuals.

1231. Wolseley, Roland E. *The Journalist's Bookshelf: An Annotated and Selected Bibliography of United States Journalism,* 7th edition. Philadelphia, Pa.: Chilton Book Co., 1961. xxi, 225 pp. LC 55—10927.

A selected, annotated bibliography of some 1,300 titles, including newer items than can be found in Price, *The Literature of Journalism* (1225).

1232. *World Communications: Press, Radio, Television, Film,* 4th edition. Paris: UNESCO, Department of Mass Communication, 1964. 380 pp.

Survey of mass communications throughout the world. Statistical data. Selective bibliography.

Note: Newspapers are listed frequently in union and other lists of periodicals.

CHAPTER 21.

NEWSPAPER INDEXES

Few daily newspapers publish their own indexes. Some provide them only for use by their own staffs. Others have a "morgue" which may be made accessible to researchers by special permission. Published indexes usually reference only one particular edition for each day.

Some research institutes have large collections of clippings from newspapers and periodicals arranged by subject matter. There is no published list of such clipping collections.

1233. CHRISTIAN SCIENCE MONITOR: Subject Index of the Christian Science Monitor. 1960 —. M; SA and A cums.

Covers the several regional editions.

1234. *La Stampa* and *La Stampa Sera* (Turin). *Index.*
Published by the Joint Publications Research Service. See *JPRS Reports* (543).

1235. *Le Monde* (Paris). *Index.*
Published by the Joint Publications Research Service. See *JPRS Reports* (543).

1236. *New York Daily Tribune Index, 1875–1906.* New York: Tribune Assoc., 1876–1907. 31 vols.
Less inclusive coverage than the *New York Times Index.*

1237. NEW YORK TIMES INDEX. 1913 –. SM, M, Q, and A.
Covers every subject reported in the newspaper, based on the final late city edition. Much information is in the form of brief abstracts condensed from news stories. The semimonthly issues constitute a news summary for two-week periods, and the annual edition summarizes the news for the previous year. Each abstract is followed by references to the date, page, and column of the original story. Book reviews are listed.

Information is classified under more than 50,000 main headings, including some 3,500 subject headings, 950 geographic headings, 5,000 association and institution names, 5,000 companies, and 30,000 personal names. Another 25,000 personal names appear in special lists; i.e., book reviews, deaths, longevity, murders. Topics such as Vietnam are covered in a dozen or more pages of the annual Index.

See the *New York Times* (1247) for details of its national and international coverage.

1238. _____. *1863–1874.* (Prior Series Vol. 2.) New York: R. R. Bowker Co., 1966. 1052 pp.
The volume consists of reproductions of indexes originally printed for staff use over periods of three months to a year. Not cumulated. Previously available only on microfilm.

Volumes for 1851–1862 and 1905–1912 are scheduled for publication in 1968.

1239. Times, London. INDEX TO THE TIMES. 1906 –. BM (since 1957).
Published under the titles of *The Annual Index* (1906–1913) and *The Official Index* (1914–1957). Similar in coverage and organization to the *New York Times Index*, but covers all daily editions. Coverage includes book reviews.

The Index covered the *Times Literary Supplement* (1541) from 1906–1921.

1240. _____. *Palmer's Index to the Times Newspaper, 1790–1941.* London: Palmer, 1868–1943. (Reprinted by Kraus, New York, 1965.)
Much shorter than *The Official Index* (1239) covering the same period. Biographical data are indexed under "Deaths."

1241. WALL STREET JOURNAL INDEX. 1967 –. M. Dow Jones & Co., Inc., 30 Broad St., New York, N. Y. 10004.
Compiled from the final Eastern edition. Part 1: Corporate News. Part 2: General News.

CHAPTER 22.

LEADING NEWSPAPERS

Section A. United States

1242. *Baltimore Sun* (Baltimore, daily and Sunday).
Known for its high editorial quality.

1243. *Chicago Tribune* (Chicago, daily and Sunday).
Noted for its conservatism and "anti-internationalism." Though staunchly Republican it opposed many Eisenhower foreign policies.

1244. *Christian Science Monitor* (Boston, daily).
Excels in providing news illuminated by background stories and analysis of the "why" and the "whither" of spot news. Stresses broad coverage of national and world affairs. The *Monitor* has won profound respect among editors and reporters for its fairness, restraint, and skill in making complex news understandable. Despite its name it is a regular daily newspaper and contains only one major religious article a day.

1245. *Los Angeles Times* (Los Angeles, daily and Sunday).
Since the early 1960's this paper has become one of the leading newspapers of the country. It furnishes extensive and intensive reporting on national and international events and developments, partly in cooperation with the *Washington Post* and partly through its own worldwide network of excellent reporters. Editorial page is independent and strong. Challenging cartoons.

1246. *New York Post* (New York, daily).
Pronounced liberal.

1247. *New York Times* (New York, daily and Sunday).
This paper is famous for its wide domestic and especially its international news service, with its own staff of correspondents in many parts of the world, and its full Washington and United Nations news coverage. Publishes the full text of numerous documents, including important treaties and pronouncements on international and foreign affairs contained in speeches and press conferences by American presidents and secretaries of state, United Nations leaders, heads of state and foreign ministers and political leaders in the United States and elsewhere. Obituaries carry extensive biographical data.

Section IV of the Sunday edition, entitled Review of the Week, contains a concise summary of the news of the week. It also reprints outstanding cartoons published in the nation's press and foreign newspapers. Includes a Science section.

The Business and Financial section carries a large assortment of domestic and foreign economic news and interpretative reports, covering both industrially advanced and developing countries. The Drama, Dance and Movie section has many items related to international and foreign affairs. The weekly Book Review section has a number of reviews, written by specialists; the book reviews in the daily paper are staff written, frequently by persons who review books on many subjects and have only general knowledge of the topics. Editorials are solid and sound, usually unexciting though there has been some change toward critical attitudes on public questions in recent years.

Important columnists include (formerly) Arthur Krock, James Reston, and C. L. Sulzberger.

The Letters to the Editor include many thought-provoking letters, often replete with factual information furnished by experts in their field.

The extent and quality of the various features of this newspaper make it an excellent, and often the best, source for research, especially with the help of its outstanding *Index*. (1237).

1248. *St. Louis Post-Dispatch* (St. Louis, daily and Sunday).
Thoughtfully written and edited. Superior Washington and foreign coverage. Bill Mauldin cartoons.

1249. *Wall Street Journal* (New York, Chicago, and Riverside, California, 5 days a week).
Important source of American and international economic and financial news and of considered editorial comment. This well-informed paper also publishes some non-economic news and reports on American and international affairs.

1250. *Washington Post and Times Herald* (Washington, D. C., daily).
Good coverage of international news, the Washington diplomatic scene, and the activities of Congress and the many government departments and agencies whose activities bear on American foreign policy. Challenging editorial page.

Section B. American and Foreign Newspapers of International Importance

While it may be difficult to get a unanimous judgment on a list of the world's outstanding newspapers a number of them have a deserved reputation for excellence among students of international affairs and journalism. This list usually includes the *Neue Zürcher Zeitung* (Zürich), *Frankfurter Allgemeine Zeitung* (Frankfurt am Main), the *New York Times,* the *Christian Science Monitor*, the *Guardian* (Manchester), *Le Monde* (Paris), *Asahi Shimbun* (Tokyo), *La Prensa* (Buenos Aires), *The Times* (London), *Dagens Nyheter* (Stockholm), *Aftonbladet* (Oslo), *Le Figaro* (Paris), *New York Herald Tribune* (ceased), and *Politiken* (Copenhagen). This particular list, in this order, was prepared a few years ago by seven professors in the Syracuse University School of Journalism. It was based upon several criteria, including continuity of editorial tradition, the influence exercised by the paper, its network of correspondents, and similar factors. Newspapers may, however, fall upon bad times politically, like *La Prensa* under Peron or the *Frankfurter Zeitung* under Hitler, and care should be exercised to evaluate a given newspaper for a particular historical period. It is not possible to judge a newspaper's political affiliation, slant, or direction by its name. The *Morning Star* of London, for instance, was named the *Daily Worker* until 1966. Under its new name it still serves as the newspaper of the English Communist Party.

Certain newspapers are of special importance not through their excellence, but rather because of their geographic or political setting. They are noticed and studied in regard to international affairs because they represent governments or political and economic groups. Nasser's "mouthpiece" may not be on the list of the ten best newspapers but its contents are noted, analyzed, and searched for indications of his policies and plans.

For extended lists of foreign newspapers and their political or other affiliations in one convenient volume see the latest edition of *Political Handbook and Atlas of the World* (1024). For judgments of the current importance or direction of a given foreign newspaper or periodical consult the index of the *New York Times*, where correspondents often comment on the political affiliation or characteristics of the foreign press. Similar judgments are expressed in the introductory notes of the monthly *Atlas* (242) which specializes in reprinting articles and editorials from foreign newspapers and periodicals. Surveys of the press in various foreign countries are found frequently in the *Journalism Quarterly* (393).

CHAPTER 23.

TRANSLATIONS FROM THE FOREIGN PRESS

For translations from foreign newspapers see:

Africa Digest (278), *Atlas* (242), *Current Digest of the Soviet Press* (125), and *Survey of the China Mainland Press* (listed under 549).

The Foreign Broadcast Information Service, *FBIS Daily Report, Foreign Radio Broadcasts* (548) furnishes full translations, excerpts, and summaries of foreign radio broadcasts, news agency transmissions, and newspapers published in all parts of the world.

APPENDIX 1.

STANDARD HISTORIES

1251. *American Nation: A History from Original Sources by Associated Scholars.* Albert Bushnell Hart, ed. New York and London: Harper, 1904–1918. 28 vols.
A standard history. Each volume written by a specialist. Bibliography. Separate index volume for the whole series.

1252. *Cambridge History of the British Empire.* J. Holland Rose, A. P. Newton, and E. A. Benians, gen. eds. New York: Macmillan: and Cambridge, England: Cambridge University Press, 1929–1959. 8 vols.
Biographies at the end of each volume.

1253. *Cambridge Modern History.* A. W. Ward et al., eds. New York: Macmillan; and Cambridge, England: Cambridge University Press, 1902–1926. 13 vols. and atlas. LC 4–21616.
Standard modern history. Bibliographies. Detailed index. Planned by the late Lord Acton.

1254. Commager, Henry Steele. *Documents of American History,* 7th edition. New York: Appleton–Century–Crofts, 1963.
Volume 1: To 1898; 632 pp. Volume 2: Since 1898; 739 pp.

1255. Gebhardt, Bruno. *Handbuch der deutschen Geschichte,* 8th edition. Herbert Grundmann, ed. Stuttgart, Germany: Union Deutsche Verlagsgesellschaft, 1954–1960. 4 vols.
German history by several scholars. From prehistory to the end of World War II. Bibliographies.

1256. *Histoire générale des civilisations.* Maurice Crouzet, ed. Paris: Presses Universitaires de France, 1953–1957. 7 vols.
A French standard work on worldwide history.

1257. Mann, Golo. *Propyläen Weltgeschichte.* 1960 –. 10 vols. (in progress).
Western history; cultural developments.

1258. *Oxford History of England,* 2d edition. Sir George Clark, ed. Oxford: Clarendon Press, 1937–1962. 14 vols.
Selective bibliographies.

1259. *The Rise of Modern Europe.* William L. Langer, ed. New York: Harper, 1934. 20 vols.
From 1250 A.D. to the end of World War II. Written by specialists. Bibliographic essays for each period of history.

APPENDIX 2.

NEW AND CEASED PUBLICATIONS

There is a continuous need for information on current changes in reference and bibliographic works. Old and established reference books appear with new names and sometimes with different editorial policies. New editions may change their approach and purpose while additional volumes become part of a series of reference works whose publication is "in progress" over a long period of time.

New periodicals appear frequently and old ones cease to exist. Some are superseded by journals with new names, of different scope or purpose. To keep current with these changes in the field of reference and bibliography it is necessary to consult professional library journals and academic periodicals in the specialized subject matter fields. The following list of periodicals is not complete but it does suggest the kind of references needed to keep informed of new and ceased publications.

1260. BIBLIOGRAPHY, DOCUMENTATION, TERMINOLOGY (8).
Includes worldwide reports on new publications.

1261. BRITISH NATIONAL BIBLIOGRAPHY (1173).
Lists and describes new British reference works (as well as other books) and the first issue of new periodicals and journals with new titles.

1262. BULLETIN OF BIBLIOGRAPHY AND MAGAZINE NOTES. 1897 —. 3 x y. $7.00. F. W. Faxon Co., Inc., 515—525 Hyde Park Ave., Boston, Mass. 02131.
Features: Births, Deaths and Magazine Notes; A Record of New Titles; Changed Titles; and Deaths in the Periodical World. This is a nonannotated list. For further information on specific titles listed, send a stamped, self-addressed envelope to the editor, Bulletin of Bibliography. Also contains book reviews.

1263. COLLEGE AND RESEARCH LIBRARIES. 1939 —. BM. $15.00. Assoc. of College and Research Libraries, 50 E. Huron St., Chicago, Ill. 60611.
This journal publishes articles on "New Periodicals of 196-," in Part I of the September issue and Part II of the March issue. Various authors, edited by Dorothy Jones Glasby. Includes periodical articles edited by Eugene P. Sheehy on "Selected Reference Books of 196- to 196-." Mr. Sheehy is the editor of the forthcoming periodical *Supplements* to the 8th edition of Winchell, *Guide to Reference Books* (603) which will cumulate the reports of new publications over a longer period of time.

1264. NEW SERIAL TITLES (see 575).
The section on Changes in Serials notes changes of serials regardless of date of beginning, including suspensions, resumptions, and cessations.

1265. STECHERT—HAFNER BOOK NEWS. 1946 —. M.
The feature, The New Books, contains a section on "General Reference and Bibliography." See also section on Periodicals and Other Serials.

1266. UNESCO BULLETIN FOR LIBRARIES. 1950 —. BM.
Provides an annotated list of new publications in each issue. Its feature, News and Information, should be consulted for additional bibliographic news.

1267. THE WILSON LIBRARY BULLETIN. 1927 –. M, 10 x y. $6.00. H. W. Wilson Co., 950 University Ave., Bronx, N. Y. 10017

Regular feature articles on Current Reference Books, contributed by Frances Neel Cheney. The various items are annotated in detail.

This journal should be watched for special articles on bibliography. See, for instance, the April 1966 issue with contributions on "Bibliographic Organization in the Federal Government" by Herbert Holzbauer, "Bibliographic Organization at the International Level" by Herbert Coblans, "Bibliographic Organization in the Humanities" by Conrad H. Rawski, and "Bibliographic Organization in the Social Sciences" by Dan Bergen.

A cumulative list of Ceased Periodicals is found in Ulrich's, *Guide* (580), pp. 647–654. Corresponding sections are found in earlier editions. Sometimes the list indicates the name of the superseding periodical, if any.

INDEX, ABSTRACTS AND OTHER JOURNALS

1. AMERICA: HISTORY AND LIFE (63).
   See section on General Bibliography and Research Aids.
2. HISTORICAL ABSTRACTS (67).
   Includes a section on Bibliographical News.
3. INTER-AMERICAN REVIEW OF BIBLIOGRAPHY (120).
4. INTERNATIONAL AFFAIRS (London) (251).
   Includes announcements of new periodicals and reference books.
5. INTERNATIONAL INFORMATION SERVICE (79).
   See section on Atlases, Yearbooks, Bibliographies, Directories.
6. INTERNATIONAL STUDIES (Bombay) (254).
7. LATIN AMERICAN RESEARCH REVIEW (311).
8. NEWSLETTER. 1960 –. SA. American Association for the Advancement of Slavic Studies, University of Illinois, Urbana, Ill. 61803. (Membership).
   New periodicals and serials are announced in the section on Institutional Developments.
9. POPULATION INDEX (91).
   Publishes Lists of New Periodicals and of Official Statistical Publications.

APPENDIX 3

ADDENDA

Data on the following publications were received too late to be included in the main body of this work. Therefore, they are listed alphabetically in table of contents sequence.

Chapter 3, Section A

Addenda 1. COMPARATIVE POLITICS. 1968 –. Q. University of Chicago Press, 5750 Ellis Ave., Chicago, Ill. 60637.
Sponsored by the Political Science Program of the City University of New York.
Articles and book reviews devoted to the comparative analysis of political institutions and behavior.

Chapter 5, Section E

Addenda 2. *Supplement, 1961–1965, Index to Latin American Periodical Literature 1929–1960* (118). Washington, D. C.: Columbus Memorial Library, Pan American Union, 1968. 2 vols.
Indexes some 800 periodicals. Coverage includes articles in the cultural, economic, educational, historical, legal, political, and social areas.

Chapter 6, Section D

Addenda 3. OUR GENERATION. 1961 –. Q. $5.00. Our Generation, 3837 Boulevard St. Laurent, Montreal 18, Canada.
Formerly *Our Generation Against Nuclear War.*
Devoted to the research, theory, and review of the problems of peace and freedom, and directed toward presenting alternative solutions to conflict, eliminating war as a way of life. The scope of our concern is very widely defined as social change. We publish articles, and review essays on international relations, particularly disarmament, on the human and natural economy, on poverty, youth and education (Publisher's statement).

Chapter 6, Section L

Addenda 4. COMPARATIVE POLITICAL STUDIES. 1968 –. Q. $8.00, private; $12.00, institutions. Sage Publications, Inc., 275 S. Beverly Dr., Beverly Hills, Calif. 90212.
Theoretical and empirical research articles by scholars engaged in cross-national comparative study. An interdisciplinary journal, it also includes a Research Notes section which reports on current research projects, research designs, and preliminary findings. Bibliographic section and review articles (Publisher's statement).

Addenda 5. FAR HORIZONS. 1968 –. BM. $1.00; foreign $1.25. Government Printing Office, Washington, D. C. 20402.

This bimonthly newsletter is published by the Office of External Research in the Department of State for the interagency Foreign Area Research Coordination Group (FAR). The 21 U. S. Government departments and agencies represented on FAR range from AID to USIA (see list on p. 3 of the first issue of this newsletter). All of them are interested in various aspects of foreign affairs; also, through contracts or grants, they support social science research by academic and other private individuals and institutions.

This periodical publishes articles and information on government guidelines for foreign area research and on federal support of same, foreign government regulations on research, information on foreign affairs research centers, new private and government publications (including bibliographies), names in the news, announcements of meetings and conferences, pertinent activities by government departments and agencies, reports on exchanges with foreign countries, and the like.

The first issue dealt with government-academic relations and the second provided a summary of financial support for foreign area research provided by government agencies.

Chapter 7, Section A, Middle East and Arab Countries

Addenda 6. MIDDLE EASTERN AFFAIRS. 1950–63. M. Council for Middle Eastern Affairs Press, 2061 Belmont Ave., Elmont, N. Y. 11003.

Articles by experts from the West and the Middle East, reviews, and a chronology of events in more than 15 countries in the Middle East and North Africa. A review of significant current developments in every other issue; an annotated bibliography of books and periodical literature four times a year. Also texts of important documents, facts and figures, and maps.

Chapter 9, Section A

Addenda 7. THE NATIONAL CATHOLIC REPORTER. 1964 –. W. $8.00. National Catholic Reporter, Box 281, Kansas City, Mo. 64141.

Edited by Roman Catholic laymen. Liberal in political and economic affairs which are stressed in addition to religious topics. Strong ecumenical tendency. Wide coverage on international affairs.

Chapter 10, Section D

Addenda 8. Library of Congress, African Section. *A List of American Doctoral Dissertations on Africa.* Washington, D. C.: Government Printing Office, 1962. 69 pp. LC 2.2:Af 8 18.

Covers doctoral dissertations accepted by universities in the United States and Canada from the late-19th century through the academic year 1960–61. The entries include notations of subsequent publication, location of abstracts, and other pertinent information.

Chapter 11, Section D. Political Science and International Relations

Addenda 9. Pogany, András H. and Hortenzia Lers Pogany. *Political Science and International Relations. Books Recommended for the Use of American Catholic Colleges and University Libraries.* (Seton Hall Bibliography Series, Vol. I.) Metuchen, N. J.: Scarecrow Press, 1967. 387 pp. LC 67–10196.
More than 5,800 titles covering the years 1955 through 1966. Author and subject indexes.

Addenda 10. *Political Elites: A Select and Computerized Bibliography.* Carl Beck and J. Thomas McKechnie, comps. Cambridge, Mass.: Massachusetts Institute of Technology Press, 1968.
Focuses on symbols and elites in world politics.

Chapter 11, Section E. Africa

Addenda 11. Department of Labor, Bureau of Labor Statistics. *Bibliography on Labor in Africa, 1960–64.* Washington, D. C.: Government Printing Office, 1966. 121 pp. LC L 2.3:1473.
This bibliography covers mainly references published between 1960 and 1965, arranged alphabetically by country and by author, and classified under five broad topics.

Addenda 12. Library of Congress, African Section. *French-Speaking West Africa, A Guide to Official Publications.* Washington, D. C.: Government Printing Office, 1967. 201 pp. LC 2.8:Af 8/967.
Lists the published government records from the mid-19th century to the present. It includes publications of the federation of French West Africa, its eight component colonies (later territories), the French administration in the mandated territory (later trust territory) of Togo, and documents of the autonomous and national governments of each state. Also included are selected League of Nations and United Nations publications on Togo, French documents, pertaining to French-speaking West Africa, and material issued by the French Union, the French Community, and the Organization commune africaine et malgache (OCAM).

Addenda 13. Library of Congress, General Reference and Bibliography Division. *Madagascar and Adjacent Islands, A Guide to Official Publications.* Washington, D. C.: Government Printing Office, 1965. 58 pp. LC 2.8:M 26.
Covers Madagascar; the Comoro Islands; and Reunion, Mauritius, and Seychelles. Includes publications of local governments and a selection of documents issued by the French and British Governments.

Chapter 11, Section E. Asia

Addenda 14. Department of the Army. *Communist China: A Strategic Survey, A Bibliography.* Washington, D. C.: Government Printing Office, 1966. 143 pp.
Prepared under the direction of the Chief of Staff, U. S. Army. Annotated bibliography of books, articles, studies, and documents dealing with the economic, sociologic, military, and political aspects of Communist China. Appended maps, charts, and data.

Addenda 15. Department of the Army. *Ryukyu Islands, A Bibliography.* Washington, D. C.: Government Printing Office, 1967. 105 pp. LC D 101.22:550—4.
Intended to be of assistance to many people—students, scholars, private groups, researchers, academic organizations, and businesses—who have interest in the Ryukyu Islands.

Chapter 11, Section E. Latin America

Addenda 16. *Latin American Studies: Selected General Bibliographical and Research Aids.* Robert Haro, comp. Berkeley, Calif.: University of California Library, 1966.

Chapter 11, Section E. Soviet Russia and Eastern Europe

Addenda 17. Library of Congress. *East Germany, A Selected Bibliography.* Washington, D. C.: Government Printing Office, 1967. 133 pp. LC 35.2:G 31/967.
A selected bibliography of books and articles, published between 1958 and 1966, relating to East Germany.

Chapter 11, Section F, Communications

Addenda 18. Voos, Henry. *Organizational Communication: A Bibliography.* New Brunswick, N. J.: Rutgers University Press, 1967. LC 67—63681.
A systematic review of the literature of research relating to communication within and among groups.

Chapter 13, Section C, Asia

Addenda 19. *South Asian History, 1750—1950. A Guide to Periodicals, Dissertations and Newspapers.* Margaret H. Case, ed. Princeton, N. J.: Princeton University Press, 1967. 575 pp. LC 67—21019.
Includes an annotated and indexed list of over 5,000 articles from 351 periodicals and 26 books of collected essays and encyclopedias.

Chapter 13, Section E

Addenda 20. *Yearbook on International Communist Affairs.* Milorad M. Drachko-vitch, ed. Stanford, Calif.: Hoover Institution, Stanford University. LC 67–31024. Published annually since 1966. Designed to aid professional scholars, teachers, students, and nonspecialists. The Yearbook is the first comprehensive, continuous publication in English concerning the international political activities of the various Communist parties and their interparty relations. It is intended to provide recent data and to fill information gaps. Its ten sections include: Introductory Essay; Profiles of Individual Communist Parties; Chronology; International Gatherings; International Communist Front Organizations; Fourth (Trotskyist) International; Documents; Biographies; Bibliography (in English, Russian, French, and German).

Chapter 13, Section G

Addenda 21. Department of State. *African Programs of U. S. Organizations, A Selective Directory.* Washington, D. C.: Government Printing Office, 1965. 132 pp. LC S 1.116:43.
Description of the current programs of 724 American nongovernmental organizations and institutions interested in Africa, including universities, foundations, missionary societies, business firms, and private nonprofit institutions whose activities are concerned wholly or in part with Africa.

Chapter 17

Addenda 22. Federal Register, National Archives and Records Service, General Services Administration. *Public Papers of the Presidents of the United States.* Washington, D. C.:Government Printing Office, 1957 –.
The series was begun in 1957 in response to a recommendation of the National Historical Publications Commission. An extensive compilation of messages and papers of the Presidents, covering the period 1789 to 1897, was assembled by James D. Richardson and published under congressional authority between 1896 and 1899. Since that time various private compilations were issued, but there was no uniform, systematic publication comparable to the *Congressional Record.* Many Presidential papers could be found only in mimeographed White House releases or as reported in the press.
There are 22 volumes so far, covering the period April 12, 1945 to December 31, 1966 (the administrations of Truman, Eisenhower, Kennedy, and Johnson).
Proclamations, executive orders, and similar documents required by law to be published in the *Federal Register* and *Code of Federal Regulations* are not repeated. Instead, they are listed by number and subject under the heading "Appendix B" in each volume.
Presidential reports to Congress are listed in "Appendix C" of each volume.
Subject index. List of Items precedes the text (information furnished in the publication).

Addenda 23. WEEKLY COMPILATION OF PRESIDENTIAL DOCUMENTS. (Federal Register, National Archives and Records Service, General Services Administration.) 1965 −. W. $6.00. Government Printing Office, Washington, D. C. 20402.

Contains transcripts of the President's news conferences, messages to Congress, public speeches, remarks and statements, and other Presidential material.

Includes an Index of Contents and a Cumulative Index to Prior Issues. Cumulation of this index terminates at the end of each quarter and begins anew with the following issue. Semiannual and annual indexes are published separately.

APPENDIX 4

ADDRESSES OF PUBLISHERS

American Private Publishers

Abelard-Schuman
6 W. 57th St.
New York, N. Y. 10019

Academic Press, Inc.
111 Fifth Ave.
New York, N. Y. 10003

Aldine Publishing Co.
320 W. Adams St.
Chicago, Ill. 60606

American Behavioral Scientist
A Division of Sage Publications
275 Beverly Dr.
Beverly Hills, Calif. 90212

American Bibliographical Center—Clio Press
Riviera Campus, 2010 A.P.S.
Santa Barbara, Calif. 93103

American Data Processing, Inc.
4th Floor, Book Bldg.
Detroit, Mich. 48226

American Historical Association
400 A St., S.E.
Washington, D. C. 20003

American Library Association
50 E. Huron St.
Chicago, Ill. 60611

American Political Science Association
1726 Massachusetts Ave., N.W.,
Washington, D. C. 20006

American Universities Field Staff, Inc.
366 Madison Ave.
New York, N. Y. 10017

Americana Corp. (a subsidiary of Grolier
Inc.)
575 Lexington Ave.
New York, N. Y. 10022

Appleton-Century-Crofts
60 E. 42d St.
New York, N. Y. 10017

Asia Publishing House
29 E. 10th St.
New York, N. Y. 10003

Association of American Geographers
1146 16th St., N.W.
Washington, D. C. 20036

Ayer, N. W., and Son
W. Washington Sq.
Philadelphia, Pa. 19106

Barnes & Noble, Inc.
105 Fifth Ave.
New York, N. Y. 10013

Bedminster Press, Inc.
Vreeland Ave.
Totowa, N. J. 07512

Bowker, R. R., Co.
1180 Ave. of the Americas
New York, N. Y. 10036

Brookings Institution
1775 Massachusetts Ave., N.W.
Washington, D. C. 20036

Cambridge University Press
32 E. 57th St.
New York, N. Y. 10022

Catholic University of America Press
620 Michigan Ave., N.E.
Washington, D. C. 20017

Cattell, Jaques Press
Box 5001
Tempe, Ariz. 85281

Chandler Publishing Co.
124 Spear St.
San Francisco, Calif. 94105

Chilton Book Co.
401 Walnut St.
Philadelphia, Pa. 19106

Columbia University Press
440 W. 110th St.
New York, N. Y. 10025

Congressional Staff Directory
300 New Jersey Ave., S.E.
Washington, D. C. 20003

Cornell University Press
124 Roberts Pl.
Ithaca, N. Y. 14850

Council on Foreign Relations, Inc.
58 E. 68th St.
New York, N. Y. 10021

Duke University Press,
Box 6697, College Station
Durham, N. C. 27708

Dutton, E. P., & Co.
201 Park Ave. S.
New York, N. Y. 10003

East-West Center Press
177 East-West Rd.
Honolulu, Hawaii 96822

Edwards Brothers
2500 S. State St.
Ann Arbor, Mich. 48104

Encyclopaedia Britannica, Inc.
425 N. Michigan Ave.
Chicago, Ill. 60611

Faxon, F. W., Co., Inc.
515-525 Hyde Park Ave.
Boston, Mass. 02131

Foreign Policy Association
345 E. 46th St.
New York, N. Y. 10017

Free Press of Glencoe, Inc.
866 Third Ave.
New York, N. Y. 10022

Gale Research Co.
1400 Book Tower
Detroit, Mich. 48226

Governmental Research Association
4 Washington Sq. N.
New York, N. Y. 10003

Hafner Publishing Co., Inc.
31 E. 10th St.
New York, N. Y. 10003

Hall, G. K., & Co.
70 Lincoln St.
Boston, Mass. 02111

Hammond, Inc.
Hammond Bldg.
Maplewood, N. J. 07040

Harper & Row, Publishers
49 E. 33d St.
New York, N. Y. 10016

Harvard University Press
79 Garden St.
Cambridge, Mass. 02138

Holt, Rinehart & Winston, Inc.
383 Madison Ave.
New York, N. Y. 10017

Hoover Institution on War, Revolution
and Peace
Stanford University
Stanford, Calif. 94305

Houghton Mifflin Co.
2 Park St.
Boston, Mass. 02107

Human Relations Area Files (HRAF) Press,
see Taplinger Publishing Co., Inc.

Indiana University Press
10th and Morton Sts.
Bloomington, Ind. 47401

Institute of Pacific Relations, New York.
Write in care of the University of British
Columbia, Vancouver, B.C., Canada

Irwin, Richard D., Inc.
1818 Ridge Rd.
Homewood, Ill. 60430

Jewish Publication Society of America
222 N. 15th St.
Philadelphia, Pa. 19102

Johnson Reprint Corp.
111 Fifth Ave.
New York, N. Y. 10003

Kallman Publishing Co.
1614 W. University Ave.
Gainesville, Fla. 32601

Kraus Reprint Corp.
16 E. 46th St.
New York, N. Y. 10017

Lippincott, J. B., Co.
E. Washington Sq.
Philadelphia, Pa. 19105

Little, Brown and Co.
34 Beacon St.
Boston, Mass. 02106

Louisiana State University Press
Baton Rouge, La. 70803

Macmillan Co.
60 Fifth Ave.
New York, N. Y. 10011

Marquis, A. N., Co., Inc.
210 E. Ohio St.
Chicago, Ill. 60611

Massachusetts Institute of Technology Press
50 Ames St.
Cambridge, Mass. 02142

Massachusetts Institute of Technology
Publications Office
77 Massachusetts Ave.
Cambridge, Mass. 02139

McGraw-Hill Book Co.
330 W. 42d St.
New York, N. Y. 10036

Michigan State University Press
Box 550
East Lansing, Mich. 48823

Nelson, Thomas, & Sons
Copewood and David Sts.
Camden, N. J. 08103

New York University Press
32 Washington Pl.
New York, N. Y. 10003

Northwestern University Press
1735 Benson Ave.
Evanston, Ill. 60201

Oceana Publications, Inc.
40 Cedar St.
Dobbs Ferry, N. Y. 10522

Oxford University Press
200 Madison Ave.
New York, N. Y. 10016

Penguin Books, Inc.
3300 Clipper Mill Rd.
Baltimore, Md. 21211

Pergamon Press, Inc.
122 E. 55th St.
New York, N. Y. 10022

Philosophical Library, Inc.
15 E. 40th St.
New York, N. Y. 10016

Praeger, Frederick A., Inc.
111 Fourth Ave.
New York, N. Y. 10003

Prentice-Hall, Inc.
Englewood Cliffs, N. J. 07632

Princeton Research Publishing Co.
20 Nassau St.
Princeton, N. J. 08540

Princeton University Press
Princeton, N. J. 08540

Public Administration Service
1313 E. 60th St.
Chicago, Ill. 60637

Public Affairs Press
419 New Jersey Ave., S.E.
Washington, D. C. 20003

Rand Corp.
1700 Main St.
Santa Monica, Calif. 90406

Rand McNally & Co.
Box 7600
Chicago, Ill. 60680

Rowman & Littlefield, Inc.
84 Fifth Ave.
New York, N. Y. 10011

Rutgers University Press
30 College Ave.
New Brunswick, N. J. 08903

Sage, Russell Foundation
230 Park Ave.
New York, N. Y. 10017

St. Martin's Press, Inc.
175 Fifth Ave.
New York, N. Y. 10010

Scarecrow Press, Inc.
52 Liberty St.
Metuchen, N. J. 08840

Scribner's, Charles Sons
597 Fifth Ave.
New York, N. Y. 10017

Sloan, Ruth Associates, Inc.
2500 Virginia Ave., N.W.
Washington, D. C. 20037

Stanford University Press
Stanford, Calif. 94305

Taplinger Publishing Co., Inc.
29 E. 10th St.
New York, N. Y. 10003

Taylor Publishing Co.
6320 Denton Dr.
Dallas, Tex. 75235

Telberg Book Corp.
544 Ave. of the Americas
New York, N. Y. 10011

Twentieth Century Fund
41 E. 70th St.
New York, N. Y. 10021

Universal Reference System, see Princeton
Research Publishing Co.

University Microfilm Library Service
300 N. Zeeb Rd.
Ann Arbor, Mich. 48106

University of Arizona Press
P. O. Box 3398, College Station
Tucson, Ariz. 85719

University of California Press
Berkeley, Calif. 94720

University of Chicago Press
5750 Ellis Ave.
Chicago, Ill. 60637

University of Florida Press
15 N.W. 15th St.
Gainesville, Fla. 32601

University of Illinois Press
Urbana, Ill. 61801

University of Kentucky Press
Lexington, Ky. 40506

University of Miami Press
Drawer 9088
Coral Gables, Fla. 33124

University of Michigan Press
615 E. University
Ann Arbor, Mich. 48106

University of Minnesota Press
2037 University Ave., S.E.
Minneapolis, Minn. 55455

University of New Mexico Press
Albuquerque, N. M. 87106

University of Pennsylvania Press
3729 Spruce St.
Philadelphia, Pa. 19104

University of Wisconsin Press
P. O. Box 1379
Madison, Wis. 53701

Warne, Frederick, & Co., Inc.
101 Fifth Ave.
New York, N. Y. 10003

Wayne State University Press
Detroit, Mich. 48202

Who's Who in American Education, Inc.
P. O. Box 1898, 701 Main St.
Hattiesburg, Miss. 39401

Wilson, H. W., Co.
950 University Ave.
Bronx, N. Y. 10452

World Trade Academy Press, Inc.
50 E. 42d St.
New York, N. Y. 10017

Yale University Press
92A, Yale Station
New Haven, Conn. 06520

U. S. Government Agencies Concerned with Book Publications

Addresses of U. S. Government agencies concerned with book publishing are listed in:

LITERARY MARKET PLACE. The Business Directory of American Book Publishing, 1967–1968. R. R. Bowker Co., New York.

The addresses of *all* U. S. Government agencies are found in the UNITED STATES GOVERNMENT ORGANIZATION MANUAL (1193).

Detailed information on libraries in government agencies is included in the:

AMERICAN LIBRARY DIRECTORY. Eleanor F. Steiner-Prag, comp. R. R. Bowker Co., New York, 1966. Biennial editions.

The United Nations and Other Public International Organizations

United Nations, United Nations Publications, Rm. 1059, New York, N. Y. 10017.

International Court of Justice, Peace Palace, The Hague, Netherlands.

UNESCO, UNESCO House, Place de Fontenoy, Paris (7ᵉ), France.

Pan American Union, Washington, D. C. 20006.

For addresses of other public international organizations see Chapter 13, Section H.

INDEX OF NAMES

Note: Authors, editors, and compilers of books are included in the following index. Persons associated with periodical publications are not included.

The italic number following the name is the entry number.

INDEX OF TITLES

Note: The italic number following the title is the entry number.

Other publications of ABC-CLIO in

• reference

• history

• bibliography

• political science

Two new books

☐ **BIBLIOGRAPHY AND THE HISTORIAN**
Dagmar Horna Perman, editor. This work presents the analytical views of twenty-three eminent scholars on the needs of the history profession in the fields of computer technology and automated data collection for storage, retrieval and dissemination of information. viii, 176 pages, 1967. $6.00 clothbound, $3.75 paperbound.

☐ **AUSTRIAN HISTORICAL BIBLIOGRAPHY 1965**
Eric H. Boehm and **Fritz Fellner,** editors. This is the first volume of an annual series which will provide complete bibliographical coverage of Austrian historical studies and recent affairs. It also contains bibliographical materials published in Austria on the history of other countries of the world. 120 pages, 1968. $19.00 clothbound.

A standard directory

☐ **HISTORICAL PERIODICALS**
An Annotated World Directory of Historical and Related Serial Publications in the Humanities and Social Sciences. **Eric H. Boehm** and **Lalit Adolphus,** editors. The only worldwide guide in its field. xix, 620 pages, 1961. $27.50 clothbound.

Twentieth Century Series

☐ No. 1 **GERMAN NATIONAL SOCIALISM,** 1919-1945. **Martin Broszat.** The first English-language translation of this work which was designed to be a standard source of background information on National Socialism. viii, 154 pages, 1966. $5.50 clothbound, $2.75 paperbound.

☐ No. 2 **WE SURVIVED. Fourteen Histories of the Hidden and Hunted of Nazi Germany.** **Eric H. Boehm.** "A collection of adventure stories which are as exciting as any to come out of the war." The Hartford Courant. xiii, 316 pages, 1966. $5.85 clothbound, $2.75 paperbound.

☐ No. 3 **INTERNATIONAL RELATIONS RESEARCH – Problems of Evaluation and Advancement. E. Raymond Platig.** A new and definitive work on the study and research in international relations and related foreign area studies. xiv, 211 pages, 1967. $6.50 clothbound, $3.75 paperbound.

Bibliography and Reference Series
All Paperbound

☐ No. 1 **BLUEPRINT FOR BIBLIOGRAPHY –** A System for the Social Sciences and Humanities. Eric H. Boehm. ii, 22 pages. 1965. $2.

☐ No. 2 **BIBLIOGRAPHIES ON INTERNATIONAL RELATIONS AND WORLD AFFAIRS –** An Annotated Directory. Eric H. Boehm. ii, 33 pages. 1965. $4.

☐ No. 3 **LIST OF PERIODICALS.** Publications from which articles are abstracted for "America: History and Life" and "Historical Abstracts." 16 pages. 1967. Free.

☐ No. 4 **A BIBLIOGRAPHY OF LIBRARY DIRECTORIES** combined with **A BIBLIOGRAPHY OF LIBRARY SCIENCE DICTIONARIES,** 1967 editions. **Richard C. Lewanski.** 49 pages. 1967. $3.85.

☐ No. 5 **RESEARCH IN THE SOCIAL SCIENCES AND HUMANITIES. Lyman H. Legters.** The research program under Title VI of the National Defense Education Act. 31 pages. 1967. $3.

☐ No. 6 **REFERENCE WORKS: HISTORY AND RELATED FIELDS. Inge P. Boehm** and **Alexander S. Birkos,** editors. An annotated and indexed collection of works cited in volumes 1-10 of "Historical Abstracts." vi, 58 pages. 1967. $3.75.

☐ No. 7 **THE CUE SYSTEM FOR BIBLIOGRAPHY AND INDEXING. Eric H. Boehm.** The theory and application of an alphabetic system with a high mnemonic potential. 45 pages. 1967. $3.

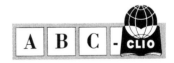

AMERICAN BIBLIOGRAPHICAL CENTER
CLIO PRESS

Riviera Campus, 2010 Alameda Padre Serra
Santa Barbara, California 93103

Publishers of • AMERICA: HISTORY AND LIFE • HISTORICAL ABSTRACTS